"True science is never dogmatic. It follows the evidence of eyes and ears wherever it may lead. William Dembski argues, convincingly, that the evidence at hand, particularly in biology and biochemistry, leads inexorably to the conclusion that life could not exist without an intelligent designer. If Dembski is right—and I believe he is—then it is unscientific to deny the existence of God.

"By making this argument so carefully and so well, Dembski has performed a real service not only for science but also for theology, which has long been intimidated by the aggressive 'scientific' claim that reason is the enemy of faith. It is not, and Dembski shows us why it is not."

THOMAS G. WEST, professor of politics at the University of Dallas, senior fellow with the Claremont Institute, author of *Vindicating the Founders: Race, Sex, Class, and Justice in the Origins of America*

"Intelligent design is moving quickly to replace Darwinian evolution as the central guiding principle of biological science. This book is a clear and thought-provoking analysis of the theological, philosophical and scientific aspects of intelligent design by one of its leading proponents. Everyone interested in the coming revolution should read it."

JONATHAN WELLS, postdoctoral biologist and senior fellow at the Discovery Institute, Seattle

---

"With graduate degrees in mathematics, philosophy and theology, William Dembski is uniquely qualified to address the question of whether divine design is detectable in the realm of nature. His groundbreaking work in design theory is philosophically significant in its own right, but in this book Dembski goes beyond theory to application, claiming that his method, when applied to the natural world of living things, shows in a rigorous way that biological organisms are products of intelligent design.

"Bold and provocative, Dembski's book challenges the conventional wisdom which says that while science may have input into theology, theology has no input into science. Sooner rather than later, the doyens of contemporary science and religion dialogue will no longer be able to ignore the position Dembski represents, for his work is simply too good for his challenge to stand unanswered."

WILLIAM LANE CRAIG, fellow of Discovery Institute's Center for the Renewal of Science and Culture

---

"There are many things I admire about this book: its thoughtfulness, its philosophical and theological acumen, its willingness to face all difficulties. But the most important contribution is the effort to return the notion of design to its proper standing in science--that is, to bring science back under the rubric of rationality. Naturalism under the guise of science makes a lot of assumptions that it will now be forced to defend instead of assert."

JACK COLLINS, Ph.D., associate professor of Old Testament, Covenant Theological Seminary, St. Louis, Missouri

"The toppling of the Berlin Wall will seem small in comparison with the impending demolition of scientific naturalism. Most of us have heard but a rumor of this event with our ears; Dembski is one of those making it happen. Will this be a bad thing? No, a good one. The collapse of the idea that nature is blind, purposeless and 'all there is' will not destroy the scientific study of nature but allow it to come into its own.

"As a philosopher of the natural moral law, I have particular reason to extol Dembski's work. There would be little point in speaking of a 'law written on the heart' if conscience were merely a meaningless byproduct of selfish genes. Dembski strengthens the case for saying that our deepest moral inclinations not only look designed, they are."

J. BUDZISZEWSKI, departments of government and philosophy, The University of Texas, author of *Written on the Heart: The Case for Natural Law*

"*Intelligent Design* is a critical resource for anyone who wants to understand the reemergence of the design argument. Dr. Dembski has taken the key concepts from his seminal but highly technical work *The Design Inference* and made them accessible to the average reader. Furthermore, he has placed these arguments in their historical setting, allowing the reader to understand the early development of the design argument, the reasons for its demise for almost 150 years, and the critical new insights, which Dr. Dembski has helped to fashion, that are responsible for the return of the design argument as an intellectually compelling alternative to naturalism."

WALTER L. BRADLEY, professor of mechanical engineering, Texas A&M University

---

"The past twenty years of laboratory research in the biological sciences have unveiled incredible mysteries of nature. Those scientists that have participated in these endeavors have been awestruck not only by the beauty of nature at the molecular level but also by the complexity of even the simplest of cells. In fact, scientists adhering to strict Darwinism must remind themselves that what they see is only 'apparent' design. In Bill Dembski's first book, *The Design Inference*, he laid out the logic for discriminating 'real' from 'apparent' design. In this new work Dr. Dembski unpacks the meaning of 'intelligent design' from the historical, philosophical and theological perspectives. I would encourage even those of my colleagues who disagree with its implications to read and consider the arguments presented in this volume. It promises to be provocative, controversial, but central to the ultimate question of science and religion."

SCOTT A. MINNICH, Ph.D., associate professor, department of microbiology, molecular biology and biochemistry, University of Idaho

---

"If philosophic naturalism is the disease, and I am confident it is, Dembski's *Intelligent Design* is surely the cure. Extending the argument of his *Design Inference* Dembski here traces, in lucid accessible language, the fate of the inference to intelligent cause in Western thought since Bacon. His intellectual history is meticulous, and the positive case he advances for reintroducing design has implications that are radical and far reaching. In his exposition, Dembski exemplifies the finest traditions of the American public intellectual—he assumes that ordinary people, given evidence and argument, are perfectly capable of making reasoned decisions on big questions that matter."

JOHN ANGUS CAMPBELL, professor, department of communication, University of Memphis

William A. Dembski

Intelligent Design

The Bridge

Between

Science &

Theology

InterVarsity Press
Downers Grove, Illinois

InterVarsity Press
P.O. Box 1400, Downers Grove, IL 60515
World Wide Web: www.ivpress.com
E-mail: mail@ivpress.com

InterVarsity Press® is the book-publishing division of InterVarsity Christian Fellowship/USA®, a student movement active on campus at hundreds of universities, colleges and schools of nursing in the United States of America, and a member movement of the International Fellowship of Evangelical Students. For information about local and regional activities, write Public Relations Dept., InterVarsity Christian Fellowship/USA, 6400 Schroeder Rd., P.O. Box 7895, Madison, WI 53707-7895.

ISBN 0-8308-1581-3

Printed in the United States of America ∞

Library of Congress Cataloging-in-Publication Data

Dembski, William A., 1960–
    Intelligent design : the bridge between science & theology /
William A. Dembski.
        p.   cm.
    Includes bibliographical references and index.
    ISBN 0–8308–1581–3 (pbk. : alk. paper)
    1. Religion and science. 2. God—Proof, Cosmological.
3. Naturalism.   I. Title.
BL240.2.D46   199999–37141
215—dc21   *CIP*

25	24	23	22	21	20	19	18	17	16	15	14	13	12	11	10	9	8	7	6			
20	19	18	17	16	15	14	13	12	11	10	09	08	07	06	05	04	03	02	01			

*True fortitude of understanding
consists in not suffering what we know,
to be disturbed by what we do not know.*
WILLIAM PALEY

To my beloved wife, Jana
PROVERBS 31:10–31

Contents

Foreword

It's often the most obvious things that elude us, things that, in retrospect, we smack our foreheads and moan, "Why didn't I think of that?" Even a topic's practical importance seems to have little bearing on the likelihood that an insight will occur to us. I bet the friends of the fellow who invented the alphabet could have kicked themselves. Once they were told of it, the concept of using written marks (letters) to stand for sounds and strings of letters to stand for the sounds of words, the idea must have appeared utterly simple—as it does to us today. The progress afforded by a written alphabet is enormous. Yet the discovery escaped great civilizations such as China, where written communication still uses cumbersome pictographic characters.

Other examples of obvious-in-retrospect ideas include the place-value system of arithmetic and the concept of zero. Together they allow modern schoolchildren to easily solve problems that in ancient times required considerable effort using Roman numerals. In the sciences the medieval philosopher Jean Buridan's easily grasped idea of impetus, a forerunner of the modern concept of momentum, arguably started modern physics. And when he first heard of natural selection, Thomas Huxley is reputed to have exclaimed, "How stupid of me not to have thought of it!"

When I first read William Dembski's work on detecting intelligent design, I knew just how Huxley felt. The idea of intelligent design has, of course, been around for a long time. But until Dembski, thinking about how we detect design was like writing before the alphabet or calculating before Arabic numerals. Indeed, in the past, ascribing something to design often seemed a matter of mere taste. Sometimes the nail was struck head on. But other times a thumb was hit instead. Socrates, for example, thought that the progression of the seasons, of day and night, of rain and dry weather, pointed toward design. But what else could follow day except night? What could come after drought but rain?

How then can we reliably detect design? Dembski's insight, first elaborated in his scholarly monograph *The Design Inference* and explained here for a broader readership, is that we recognize design in what he calls "specified complexity" or equivalently "specified small probability." In other words, we apprehend design in highly improbable (complex) events that also fit some independently identifiable pattern (specification).

For example, if we turned a corner and saw a couple of Scrabble letters on a table that spelled AN, we would not, just on that basis, be able to decide if they were purposely arranged. Even though they spelled a word, the probability of getting a short word by chance is not prohibitive. On the other hand, the probability of seeing some particular long sequence of Scrabble letters, such as NDEIRUABFDMOJHRINKE, is quite small (around one in a billion billion billion). Nonetheless, if we saw that sequence lined up on a table, we would think little of it because it is not specified—it matches no recognizable pattern. But if we saw a sequence of letters that read, say, METHINKSITISLIKEAWEASEL, we would easily conclude that the letters were intentionally arranged that way. The sequence of letters is not only highly improbable, but it also matches an intelligible English sentence. It is a product of intelligent design.

Now that isn't hard, is it? It is as easy as adding 46 to 54 to get 100. But of course before the place-value system it was rather difficult to add XLVI to LIV to get C. And before Dembski, rationally justifying a conclusion of intelligent design was an awkward, tentative affair. Elegant tools make us all feel smarter.

Dembski invented the tools, but he has not taken all the fun. The best is yet to come. The real excitement will be in applying design theory to a range of subjects. Intelligent design theory has implications for virtually all humane studies, including philosophy, theology, literary criticism, history and more. It promises to be a clarifying lens through which to view issues of interest to the public in general and to Christians in particular, as this book itself demonstrates.

For a scientist such as myself, however, design theory is most exciting as a tool to probe nature. Intelligent design theory requires data from the physical world to assess the probability of an event, so our appreciation of the design of life and the universe will necessarily depend on the state of our science, which, as the history of science shows, can fluctuate. After the publication of Darwin's *Origin of Species*, the fortunes of intelligent design appeared dim. Apparently an unintelligent process—natural selection—could account for the complexity of the biological world. Moreover, to nineteenth century scientists the universe appeared a cold, bland place, indifferent to human life. With the progress of science in the twentieth century, however, the design argument has made a remarkable comeback, starting with that apparently dull universe.

In 1913 Lawrence Henderson's *The Fitness of the Environment* pointed out the surprisingly felicitous properties of water, oxygen, carbon dioxide and other chemicals for life. Henderson's work has recently been extended by Michael Denton, who shows in *Nature's Destiny* that human life precariously depends upon such things as the chemistry of molybdenum (necessary for nitrogen fixation). The middle part of our century saw increasing evidence for the Big Bang hypothesis, with the specter of a beginning to the universe, which ruled out countless chance events that might have been possible in an infinite, eternal universe. The universe got much cozier in 1973 with the publication of Brandon Carter's seminal paper "Large Number Coincidences and the Anthropic Principle in Cosmology." Since then a gaggle of scholarly articles and popular books have recorded the ways in which the universe is fine-tuned for life, ranging from the strength of the gravitational constant to the values of the resonance levels of carbon nuclei to the frequency of supernovae. Eyebrows have been raised.

Intelligent design has lately been making forays into biology too. The problem of the origin of life, once thought to be solvable in the heady days after Stanley Miller's famous experiments, has sunken back into intractability. It is not just that we have no answer for life's origin; rather, as Thaxton, Bradley and Olsen rigorously showed in *The Mystery of Life's Origin*, the chemical and physical knowledge we have gained as a result of four decades' work itself shows the implausibility of unintelligent causes for life. Further, as I have argued in *Darwin's Black Box*, the progress of science has also pointed to design at the cellular basis of life, where molecular machines of stunning complexity carry out life's most basic tasks.

Of course coming to a rigorous conclusion of design in any of these cases means probing nature's complexity and a lot of lab work to refine probability estimates. None of that is likely to be easy. Still, although it is difficult to predict the (frequently nonlinear) advance of science, the arrow of progress indicates that the more we know, the deeper design is seen to extend. I expect that in the decades ahead we will see the contingent aspects of nature steadily shrink. And through all of this work we will make our judgments about design and contingency on the theoretical foundation of Bill Dembski's work.

Michael J. Behe
Department of Biological Sciences
Lehigh University

Preface

Intelligent design is three things: a scientific research program that investigates the effects of intelligent causes; an intellectual movement that challenges Darwinism and its naturalistic legacy; and a way of understanding divine action. Intelligent design therefore intersects science and theology. Although the intelligent design movement continues to gain momentum in the culture at large, scientists and theologians remain skeptical about its merits. Many scientists think intelligent design makes for bad science (that it's just creationism in disguise), whereas many theologians think it makes for bad theology (that it misunderstands divine action). This book argues that these perceptions are mistaken and that intelligent design is just what the doctor ordered for both science and theology.

The Focus: Detecting Design in the Universe

In its treatment of design this book focuses not so much on whether the universe as a whole is designed but on whether we are able to detect design within an already given universe. The universe provides a well-defined causal backdrop (physicists these days think of it as a *field* characterized by *field equations*). Although one can ask whether that causal backdrop is itself designed, one can as well ask whether events and objects occurring within that backdrop are designed. At issue here are two types of design: (1) the design of the universe as a whole and (2) instances of design within the universe. An analogy illustrates the difference. Consider an oil painting. An oil painting is typically painted on a canvas. One can therefore ask whether the canvas is designed. Alternatively one can ask whether some configuration of paint on the canvas is designed. The design of the canvas corresponds to the design of the universe as a whole. The design of some configuration of paint corresponds to an instance of design within the universe.

Though not perfect, this analogy is useful. The universe is a canvas on which is depicted natural history. One can ask whether that canvas itself is designed. On the other hand, one can ask whether features of natural history depicted on that canvas are designed. In biology, for instance, one can ask whether Michael Behe's irreducibly complex biochemical machines are designed. Although design remains an important issue in cosmology, the focus of the intelligent design movement is on biology. That's where the action is. It was Darwin's expulsion of design from biology that made possible the triumph of naturalism in Western culture. So, too, it will be intelligent design's reinstatement of design within biology that will be the undoing of naturalism in Western culture.

The Goal: Showing How Design Unseats Naturalism

The guiding question throughout this book is, If naturalism is false, how could we know it? The key to overturning naturalism is design, and not just the design of the universe taken as a whole but design within the universe, and especially within biology. Whereas the origin and early evolution of the universe remain speculative, the causal backdrop for life is well-defined. The nuts and bolts of life occur at the level of biochemistry. Biochemistry provides the causal backdrop against which design in biology must be decided. The aim of this book then is to show how detecting design within the universe, and especially against the backdrop of biology and biochemistry, unseats naturalism. To do this I shall review some of my own research on detecting design. I shall show that detecting design within the universe follows a well-defined methodology. Moreover, when applied to the irreducibly complex biochemical systems of Michael Behe, this methodology convincingly demonstrates design.

The implications of intelligent design are radical in the true sense of this much overused word. The question posed by intelligent design is not how we should do science and theology in light of the triumph of Enlightenment rationalism and scientific naturalism. The question rather is how we should do science and theology in light of the impending collapse of Enlightenment rationalism and scientific naturalism. These ideologies are on the way out. They are on the way out not because they are false (although they are that) or because they have been bested by postmodernity (they haven't) but because they are bankrupt. They have run out of steam. They lack the resources for making sense of an information age whose primary entity is information and whose only coherent account of information is design.

An Overview: Answering Questions About Intelligent Design

Who will want to read this book? Certainly anyone interested in the creation-evolution controversy, the relation between science and theology, the nature of divine action, and the cultural implications of intelligent design. Except for chapter six this book is accessible to the general reader (chapter six is on information theory, and some mathematics is unavoidable). Several of the chapters are adapted from previously published articles. I've presented most of the ideas contained here in public lectures. I've seen how these ideas play out under fire. The chapters are therefore tailored to questions people are actually asking about intelligent design.

This book breaks into three parts. Chapters one through three set the stage. The first chapter massages our intuitions about design, the next two show how modernity has undermined those intuitions. Chapters four through six examine the philosophical and scientific basis for intelligent design. This is the heart of the book, and readers interested in a popular formulation of my ideas in *The Design Inference* (Cambridge, 1998) will want to turn here. Chapters seven and eight properly conclude the book, showing how science and theology relate coherently and how intelligent design establishes the crucial link between the two. The appendix then answers any residual reservations the reader may have about design. The three parts together with the appendix provide a unified framework for understanding the relation between science and theology.

A Chapter-by-Chapter Summary

Chapter One: Recognizing the Divine Finger. The book begins by examining the use of biblical signs to guide human decision-making. Gideon, for instance, looked for a sign from God to decide whether to go to war with Midian. Among the ancients decision-making through the use of signs followed a well-defined logic. This chapter unpacks that logic. The logic of signs not only remains compelling for today but also provides the basis for how one detects intelligent causes and therefore design. When intelligent causes act, they leave behind a characteristic trademark of their activity. Biblical signs constitute a case in point. Besides unpacking the logic of signs, this chapter also presents several case studies from Scripture of how signs guide decision-making. Of special interest is how the resurrection of Christ *signifies* that humanity itself shall ultimately be resurrected.

Chapter Two: The Critique of Miracles. The biblical logic of signs is largely regarded as passé. Why? Between 1650 and 1850, in the period from Spinoza to Schleiermacher, the rational foundations of the Christian faith were fundamentally altered. Whereas it had been unproblematic for faith and reason to work together so that reason could supply evidence for faith, in the period from Spinoza to Schleiermacher the very notion that evidence of any sort could support the Christian faith was increasingly abandoned. Miracles, which had been regarded as particularly powerful evidence for faith, were now regarded as incoherent. The arguments by Spinoza, Hume and Schleiermacher against miracles are still with us and appear in many contemporary treatments of divine action. The arguments don't work and this chapter refutes them. The core of this chapter appeared as "Schleiermacher's Metaphysical Critique of Miracles," *Scottish Journal of Theology* 49, no. 4 (1996): 443-65.

Chapter Three: The Demise of British Natural Theology. If chapter two reopens the door to divine action on the theological front, this chapter reopens it on the scientific front. The intelligent design movement is linked both conceptually and historically to British natural theology. British natural theology was the attempt by British scientists in the two centuries preceding Darwin to understand divine action scientifically. British natural theology died in the nineteenth century. A positivist conception of science that restricted science to the study of undirected natural causes effectively did away with it. That faulty conception of science is still with us, and it is the purpose of this chapter to refute it. Although natural theology was not without its problems, it contained a core idea—design—which neither positivism nor Darwinism ever adequately addressed. This chapter argues that the blanket dismissal of natural theology in the nineteenth century was not warranted and that its core idea of design remains viable. This chapter appeared as "Not Even False? Reassessing the Demise of British Natural Theology," *Philosophia Christi*, 2d series, 1, no. 1 (1999): 17-43.

Chapter Four: Naturalism and Its Cure. The ancients understood the logic by which God becomes recognizable in creation. The modern theological critique of miracles and the modern scientific critique of natural theology upset that premodern logic. This chapter examines the root cause behind those critiques—naturalism, the view that nature is fundamental and self-sufficient. Having examined naturalism, this chapter considers how naturalism is best challenged. It argues that intelligent design provides the most effective challenge to naturalism to date. Most Christians accept that God by wisdom created the world and that therefore God is a designer and the world is designed. But many Christians also accept that God's design is accessible only through the eyes of faith. This chapter argues that God's design is also accessible to scientific inquiry. The crucial point of this chapter is that design is *empirically detectable,* that is, we can detect it through observation. This chapter expands my introduction to *Mere Creation: Science, Faith & Intelligent Design* (InterVarsity Press, 1998).

Chapter Five: Reinstating Design Within Science. How is design empirically detectable? This chapter answers that question. In order to detect design two features must be present, complexity and specification. Complexity guarantees that the object in question is not so simple that it can readily be attributed to chance. Specification guarantees that the object exhibits the right sort of pattern associated with intelligent causes. A single letter of the alphabet is specified without being complex. A long sequence of random letters is complex without being specified. A Shakespearean sonnet is both complex and specified. *Specified complexity* is how we detect design empirically. This chapter explains specified complexity and shows how it applies to Michael Behe's irreducibly complex biochemical systems. This chapter also argues that science must be expanded to include intelligent design. The argument here forms the basis for my book *The Design Inference* as well as for several of my popular articles on design. In particular, this chapter expands my article "Reinstating Design Within Science," *Rhetoric & Public Affairs* 1, no. 4 (1998): 503-18.

Chapter Six: Intelligent Design as a Theory of Information. For many in the scientific community, intelligent design represents yet another ill-conceived attempt by creationists to straightjacket science within a religious ideology. But in fact intelligent design can be formulated as a scientific theory having empirical consequences and devoid of religious commitments. Intelligent design can be unpacked as a theory of information. Within such a theory, information becomes a reliable indicator of design as well as a proper object for scientific investigation. This chapter identifies the specified complexity of chapter five with a powerful extension of Shannon information. Having drawn the connection between specified complexity and information, this chapter presents a conservation law governing the origin and flow of information. From this law it follows that information is not reducible to natural causes and that the origin of information is best sought in intelligent causes. Intelligent design thereby becomes a theory for detecting and measuring information, explaining its origin and tracing its flow. An abridged version of this chapter appeared as "Intelligent Design as a Theory of Information," *Perspectives on Science and Christian Faith* 49, no. 3 (1997): 180-90.

Chapter Seven: Science and Theology in Mutual Support. Over the last hundred years science and theology have been increasingly characterized in terms of either a warfare or partition metaphor (i.e., either they're in unresolvable conflict, or they're so different that no substantive communication can exist). The aim of this chapter is to show that science and theology, though distinct and not capable of resolving each other's claims with mathematical certainty, are capable nonetheless of providing epistemic support for each other's claims. Within an interdisciplinary dialogue, epistemic support asks whether claims in one discipline can help justify claims in another discipline. This chapter develops a notion of epistemic support that is appropriate for fostering a genuinely productive interdisciplinary dialogue between science and theology. It then shows that such a relation of epistemic support exists between the Big Bang and divine creation. This chapter extends my article with Stephen Meyer titled "Fruitful Interchange or Polite Chitchat? The Dialogue Between Theology and Science," *Zygon* 33, no. 3 (1998): 415-30.

Chapter Eight: The Act of Creation. This chapter treats divine action as a lens for understanding intelligent causation and hence design. Within theism God is the ultimate reality. Consequently, whenever God acts, there can be nothing outside of God that compels God's action. God is not a billiard ball that must move when another billiard ball strikes it. God's actions are free, and though God responds to creation, God does not do so out of necessity. Within theism, therefore, divine action is not reducible to some more basic mode of causation. Indeed within theism divine action is the most basic mode of causation since any other mode of causation involves creatures which themselves were created in a divine act. Intelligent design thus becomes a unifying framework for understanding both divine and human agency and illuminates several long-standing philosophical problems about the nature of reality and our knowledge of it. A version of this chapter was presented at the second Millstatt Forum in Strasbourg, France (August 10, 1998).

Appendix: Objections to Design. The appendix answers the main objections to design that were not addressed in the preceding chapters. I list nine of them: (1) Invoking design is merely a stopgap for ignorance (god-of-the-gaps); (2) Design explains everything and so explains nothing; (3) Design is just scientific creationism cloaked in newer and more sophisticated terminology (here I'm indebted to Mark DeForrest for sharing with me an unpublished manuscript on the difference between intelligent design and scientific creationism); (4) Design cannot be scientific because science trades solely in naturalistic explanations (i.e., the methodological naturalism objection); (5) Design is refuted by all the examples of imperfect design in nature; (6) Design can be explained by appealing to chance (i.e., the selection effect argument); (7) Design is a purely mathematical construct and hence cannot speak meaningfully to biological reality; (8) David Hume's objection—to infer design in nature depends on either a failed argument from analogy or a vacuous inductive generalization based on a sample of size zero; and (9) Design can be inferred only for mundane designers, like humans or extraterrestrials, but not for transcendent designers. None of these objections works. The appendix shows why.

My Thanks

My debts to colleagues are many. Stephen Meyer and Paul Nelson stand out. I've been collaborating with them now for seven years on writing projects, academic conferences and media events, all relating to intelligent design. Our much advertised book *Uncommon Descent: The Intelligent Design of Biological Systems* will appear shortly after this one (at least that's the hope). Steve and Paul have exercised an unmatched influence in shaping my thoughts about design. Their continual prodding and testing of my ideas have proven a constant source of refreshment to my own research.

After Steve and Paul, my closest colleagues are Michael Behe, Phillip Johnson, Jay Richards and Jonathan Wells. I'm especially grateful to Mike for writing the foreword to this book. His book *Darwin's Black Box* has proven a tremendous resource for the intelligent design movement. Indeed the case I make in this book would have been much more difficult without the opening he provided. Phil Johnson is the de facto leader of the intelligent design movement. Phil's unyielding refusal to confuse science with naturalism and his unqualified commitment to let science go wherever the evidence leads have been good medicine for me ever since the publication of his book *Darwin on Trial*. Jay Richards and Jonathan Wells are rising stars in the intelligent design movement. They are not just wonderful conversation partners but also courageous comrades in arms. Intelligent design is controversial stuff. It is not for those who want safe academic careers or packaged tours of life. Jay and Jonathan have recognized as much and are willing to pay the price. For that I commend them.

Work on this book proceeded at the same time I was writing *The Design Inference*. The present book can thus be viewed as a commentary on *The Design Inference*. Whereas I lay out the formal apparatus for detecting design in *The Design Inference*, I summarize that book and lay out its cultural and theological implications in this book. It's therefore fitting that the first chapters of this book were written during my time at Princeton Theological Seminary. Of the faculty there, I'm especially grateful to Diogenes Allen, James Deming, James Loder, Bruce McCormack and Wentzel van Huyssteen. Chapters two, three, four and seven of this book arose out of seminars, lectures and private conversations with them.

Next I want to commend the Discovery Institute and especially its Center for the Renewal of Science and Culture of which I am a fellow (www.discovery.org/crsc). Bruce Chapman, the president of Discovery, and John West, the associate director of the center, have been a constant encouragement to me. They, along with Steve Meyer, who directs the center, have a well-conceived strategy for bringing intelligent design into the cultural mainstream. The center's research fellowship program is part of that strategy. Without a research fellowship from the Discovery Institute, I would have been considerably hampered in my own research. Academic jobs for card-carrying design theorists are still hard to come by. That will change, but during the interim the Discovery Institute is making it possible for research on design to proceed apace. I also want to thank the staff at the Discovery Institute, especially Doug Bilderback, Rob Crowther and Ginny Richards.

Others who have contributed significantly to this book include Douglas Axe, Stephen Barr, David Berlinski, John Bloom, Harold Booher, Walter Bradley, Jay Budziszewski, Jon Buell, John Angus Campbell, Rodney Clapp, Jack Collins, Robin Collins, Chuck Colson, Michael Corey, William Lane Craig, Mark DeForrest, Michael Denton, David DeWolf, Fieldstead & Co., Foundation for Thought and Ethics, Hugh Gauch, George Gilder, Bruce Gordon, Charles Harper, Stephen Jones, Bob Kaita, Rob Koons, Rich McGee, John Warwick Montgomery, J. P. Moreland, Robert Newman, Notre Dame's Center for Philosophy of Religion, Dean Overman, James Parker III, Pascal Centre (at Redeemer College, Ancaster, Ontario, Canada), Nancy Pearcey, Phylogenists, Alvin Plantinga, Del Ratzsch, Hugh Ross, Jeff Schloss, Fred Skiff, Charlie Thaxton, Jitse van der Meer, Howard Van Till, John Wiester, Oliver Wilder-Smith, Robert Wood and Tom Woodward.

Of these I want to thank especially the Pascal Centre (for supporting me financially with a research grant during the very early stages of the writing of this book), Rob Koons (for spurring me to write what ultimately became chapter six for a conference he organized titled "Naturalism, Theism and the Scientific Enterprise" in Austin, Texas, February 22, 1997) and Oliver Wilder-Smith (for spurring me to write what ultimately became chapter eight for the second Millstatt Forum in Strasbourg, France, August 10, 1998).

Finally I wish to commend my family for always standing behind me in my work on intelligent design. Above all I wish to commend my beloved wife, Jana, to whom this book is dedicated. I'm grateful for her love, support and prayers. The reference to Proverbs 31:10-31 in the dedication is entirely deserved.

William A. Dembski
Irving, Texas

Part 1

Historical Backdrop

1

Recognizing the Divine Finger

1.1 Homer Simpson's Prayer

In an episode of the animated television series *The Simpsons*, Marge tries to tell her husband Homer that she is pregnant with their third child. "Can't talk now—praying," he interrupts.

> Dear Lord, the gods have been good to me and I am thankful. For the first time in my life everything is absolutely perfect the way it is. So here's the deal: you freeze everything as it is and I won't ask for anything more. If that is okay, please give me absolutely no sign. [pause] Okay, deal. In gratitude, I present to you this offering of cookies and milk. If you want me to eat them for you, please give me no sign. [pause] Thy will be done.[1]

What's wrong with Homer's prayer? Assuming God is the sovereign ruler of the universe, what is to prevent God from answering Homer's prayer by providing no sign? Granted, usually when we want God to confirm something, we look for something extraordinary, some sign that leaves no doubt about God's will. But presumably God could have made it thunder when Homer asked God to freeze everything and God could have made the earth to quake when Homer asked to eat those cookies and milk. Presumably it is just as easy for God to confirm Homer's prayer with no sign as to disconfirm it with a sign. What then is wrong with Homer's prayer?

Certainly Homer's prayer is self-serving. He clearly wants his life to stay the same, and he also wants to consume those cookies and milk. Since signs are by definition rare, by asking for no sign Homer is virtually guaranteeing that the cookies and milk will be his to consume. As for his life staying unchanged, that's a different matter. Homer's wife Marge is after all pregnant with their third child, a fact that in short order will destroy the "absolute perfection" of Homer's life. Nonetheless if we omit Homer's self-interest, it's not immediately evident what's wrong with his prayer. In the case of the cookies and milk, Homer wants God to confirm a course of action by the absence of a sign. Logically this is equivalent to God confirming the opposite course of action with a sign. "If you want me to eat these cookies and milk, give me no sign" is logically equivalent to "If you give me a sign, then you don't want me to eat these cookies and milk."[2]

There is, however, an asymmetry between tying a course of action to a sign and tying it to no sign. To see this, consider what would have happened if Homer's prayer had gone something like this:

> I present to you this offering of cookies and milk. If you want me to eat them for you, please give me no sign. [loud thunder] Since it's raining outside, I expected the thunder. Thank you for giving me no sign. [powerful earthquake] Since we live on a geological fault, mild tremors aren't out of the ordinary. Thanks for giving me no sign. [radio comes on unexpectedly and the announcer describes the carcinogenic effects of cookies and milk] This part of the country is known for weird atmospheric disturbances, so thanks for giving me no sign. [loud voice exclaims, "Homer, you big dummy, this is God—don't eat those cookies and milk!"] Whoa. Back in my teenage years I used to drop acid. I've had flashbacks and weird mystical experiences ever since. So, God, thank you for giving me no sign. Amen.

The prayer being ended and no sign being given, Homer consumes the cookies and milk.

What's wrong with this prayer? Certainly it seems that Homer is rationalizing away a whole series of signs. By asking for the absence of a sign to confirm eating the cookies and milk, Homer is equivalently asking for a sign to disconfirm eating the cookies and milk. Such signs seem to have been given to him in abundance, and yet Homer rationalizes each of them. Here then is the problem in seeking confirmation through the absence of a sign. By praying for the absence of a sign, Homer fails to *specify* a sign. Thus any putative sign that comes along is easily rationalized—"that's not the sort of sign I was looking for."

Likewise, praying for a sign to confirm something is useless unless the sign is specified. Only if a sign is specified can we avoid rationalizing it once it occurs. So long as no sign is specified, the instruction *give me no sign to confirm eating these cookies and milk* is not only logically but also functionally equivalent to *give me a sign to disconfirm eating these cookies and milk*. So long as no sign is specified, it won't be clear whether an event actually does constitute a sign or is merely a coincidence. Indeed a sign is not properly a sign unless it is specified.

To see this, consider the sign that would have convinced the atheist philosopher Norwood Russell Hanson to become a theist:

> I'm not a stubborn guy. I would be a theist under some conditions. I'm open-minded. . . . Okay. Okay. The conditions are these: Suppose, next Tuesday morning, just after breakfast, all of us in this one world are knocked to our knees by a percussive and ear-shattering thunderclap. Snow swirls, leaves drop from trees, the earth heaves and buckles, buildings topple and towers tumble. The sky is ablaze with an eerie silvery light, and just then, as all of the people of this world look up, the heavens open, and the clouds pull apart, revealing an unbelievably radiant and immense Zeus-like figure towering over us like a hundred Everests. He frowns darkly as lightning plays over the features of his Michelangeloid face, and then he points down, *at me*, and explains for every man, woman and child to hear: "I've had quite enough of your too-clever logic chopping and word-watching in matters of theology. Be assured Norwood Russell Hanson, that I do most certainly exist!"[3]

Hanson has here specified a sign and connected it to personal faith in God. If that sign were to happen, Hanson would be obligated to become a theist. Contrast this with Homer Simpson. Homer connects eating cookies and milk to an unspecified sign. Because Homer specifies no sign, anything that happens can be rationalized to permit eating the cookies and milk.

Although Hanson was clearly having a bit of fun, his challenge illustrates several important truths about signs in guiding human decision-making. First, a sign must be clearly specified—otherwise it can be rationalized away. Second, the sign must be extraordinary. That's not to say it need constitute a miracle. But it must depart from the ordinary course of events. Third, the sign must be clearly tied to some decision. Thus if the sign happens, it must be clear what is to be done or believed. In Hanson's case he would be obliged to believe in God if the sign he requested came to pass. Finally, signs are contingent. In other words, they can happen but don't have to happen. Free agents produce signs and are just as capable of granting them as withholding them. It follows that the absence of a sign provides no guide to decision-making. Thus if the sign Hanson requested does not come to pass, its absence justifies neither belief nor unbelief in God. In chapter five we shall see how these truths about signs provide the basis for how to detect intelligent causes and therefore design. The search for signs is the search for an intelligent agent.

1.2 Signs in Decision-Making

Let us now examine these truths about signs more closely. We will call the agent who looks for a sign the *sign-seeker.* Moreover, we will call the agent from whom the sign is sought the *sign-giver.* The sign-seeker looks for a sign from the sign-giver in order to reach a decision. To leave no doubt about which sign corresponds to which decision, the sign-seeker specifies a sign. In specifying a sign the sign-seeker makes clear which events conform to the sign and which don't. For instance, if the sign specified by the sign-seeker is obtaining a million dollars, then winning a million dollars at a lottery or inheriting a million dollars would both be instances of the sign. On the other hand, going bankrupt would contradict the sign. Note that signs can have time limits. Thus if the sign does not happen within the specified time limit, the sign becomes null and void.

Having specified a sign, the sign-seeker needs to connect that sign to a decision. The sign and the decision will therefore be connected in the following sort of conditional, what I call a *test-conditional:*

If the sign happens, then I will decide such-and-such.

Deciding such-and-such may mean committing an act, uttering a statement, embracing a belief or forming a desire. Alternatively it may mean refraining from an act, keeping silence, chucking a belief or quashing a desire. Just as the sign needs to be specified, so does the decision. In specifying the decision the sign-seeker must be clear which courses of action or beliefs conform to the decision and which do not. For instance, if the decision specifies donating a million dollars to education, then giving the million to either one's high school or one's college would both count. Blowing the million gambling in Las Vegas, on the other hand, would not.

Both the sign and the decision need to be precisely specified. If either or both are fuzzy, then decision-making based on signs becomes fuzzy as well. Only by precisely specifying both the sign and the decision can the sign-seeker's decision-making remain unbiased and disciplined. To see this, consider the following test-conditionals:

> FF: If she resists my advances, then I won't bother her.
> FC: If she resists my advances, then I'll immediately break off all contact with her.
> CF: If tonight she refuses to let me touch her, then I won't bother her.
> CC: If tonight she refuses to let me touch her, then I'll immediately break off all contact with her.

The sign-seeker here is a Lothario, and the sign-giver is the woman he hopes to seduce. The "F" and "C" labeling these conditionals stand for "fuzzy" and "clear" respectively. In the conditional labeled FF both the sign and the decision are fuzzy. Indeed a self-absorbed male convinced of his prowess is unlikely to interpret any act as resisting his advances (short of, perhaps, a knee to the groin). And how could such a self-absorbed male interpret any attention he devotes to a woman as bothering her? The conditional labeled FF is so fuzzy that it permits the Lothario to do exactly as he pleases. Contrast this with the conditional labeled CC. In this conditional both the sign and the decision are clear. The woman's steadfast refusal to let him touch her tonight will be clear. So, too, will his decision to immediately break off all contact with her.

Interestingly the conditionals labeled FC and CF, though containing a clear element, are just as fuzzy as the conditional labeled FF. Indeed the fuzziness in the sign of FC and in the decision of CF destroys any residual clarity. Consider the conditional labeled FC. Since the Lothario interprets virtually all genuine resistance as "playing hard to get," the decision to immediately break off all contact with her can be deferred indefinitely. Fuzziness in the antecedent of FC subverts the clarity in the consequent. Similarly fuzziness in the consequent of CF subverts the clarity in the antecedent. The sign in this conditional is clear enough. But the Lothario will construe his decision not to bother her so broadly that any attempt at seduction will be considered fair game. FF, FC and CF are equally useless. Only CC provides an effective guide to decision-making.

To recap, the sign-seeker specifies a sign and a decision and then connects the two in a test-conditional: *If sign, then decision.* If the sign actually does happen, the sign-seeker is then committed to carrying out the decision. Consequently everything hinges on the sign. Let us therefore turn to the agent capable of giving the sign, namely, the sign-giver. If the sign-giver gives the requested sign, everything proceeds straightforwardly. This is simply a matter of logic. The sign-seeker accepts the conditional *if sign, then decision.* If the sign-giver gives the sign, the sign-seeker is then obligated to follow through with the decision.[4]

By giving the sign, the sign-giver presumably endorses the sign-seeker's decision. But what if the sign-giver refuses to give the sign? Does that mean the sign-giver endorses the opposite decision? Consider, for instance, the medieval practice of trial by ordeal. The sign-seeker here is the court and the sign-giver is God. The court takes someone accused of a crime and inflicts on that person a wound. If the wound heals within an allotted time, then the accused is judged innocent (note the test-conditional: *if the wound heals, then deem the accused innocent*). Normally the wound would take a long time to heal. But since God (= sign-giver) is capable of healing the wound much more quickly, swift healing is taken as a sign by the court (= sign-seeker) that the accused is innocent.

But what if God refuses to perform the requested sign? Does that mean the accused is guilty? Hardly. God is a free agent and under no obligation to act when a human court says to act. Indeed God may so despise trials by ordeal that he refuses utterly to provide the signs they request. Trials by ordeal attempt to force God's hand. A sign-giver, however, is always free not to give a sign. Moreover, that refusal to give a sign must properly be interpreted as *silence* and not as endorsing some course of action. If the sign-giver gives the requested sign, the sign-seeker will not only reach a decision but will also be justified thinking the sign-giver endorsed that decision. On the other hand, if the sign-giver does not give the requested sign, the sign-seeker is not therewith justified in forming a decision. Indeed any decision made in the absence of that sign lacks the endorsement of the sign-giver.

This asymmetry between a sign and its absence is evident throughout Scripture. Gideon, for instance, asked a sign from God to confirm whether he should go to war with Midian. The condition Gideon put to God was of the form *If you make the fleece in my barn on alternate nights wet and dry, then I'll wage war against Midian*. Because God performed the sign, Gideon went to war with Midian. (Note that my intent with the Gideon story and the examples that follow is not to argue for the historicity of such Scriptural narratives but simply to show how they illustrate the use of signs and therewith the detection of design.)

In contrast to the Gideon story we read throughout Scripture of cases where God keeps silent and refuses to provide a requested sign. For instance, toward the end of Saul's life God no longer responded to Saul's requests for signs: "When Saul inquired of the LORD, the LORD answered him not, neither by dreams, nor by Urim, nor by prophets" (1 Samuel 28:6 KJV). God's silence was God's judgment on Saul's persistent disobedience. Throughout Scripture God's silence mirrors human alienation from God. Often human arrogance elicits God's silence. Scripture, for instance, commands not to tempt God by requiring God to perform signs on demand. Arrogant persons who demand such signs should not expect to receive them. When the Pharisees demanded of Jesus a sign from heaven, Jesus responded: "A wicked and adulterous generation seeketh after a sign; and there shall no sign be given unto it" (Matthew 16:4 KJV).

In this text Jesus does not repudiate all seeking after divinely given signs. What Jesus condemns is seeking after signs as a way of forcing God's hand. The Pharisees who demanded a sign from Jesus were privately hoping that Jesus would perform no sign. They had no desire to embrace Jesus as God's representative. By asking for a sign and not getting one the Pharisees would have a pretext for rejecting Jesus. Contrast this with the Gideon story. God had spoken to Gideon and told him to wage war on Midian. Gideon wanted to make sure that he had accurately heard from God. Gideon therefore put out a fleece. (The very expression "put out a fleece" has come to mean "ask for a sign.") The sign Gideon requested was meant to confirm God's word. Using signs to confirm God's word is represented throughout Scripture as a perfectly valid use of signs.

1.3 Ordinary Versus Extraordinary Signs
We've been considering the role of signs to guide decision-making. As we've seen, both sign and decision need to be clearly specified and connected in a test-conditional of the form *if sign, then decision*. Also we've

seen how the absence of a sign provides no guidance for decision-making. The final point about signs that we now need to consider is their extraordinariness. For signs to guide decision-making effectively they need to be extraordinary. Why is this?

To see why, we need to understand the motivation for seeking a sign in the first place. An agent, whom we are calling a sign-seeker, is seeking guidance with a decision. If the sign-seeker's resources for making the right decision were adequate, he or she would have no need to seek outside guidance. The sign-seeker therefore seeks guidance out of a perceived lack or inadequacy. There's more, however. For instance, students who lack knowledge and experience seek guidance from their teachers; yet we usually don't speak of them as asking for a sign from their teachers. Students receive guidance from their teachers by receiving instruction. Now if all our guidance could be conferred simply through instruction, we would not need signs. It follows that signs, if they are to serve a necessary purpose, must guide decision-making in ways that instruction cannot.

Instruction imparts information. It explains why a given decision is correct. It makes rational discourse the arbiter of the decision. But suppose we are confronted with a decision for which rational discourse is inadequate. Suppose no amount of words can enlighten our minds about whether to decide a matter one way or the other. Suppose we are in a situation where instruction is incapable of guiding us. What then? Despite postmodern skepticism and relativism, we live in a cerebral age that regards the human intellect as the sole resource for solving our problems. By contrast, to seek a sign is to admit that human intellect alone is inadequate for reaching a decision. To seek a sign is to acknowledge one's limitations and entrust oneself to the sign-giver.

Even so, this doesn't answer why a sign needs to be extraordinary. In fact a sign does not have to be extraordinary if the sign-seeker has unmediated access to the sign-giver. With unmediated access to the sign-giver, the sign-seeker needs nothing more than a simple yes or no from the sign-giver to reach a decision: *If you say "yes," then I'll do such-and-such.* The reason signs have to be extraordinary is because in general sign-seekers do not have unmediated access to sign-givers. This is certainly the case with God.[5] But it can also be the case with human interactions.

Consider a Persian satrap who is assigned to some outlying province and must decide whether to establish peace with a neighboring barbarian tribe. The satrap, though wielding considerable local authority, is nonetheless a representative of the Persian king and thus lacks the authority to conclude a peace treaty with the barbarian tribe on his own initiative. The satrap therefore sends to the king for guidance, which the king gladly provides. In asking for guidance the satrap is not asking the king for a lesson in diplomacy. The satrap is not a pupil going to a teacher for instruction and trying to determine what in the grand scheme of things is going to be best, peace with the barbarians or war. The satrap simply wants to know the king's will, irrespective of the king's motivations or reasons.

The satrap sends to the king and the king sends back. The communication between satrap and king is not unmediated. It is mediated by scrolls, secretaries, messengers, horses, roads, inns and way stations. Oh, and one more thing—*a seal*. When the satrap receives the king's scroll detailing Persian policy toward the neighboring barbarian tribe, the first thing the satrap is going to look for is an unbroken seal. The seal confirms that the scroll actually came from the king. If intact, it confirms that the scroll was not tampered with after it left the king's hands. The seal is a sign assuring the satrap that what purports to be the king's policy actually is the king's policy. In short, the seal validates the scroll.

The seal is not optional. Because access to the king is mediated, the satrap needs to make sure that any scroll he receives is not a forgery. To ensure that the scroll is not a forgery, however, the seal needs to be uniquely the king's. To be sure, the king could confer the authority to use the seal on a deputy, but if so, the deputy would be acting in the name of the king. No one acting in a name other than the king's must be able to use the seal. Indeed it was a capital offense in ancient times to employ a king's seal without permission.

The seal is extraordinary. That's not to say the seal is supernatural, weird or mystical. But by being uniquely associated with the king's name and authority, the seal assumes a significance above any other in the realm. If the seal were easy to forge or if no penalty existed for dishonestly using it, the seal would no longer be extraordinary and would quickly lose its power to validate the king's communications to his satraps. Gresham's law in economics states that bad money drives out good. So, too, a king's seal that loses its extraordinariness loses its power to enforce the king's edicts.

The story about the satrap and the king is of course a parable. The seal is a sign, the king is the sign-giver, and the satrap is the sign-seeker. Because the satrap does not have unmediated access to the king, the seal needs to be uniquely specific to the king. If others can use the same seal, they can impersonate the king and the seal loses its power. More generally, when a sign-seeker does not have unmediated access to a sign-giver, the sign-seeker needs a sign uniquely specific to the sign-giver. In other words, the sign-seeker needs a sign that only the sign-giver could have given. If others can produce the same sign, they can impersonate the sign-giver and the sign loses its power. Since ordinary signs are easily counterfeited, only extraordinary signs fit the bill. Sign-seekers therefore look for extraordinary signs to validate their decisions.

I've been addressing here two properties of signs, *extraordinariness* and *unique specificity*. Ideally a sign should be uniquely specific to the sign-giver, just as a fingerprint is uniquely specific to a human being. For a sign to be uniquely specific, however, it must first be extraordinary. It follows that unique specificity entails extraordinariness. Thus if a sign is going to have any power to validate a decision, it must for starters be extraordinary. Once we determine that it is extraordinary, we can inquire whether the sign is uniquely associated with only one possible sign-giver. Unique specificity is the more interesting question, but extraordinariness is the question that needs to be established first. Extraordinariness is a necessary condition for a sign to validate a decision, even if it is not a sufficient condition.

To summarize, a sign-seeker seeks a sign from a sign-giver to validate a decision. The sign-seeker therefore specifies a sign and a decision and then connects the two in a test-conditional: *If sign, then decision*. To ensure that the occurrence of the sign actually results from the sign-giver and not from some other source, the sign-seeker specifies an extraordinary sign and ideally a sign uniquely specific to the sign-giver. That way, if the sign happens, the sign-seeker can have confidence that the sign-giver actually did validate the sign-seeker's decision. On the other hand, if the sign does not occur, the sign-seeker interprets this as silence from the sign-giver and has no basis for reaching a decision. This is the general scheme for validating decisions through signs, and it occurs frequently throughout Scripture. Let us turn to several examples.[6]

1.4 Moses and Pharaoh

Signs play an important role in the early chapters of Exodus. In Exodus 3 God instructs Moses to return to Egypt to lead the Israelites out of Egypt and into the land of Canaan. Moses, however, is reluctant to take on this task. Exodus 4 (KJV) begins with Moses fretting about his credibility with the Israelites: "Behold, they will not believe me, nor hearken unto my voice: for they will say, The LORD hath not appeared unto thee." For Moses to be the great liberator of the Israelites, they must first believe that God has sent Moses to liberate them. But why should they believe him? It's not enough for Moses simply to come along and tell the Israelites: "God told me to liberate you. Pack your bags; we're moving out of Egypt."

Moses was concerned about his credibility and rightly so. Moreover, God recognized Moses' credibility problem as legitimate. What was God's solution? It was not to give Moses overwhelming rhetorical skills. Nor was it to move secretly in the hearts of Moses' listeners and thereby inspire faith in their hearts. Instead it was to give Moses a set of signs so that the Israelites "may believe that the LORD God of their fathers, the God of Abraham, the God of Isaac, and the God of Jacob, hath appeared unto thee" (Exodus 4:5 KJV). These signs included transforming a rod into a snake, transforming Moses' hand from normal to leprous and, finally, transforming water into blood. (Note that the important thing about these signs is not that they are miraculous—I'm not making a case for miracles—but how they elucidate the use of signs among ancient peoples and how this use of signs connects with detecting intelligent causation.)

Moses was to return to Egypt with these signs and thereby convince the Israelites that God had actually sent him to be their liberator. The signs were to be presented sequentially so that if the one sign proved unconvincing the next would do the trick. Thus Moses was first to transform a rod into a snake, then his hand from normal to leprous, and finally water into blood. As God put it to Moses: "If they will not believe thee, neither hearken to the voice of the first sign, [then] they will believe the voice of the latter sign" (Exodus 4:8 KJV).

When Moses returned to Egypt, his main problem was to convince not the Israelites that God had sent him but rather the Egyptians. To be sure, the signs God had given Moses to validate his mission were extraordinary. Nonetheless they were not uniquely specific to God. Exodus 7 and 8 describe three signs that Moses performed: transforming a rod into a snake, transforming water into blood and making the land swarm with frogs. Yet in each case we read the following refrain: "The magicians of Egypt, they also did in like manner with their enchantments" (Exodus 7:11, 22; 8:7 KJV). The problem was that Pharaoh's magicians were capable of performing the same signs as Moses.

Well, not quite. Pharaoh's magicians were able to perform the first three signs that Moses performed before Pharaoh. But after that the magicians were unable to keep pace with Moses. His next sign was a plague of lice. The magicians tried to duplicate that plague but were unable: "And the magicians did so with their enchantments to bring forth lice, but they could not" (Exodus 8:18 KJV). How the magicians interpreted their failure is revealing: "Then the magicians said unto Pharaoh, This is the finger of God" (Exodus 8:19 KJV).

How do we recognize the "finger of God"? By witnessing something that God alone could have done, or in the language of signs, by witnessing a sign that is uniquely specific to God. Such signs have to be extraordinary. But extraordinariness isn't by itself enough if agents other than God are capable of performing the same signs. Through their occult powers, Pharaoh's magicians were able to perform the same signs as Moses. Only after Pharaoh's magicians had exhausted their occult powers were they convinced that Moses' signs could only have been sent from God.

The important point here is not the precise place where Pharaoh's magicians abandoned their occult powers and recognized the divine finger. The plague of frogs failed to convince them of the divine finger, but the plague of lice did. Should they have held out longer before recognizing the divine finger, say, till the last great plague, the death of Egypt's firstborn? The degree of extraordinariness we require before attributing a sign to God depends on what events we are willing to attribute uniquely to God. All of us seem to have some threshold beyond which we would attribute signs uniquely to God (e.g., the flamboyant sign that would have convinced the atheist Norwood Russell Hanson to turn to theism).

Although the degree of extraordinariness we require before attributing a sign to God is an important question and one to which we shall return, my aim for now is simply to illustrate the logic by which signs validate decisions in Scripture. Moses wanted to convince both the Israelites and the Egyptians that God had sent him to liberate the Israelites. The Egyptians, however, were proving recalcitrant. Pharaoh in particular was unwilling to let the Israelites leave Egypt. Yet Moses insisted that Pharaoh do just that. This was the decision Moses wanted Pharaoh to reach. The well-known plagues of Egypt were signs to help Pharaoh reach that decision.

It is significant that the plagues of Egypt did not happen out of the blue. *They were specified.* Typically Moses would warn Pharaoh which plague was coming, thereby specifying a sign. In addition the decision Moses wanted Pharaoh to reach from these signs was clearly specified: Let the Israelites leave Egypt. So corresponding to the ten plagues of Egypt were ten test-conditionals:

☐ If the river turns to blood, then Pharaoh is to let the Israelites leave Egypt.

☐ If frogs overrun Egypt, then Pharaoh is to let the Israelites leave Egypt.

☐ If lice overrun Egypt, then Pharaoh is to let the Israelites leave Egypt.

☐ If flies overrun Egypt, then Pharaoh is to let the Israelites leave Egypt.

☐ If murrain afflicts Egypt's livestock, then Pharaoh is to let the Israelites leave Egypt.

☐ If boils and blains afflict the Egyptians, then Pharaoh is to let the Israelites leave Egypt.

☐ If hail devastates Egypt, then Pharaoh is to let the Israelites leave Egypt.

☐ If locusts overrun Egypt, then Pharaoh is to let the Israelites leave Egypt.

☐ If darkness overtakes Egypt for three days, then Pharaoh is to let the Israelites leave Egypt.

☐ If all the Egyptian firstborn children die, then Pharaoh is to let the Israelites leave Egypt.

One after another, Moses urged Pharaoh to take each of these conditionals to heart. As it turned out, Pharaoh took only the last one to heart and only after it was too late. Thus only after all the Egyptian firstborn children died did Pharaoh finally let the Israelites leave Egypt. The sign did its work, but at a terrible cost.

1.5 The Philistines and the Ark
The next example I want to consider is also from the Old Testament; it's recounted in 1 Samuel 5—6.[7] Though not as spectacular as the plagues of Egypt, it is actually clearer for illustrating the logic by which signs

validate decisions. Here is the context. The Israelites have been at war with the Philistines. Wanting to ensure victory, the Israelite army brings the ark of the covenant into its camp. Although the ark's presence in the camp temporarily boosts Israelite morale, once the fighting starts, the Philistines rout the Israelites and capture the ark. First Samuel 4 therefore closes with an Israelite lament: "The glory is departed from Israel: for the ark of God is taken" (1 Samuel 4:22 KJV).

In contrast, 1 Samuel 5 opens with jubilant Philistines celebrating the capture of the ark. But their celebration doesn't last long. They move the ark to the temple of Dagon in Ashdod, and on the first night the image of Dagon falls over, and on the second it is badly mutilated. What's more, the people of Ashdod begin to suffer from painful sores. So they decide to unload the ark on their fellow Philistines in Gath. The people of Gath take the ark but likewise are afflicted with painful sores. So the people of Gath in turn try to unload the ark on their fellow Philistines in Ekron. But the wise people of Ekron refuse to have anything to do with it.

First Samuel 6 therefore begins with the Philistines calling a council of priests and diviners to figure out what to do with the ark. The question everyone asks is whether the God of Israel is afflicting the Philistines on account of the ark, or whether their affliction is simply the result of chance. Until now there have been a lot of unusual coincidences involving the ark, but nothing that decisively ties them to the God of Israel. In particular, no sign has been specified. Bad things seem to happen to the Philistines wherever the ark goes. But bad things have happened in the past. How then to make sure it is the presence of the ark among the Philistines that is responsible for the divine displeasure and the resulting string of misfortunes?

To resolve this question, the priests and diviners specified the following sign:

> Now then, get a new cart ready, with two cows that have calved and have never been yoked. Hitch the cows to the cart, but take their calves away and pen them up. Take the ark of the LORD and put it on the cart. . . . Send it on its way, but keep watching it. If it goes up to its own territory, toward Beth Shemesh, then the LORD has brought this great disaster on us. But if it does not, then we will know that it was not his hand that struck us and that it happened to us by chance. (1 Samuel 6:7-9)

This passage shows how thoroughly ancient peoples grasped the logic by which signs validate decisions. Indeed all the elements for using signs to validate decisions are present. (Again, don't let the miraculous or prophetic nature of the signs distract you; it's the logic that is important.)

The sign-seeker here is the Philistine people. The sign-giver is the God of Israel. The specified sign is that the cows go toward Beth Shemesh. The specified decision is to believe that the God of Israel afflicted the Philistines for capturing and then keeping the ark. The test-conditional that relates sign and decision appears explicitly in this passage: "If it [i.e., the ark as drawn by the two cows] goes up to its own territory, toward Beth Shemesh, then the LORD has brought this great disaster on us."

Note that this sign is indeed extraordinary. The two cows have just had calves. Their natural inclination is therefore to stay with their calves, and if separated, to join them. To move away from them, as in going toward Beth Shemesh, contradicts the cows' natural inclination. Beth Shemesh, after all, was an Israelite town outside of Philistia and removed from the calves. It's entirely *ordinary* for the cows to go to their calves. It's *extraordinary* for the cows to leave their calves and go toward Beth Shemesh.

Although the sign in this test-conditional is extraordinary, it is not uniquely specific to the God of Israel. Other factors could conceivably be responsible for the cows taking the ark to Beth Shemesh. Unique specificity is an ideal to which we aspire in our signs. We want the signs of our test-conditionals to be uniquely specific to the sign-giver from whom we are seeking a sign. In general, however, we have to make do with extraordinariness rather than unique specificity. Still, as the degree of extraordinariness increases, our confidence in the test-conditional increases as well.

Recall the sign in section 1.1 that would have convinced Norwood Russell Hanson to become a theist—skies splitting, voices from on high, a great Zeus-like apparition, etc. Certainly a being capable of providing Hanson's sign would be intelligent and powerful, but it's not at all clear that this being would be the transcendent God of theism. It's possible for technologically advanced extraterrestrials to offer us a freak show that would cause us to take seriously their claims to godhood, much as we Westerners might be able to dazzle the aborigines of Borneo into believing that we are gods through the power of our technologies. Dazzle alone, however, won't buy you theism. A God who transcends the universe has to be more than a special-effects artist. Even so, Hanson and presumably most of us would become theists if we witnessed such a sign. In general then we settle for signs that are extraordinary but less than uniquely specific to the sign-giver whose guidance we are seeking.

There is an end to the story of the Philistines and the ark. Following the advice of their priests and diviners, the Philistines "took two such cows and hitched them to the cart and penned up their calves. They placed the ark of the LORD on the cart. . . . Then the cows went straight up toward Beth Shemesh. . . . The rulers of the Philistines followed them as far as the border of Beth Shemesh" (1 Samuel 6:10-12). Having confirmed that the cows did go to Beth Shemesh, the Philistines were convinced that the God of Israel was indeed responsible for the strange disturbances in their land.

1.6 The Sign of the Resurrection

The resurrection of Jesus Christ is not only a miracle but also a sign. The word *miracle* derives from the Latin verb *mirari*, meaning "to wonder, marvel or be amazed." Truly the resurrection has amazed people throughout the centuries. Believers have been amazed at how the resurrection demonstrates the power of God. Skeptics, on the other hand, have been amazed at how people could be so gullible as to believe the resurrection. This controversy between believers and skeptics over the resurrection has been with us since the inception of Christianity (e.g., the controversy between Celsus and Origen in the third century).[8] It is unlikely to be resolved soon.

Since the question of miracles is taken up in the next chapter, I want here to consider the resurrection not as a miracle but as sign. The word *sign* derives from the Latin verb *signare*, meaning to mark, indicate or seal, and from the Latin noun *signum*, meaning a proof, confirmation or password. Whereas miracles induce wonder, signs induce conviction. The question I therefore want to consider is, What conviction is the resurrection supposed to induce in us? We can rephrase this question in the language of test-conditionals: Since the resurrection is a sign, with what decision should it be paired? Alternatively in the test-conditional *if resurrection, then decide thus-and-so*, what is the thus-and-so?

There's much more at stake with the resurrection than simply astonishing the believers and confounding the skeptics. Consider the following two passages from the New Testament:

Again [Jesus] took the Twelve aside and told them what was going to happen to him. "We are going up to Jerusalem," he said, "and the Son of Man will be betrayed to the chief priests and teachers of the law. They will condemn him to death and will hand him over to the Gentiles, who will mock him and spit on him, flog him and kill him. Three days later he will rise." (Mark 10:32-34)

You heard me [Jesus] say, "I am going away and I am coming back to you." If you loved me, you would be glad that I am going to the Father, for the Father is greater than I. I have told you now before it happens, so that when it does happen you will believe. (John 14:28-29)

Notice two things about these passages. First, Jesus, in predicting his resurrection, clearly specifies it as a sign. The resurrection is therefore not simply some incredibly unusual event that hits us out of the blue. Instead it is a specified event. Second, Jesus wants this sign to elicit a decision: "I have told you now before it happens, so that when it does happen you will believe."

What does Jesus want us to believe on account of the resurrection? From the context it's clear that Jesus intends the resurrection to ratify his entire life, actions and teachings. Now in regard to his teachings, Jesus taught many things that make perfectly good sense on their own and do not require anything like the resurrection to validate them. The golden rule (i.e., treat others as you want to be treated), for instance, is found in various formulations everywhere from Confucius to Kant. This rule makes good sense politically and ethically and does not require a miracle or sign to underwrite it.

Even so, there are things Jesus taught that would remain incredible apart from his bodily resurrection. Two stand out: (1) that Jesus has conquered death and (2) that we too shall conquer death by having our bodies resurrected. Many Eastern religions regard death not as something to be overcome but as something to be embraced. Within the Judeo-Christian tradition, however, death—bodily death—is always an enemy to be overcome. Thus within the Judeo-Christian tradition, salvation consists not in escaping the body and dissolving one's identity but rather in restoring the body and thereby reconstituting one's identity.

But why should anyone believe that after death one's body will be restored and one's identity be reconstituted? All our ordinary experience suggests the contrary. Bodies die and thereafter disintegrate. Worse yet, once they disintegrate, their constituents can be assimilated into other bodies. Cannibals appreciate this point more readily than enlightened Westerners. Yet upon reflection it becomes obvious that most of us carry in our bodies particles that once belonged to other bodies (both animal and human). Suppose someone dies in a field. The body decays and part of it gets absorbed into the field. Years later a farmer plants that field with corn. The corn in turn makes it to market. You then buy it and consume it. Part of this long-deceased person is now part of you.

It is therefore evident that the restoration of the body after death cannot be a particle–for–particle reassembly of the original body. But if our restored bodies don't use the particles that constituted us at our death, what confidence do we have that what gets restored is us? Indeed, why think that we are going to have restored bodies at all? Why not rather think that we have immortal souls that are separate from the body and that upon death permanently escape the body (as in the Platonic tradition)?

The bodily resurrection of Jesus Christ puts paid to these doubts and worries. In his bodily resurrection Jesus' corpse is revived and transformed, and the tomb that housed Jesus' corpse becomes empty. Jesus' bodily resurrection confirms that death has indeed been conquered and that we ourselves shall conquer death by having our bodies restored. Note that the bodily resurrection of Jesus Christ establishes this conviction— and not merely *the idea* of the bodily resurrection of Jesus Christ. For signs to induce conviction they actually have to occur. It is not enough to pretend that a sign has occurred or to wish that it had occurred. According to Miguel de Unamuno, "To believe in God is to yearn for His existence and, furthermore, it is to act as though He did exist."[9] The faith de Unamuno describes is not grounded in reality. The faith confirmed by signs is.

To his credit, Karl Barth appreciated this point. Despite his accommodations to biblical criticism Barth was never willing to give up the virgin birth or the resurrection. For Barth the virgin birth signified the incarnation, whereas the resurrection signified that Christ had conquered death. Observe that there is no logical necessity connecting the virgin birth to the incarnation or the resurrection to Christ's mastery over death. Adam was created from neither a human mother nor a human father, and yet Adam has never been regarded as anything other than human within the Judeo-Christian tradition. Within Christian theology, however, Jesus is regarded as God in the flesh—*Deus incarnatus*.

The virgin birth does not logically compel that Jesus is God incarnate. Nonetheless the virgin birth is the crucial sign of the incarnation, for without it we would have no grounds for thinking that God assumed flesh in Jesus and in Jesus alone. To be sure, as simply an arbitrary act of belief we might hold that Jesus was God incarnate. In de Unamuno's words, we might wish it so and act as though it were so. But people of other faiths can do the same for their messiah figures.

What distinguishes the Christian belief in the incarnation from other beliefs in other incarnations is that the Christian belief is sealed with the virgin birth.[10] Consider what the angel Gabriel said to Mary when she asked him how she could bear a child without sexual intercourse: "The Holy Ghost shall come upon thee, and the power of the Highest shall overshadow thee: therefore also that holy thing which shall be born of thee shall be called the Son of God" (Luke 1:35 KJV).

Within Hebrew thought, to call someone the Son of God was to make that person equal to God. Children, after all, have the same nature as their parents and grow up to be like their parents. The sign-giver in Jesus' conception was God, who incarnated himself in Jesus through a virgin. The virgin birth thus became the sign of the incarnation.

Likewise, Jesus' bodily resurrection became the sign that Jesus had conquered death and that we too shall conquer death by being resurrected. Again there is no logical necessity that connects Jesus' resurrection with his mastery over death or, for that matter, with our own eventual mastery over death. As a sheer possibility, Jesus, after resurrecting and ascending into heaven, might have returned to earth only to die again without resurrecting. Jesus could die a second time, and that second death could be final. Thus Jesus' resurrection does not logically guarantee that Jesus mastered death. Lazarus is a case in point. Though Jesus raised him from the dead, he presumably died again (John 11).

Jesus' resurrection is not a logical argument but a sign. The point of signs is not to confirm what rational argumentation is perfectly capable of deciding on its own. Rational argumentation, for instance, is perfectly capable of deciding whether the product of 29 and 31 is 899. Rational argumentation, however, is not capable of deciding whether Jesus resurrected—that's a matter for observation. Nor is rational argumentation capable of logically connecting Jesus' bodily resurrection with his and our own eventual mastery over death. Jesus' bodily resurrection signifies mastery over death because Jesus himself connects the two: "I have told you now before it happens, so that when it does happen you will believe."

Jesus urges his disciples to accept the test-conditional *If I resurrect, then I've mastered death and so will you.* Accepting this test-conditional requires faith. Indeed, no amount of logical argumentation can ultimately justify this conditional. At the same time, accepting this test-conditional does not require a "leap of faith"—this is not a matter of arbitrary or unexamined acceptance. Jesus' resurrection was fully observable. What's more, there is something supremely fitting about connecting his resurrection with mastery over death. Indeed, what could signify mastery over death more plainly? Jesus' resurrection constitutes an extraordinary sign, one that Jesus himself connected to mastery over death and that his disciples repeatedly verified, not only by finding his tomb empty but also by seeing and eating with Jesus after his death. Yes, the resurrection is a miracle. But more importantly it is a sign that confirms both Jesus' and our own mastery over death.

1.7 In Defense of Premodernity

Speaking to the Pharisees, Jesus said, "Ye can discern the face of the sky; but can ye not discern the signs of the times?" (Matthew 16:3 KJV). His remark is still relevant. Modernity, with its commitment to rationality and science, is wonderfully adept at discerning the regularities of nature ("the face of the sky"). On the other hand, modernity is woefully deficient at discerning the hand of God against the backdrop of those regularities ("the signs of the times"). Likewise, what is called "postmodernity" fails to discern the hand of God. Postmodernity is a reaction to modernity. Whereas modernity hopes to solve all our problems through science and technology, postmodernity renounces that hope. In place of an overarching human reason that unites science and technology, postmodernity offers a plurality of separate discourses of which none is privileged.

Neither modernity nor postmodernity supplies the resources for discerning God's hand in the world. For modernity the world is a closed nexus of cause and effect. Thus God cannot act within the world, as by giving signs. At best God is the ground of being for the world or the condition for the possibility of the world. God's relation to the world is thus not causal (God doesn't act within the world) but ontological (God gives the world its being). Within the modernist perspective it is anathema for God to act by signs and miracles. For God to act that way is to poke the divine finger into the mechanism of the world, thereby disrupting it. Thus even though humans may be inveterate sign-seekers, the God of modernity is not a sign-giver. Modernity's God answers all sign-seeking with silence.

Whereas modernity dismisses all sign-seeking from God, postmodernity allows it but then immediately restricts it to certain groups of religious believers. Yes, to a restricted group of Christians the bodily resurrection of Jesus Christ is a sign signifying Jesus' mastery over death. But postmodernity is quick to add that this sign carries no weight outside that narrowly constrained group. Christianity is but one vendor in the marketplace of ideas, and postmodernity assigns each vendor equal status. Within postmodernity signs apply strictly within a community of discourse. To speak of "the signs of the times," as Jesus does, with the intent that certain signs assume universal significance irrespective of ideological precommitments, is anathema within the postmodernist perspective. Whereas modernity asserts that the sign-giver always remains silent, postmodernity asserts that the sign-giver is irrelevant and that any signs are strictly a matter of private interpretation by the sign-seeker.[11] Deconstruction, the postmodernist move to reduce all reality to texts, epitomizes this view.

If neither modernity nor postmodernity is adequate for discerning the signs of the times, what is? By a process of elimination we seem left with what contemporary intellectuals refer to disparagingly as "premodernity." Premodernity denotes that epoch before the rise of modern science with Copernicus, Kepler and Galileo. Typically premodernity is identified with superstition, astrology, witchcraft, witch trials, alchemy, Ptolemaic epicycles, the four humors, the four elements and so on—what C. S. Lewis called the "discarded image." Now there is no question that many elements of premodernity needed to be discarded. Nonetheless premodernity had one thing going for it that neither modernity nor postmodernity could match, namely, a worldview rich enough to accommodate divine agency.

Because modernity views the world as a closed causal nexus, the modernist God can give the world its being but cannot act within it.[12] Likewise, because postmodernity views the world as a plurality of separate discourses of which none is privileged, the postmodernist God is socially constructed within a localized discourse and cannot be said to act except within such a discourse. Neither the modernist nor the postmodernist God yields divine agency in any traditional or normative sense and certainly not God as sign-giver. Premodernity, on the other hand, does allow God sufficient room to act in the world and specifically to act as sign-giver. How so?

Unlike modernity, premodernity never embraced a world where everything proceeds by natural laws. Premodernity always maintained that the natural causes described by natural laws were fundamentally incomplete and that intelligent causes had free play in the world as well. Aristotle referred to intelligent causes as "final causes," Augustine as "voluntary causes," Moses Maimonides as just that (i.e., "intelligent causes"), nineteenth-century theologians like Charles Hodge as "mental causes," and twentieth-century theologians like Austin Farrer as "intentional causes." Within the premodern worldview, natural and intelligent causes operate in tandem, with neither reducible to the other. This is as it should be, and the burden of this book is to show that natural and intelligent causes can operate in harmony without doing violence either to science or to theology.

What is a deep problem for modernity simply does not arise for premodernity. For modernity, divine action threatens ever to violate the laws of nature. Thus for modernity, divine action cannot but constitute an unwarranted intrusion into the causal structure of the world. By contrast, premodernity never regarded the world as a closed nexus of natural causes in the first place. Consequently divine action has no natural laws to violate. Within the premodern worldview the world is not under the grip of natural laws but is a stage in which natural causes form the backdrop and intelligent causes perform the primary action. Modernity absolutizes something that was never meant to be absolutized, namely natural causes and the natural laws that are said to govern them. Indeed, since the world is a divine act, freely created apart from any law, natural causes constitute a derivative mode of causation, dependent on divine action. Moreover the natural laws that govern natural causes are themselves contingent, dependent on the divine will and with a limited domain of application. In particular, natural laws were never meant to prescribe the total structure and dynamics of the world.

Premodernity, for all its faults, possessed a much keener understanding of certain aspects of the world than either modernity or postmodernity could ever hope to attain. In particular, the premodern logic of signs described in this chapter was perfectly well understood by premodern thinkers but utterly lost on modern and postmodern thinkers. My aim in this book then is to take this premodern logic of signs and make it rigorous. In doing so, I intend to preserve the valid insights of modern science as well as the core commitments of the Christian faith.

The rigorous reformulation of the premodern logic of signs is precisely what intelligent design is all about. The premodern logic of signs used signs to identify intelligent causes. Intelligent design is the systematic study of intelligent causes and specifically of the effects they leave behind. From certain observable features of the world (i.e., signs), intelligent design infers to intelligent causes responsible for those features. The world contains events, objects and structures that exhaust the explanatory resources of natural causes and that can be adequately explained only by recourse to intelligent causes. This is not an argument from ignorance. Precisely because of what we know about natural causes and their limitations, science is now in a position to demonstrate intelligent causation rigorously.[13]

Briefly, intelligent design infers that an intelligent cause is responsible for an effect if the effect is both *complex* and *specified*. A single letter of the alphabet is specified without being complex. A long sentence of random letters is complex without being specified. A Shakespearean sonnet is both complex and specified. We infer design by identifying *specified complexity*. How does specified complexity connect with the premodern logic of signs? Recall that a sign must be specified. (Homer Simpson's prayer for the absence of a sign won't do.) Also, a sign must be extraordinary. Now the simplest way to unpack what it means for a sign to be extraordinary is probabilistically: a sign is extraordinary to the degree that it is improbable. But improbability and complexity are the same notions: a combination lock becomes *more complex* the more combinations it permits; but correspondingly it becomes *more improbable* to open the lock by chance the more combinations it permits. Specified complexity is the contemporary theoretical equivalent to the premodern logic of signs. It is the topic of chapter five.

Intelligent design formalizes and makes precise something we do all the time. All of us are all the time engaged in a form of rational activity which, without being tendentious, can be described as "inferring design." Inferring design is a perfectly common and well-accepted human activity. People find it important to identify events caused through the purposeful, premeditated action of an intelligent agent and to distinguish such events from events due to natural causes. Intelligent design unpacks the logic of this everyday activity and applies it within the special sciences. There is no magic, no vitalism, no appeal to occult forces here. Inferring design is common, rational and objectifiable.[14] Intelligent design takes the premodern logic of signs and gives it teeth.

2

The Critique of Miracles

2.1 Miracles as Evidence for Faith

Between 1650 and 1850, in the period from Spinoza to Schleiermacher, the rational foundations of the Christian faith were fundamentally altered. Previously it had been unproblematic for faith and reason to work together so that reason could supply evidence for faith. But in the period from Spinoza to Schleiermacher, the very notion that evidence could rationally support the Christian faith was abandoned. The father of liberal theology, Friedrich Schleiermacher, stands at the end of this development, summing up the matter as follows in his theological treatise *The Christian Faith*: "We entirely renounce all attempt[s] to prove the truth or necessity of Christianity; and we presuppose, on the contrary, that every Christian, before he enters at all upon inquiries of this kind, has already the inward certainty that his religion cannot take any other form than this."[1]

This was not simply a matter of rejecting Thomas Aquinas's five proofs for the existence of God, or reducing the significance of the biblical miracles within Christian apologetics or stripping the Christian tradition of superstitious accretions. The problem went much deeper. This was a wholesale repudiation of the very possibility that there could be such a thing as rational support for the Christian faith. If it used to be a valid enterprise for Christians to engage non-Christians with the sort of argument, "Here are the things you should believe about God, and here are the reasons why you should believe these things," it was so no longer. Henceforth rational argumentation was to play no role in supporting the Christian faith.

Thus in the period from Spinoza to Schleiermacher we find Spinoza denying miracles and calling them a refuge of ignorance.[2] We find the eighteenth-century deists of France and Britain using Newtonian science to exclude divine intervention within the universe.[3] We find Lessing asserting that contingent facts of history are incapable of yielding eternal religious truths.[4] We find Hume challenging the notion that the universe is designed.[5] We find Kant not only rejecting Thomas Aquinas's proofs for God's existence but also turning God into a regulative ideal whose existence outside human consciousness is problematic.[6] And of course we find Schleiermacher rejecting the very notion that evidence can support Christian belief.[7]

Why this shift? That there was a shift is evident. Thomas Aquinas certainly thought reason capable of establishing at least some truths of the Christian faith.[8] John Calvin took for granted that the truth of the gospel narratives and the truth of God creating the world were evident, even though these truths could not benefit an individual apart from the salvific work of the Holy Spirit.[9] Whence came therefore the rising conviction from the seventeenth-century onward that evidence was irrelevant to Christian faith, and even more significant, that faith was better off without evidence?

In this chapter I will argue that the key to this shift in the relation between faith and evidence was a naturalistic critique of miracles initiated by Spinoza and brought to completion by Schleiermacher. The upshot of this critique was to render miracles incoherent. So long as miracles remained coherent, they could provide evidence for faith. But once they were rejected as incoherent, their evidential value was destroyed. Moreover since miracles had previously constituted the most direct evidence for divine activity in the world, the rejection of miracles became tantamount to the rejection of all evidential support for the Christian faith. In particular the idea that God could act identifiably as a designing intelligence was lost. By rendering miracles incoherent Spinoza and Schleiermacher undercut all nonnaturalistic modes of divine activity and thereby rendered design incoherent as well.

The naturalistic critique of miracles by Spinoza and Schleiermacher fails. This chapter examines that critique and refutes it. Of particular interest will be how this naturalistic critique, as initially developed by Spinoza, was later co-opted by Schleiermacher in his reconstruction of Christian theology. Schleiermacher always considered himself a Christian theologian, but his was a naturalized Christianity that left no room for evidence to support God's activity as a designing intelligence. As we shall see in chapter three, design does not require miracles. But in a naturalized world that positively excludes miracles, design becomes increasingly implausible. This chapter shows that such a naturalized world is itself implausible. I close by examining the significance of this naturalistic critique of miracles for design.

2.2 Spinoza's Rejection of Miracles

Spinoza's refutation of miracles occurs in his *Tractatus Theologico-Politicus*. The *Tractatus Theologico-Politicus* was probably the most controversial book published in 1670 and remained an object of vituperation for many succeeding decades. As Brad Gregory describes the work,

> Spinoza's *Tractatus Theologico-Politicus* provoked some of the most violent reactions to any published work of the seventeenth century. It appeared in 1670 or perhaps late in 1669, and though its title page indicated it was published in Hamburg, it had in fact been printed in Amsterdam. [Though published anonymously] the work and the identity of its author quickly became known throughout Europe. A philosopher had simply expressed his views on the relationship between philosophy, religion and politics. From the responses to the work, however, it is clear that these did not amount to *just* one more opinion among others in a period rife with religious controversy and competing theologies.[10]

At the time of its publication Christian orthodoxy was united in its condemnation of the *Tractatus*. The Reformed Synod of North Holland called for an official ban on the book. In 1674 Willem van Blijenbergh, a Dutch correspondent of Spinoza's, published a work entitled *Refutation of the Blasphemous Book Called Tractatus Theologico-Politicus*, a title that speaks for itself.[11] Blijenbergh went on to tell John Colerus, a Lutheran biographer of Spinoza, that the *Tractatus* was "full of curious but abominable discoveries, the learning and inquiries whereof must needs have been fetched from hell. Every Christian, nay, every man of sense, ought to abhor such a book. The author endeavours to overthrow the Christian religion and baffle all our hopes which are grounded upon it."[12]

The Germans, by comparison, made these Dutch attacks on the *Tractatus* look mild. A work published anonymously at Cothen in 1702 entitled *Presentation of Four Recent Worldly Philosophers* refers to "the abominable doctrines and hideous errors which this shallow Jewish philosopher has (if I may say so) shit into the world."[13]

Spinoza's critique of miracles was not the only thing about the *Tractatus* to elicit such response. His thoroughgoing attacks on the Bible and his equating of liturgy with superstition were equally inflammatory. It remains, however, that for all Spinoza's criticisms against Christian orthodoxy, none of them would have been possible without his critique of miracles in the sixth chapter of the *Tractatus*. Religion for Spinoza had to be purified by philosophy if it was to do any good. Otherwise religion would interminably flounder in the realm of superstition. Religion properly rationalized and purified had no place for sporadic interventions by a capricious deity. Miracles were therefore the chief offender, keeping the masses[14] enslaved to superstitious religion and preventing them from attaining the freedom offered by a philosophically purified religion.

Spinoza's critique of miracles was not fundamentally new. As H. van der Loos observes, protests against miracles have a long history, taking both a religious and a scientific form:

> A common belief is that miracles first became problematic and first gave rise to "protest" at the moment when a certain scientific understanding dawned. And yet there is a protest against miracles that goes back much further, namely the protest of great founders of religions themselves. In China Confucius refused to accept miracles. Buddha was opposed to magic miracles, from which he distinguished the "miracles of the revelation of man's inner self." For the Buddhist, doctrine itself formed the miracle! Mohammed rejected miracles radically; there was only one miracle, the Koran. . . . The protest of the founders of religions was not, therefore, a scientific one, but was the fruit of a criticism that sprang from the essence of their religions. According to them, miracles belonged to the lower regions, and so were in conflict with the higher spiritual spheres of their doctrines.

Besides the religious protest we very soon find a scientific protest—a certain scepticism. The extent of the opposition of Cicero (106-43 B.C.) emerges from the following words: "For nothing can happen without cause; nothing happens that cannot happen, and when what was capable of happening has happened, it may not be interpreted as a miracle. Consequently, there are no miracles. . . . We therefore draw this conclusion: what was incapable of happening never happened, and what was capable of happening is not a miracle."[15]

Spinoza essentially took Cicero's critique of miracles, cleaned it up and subsumed it under the Cartesian philosophy of his day. Spinoza's naturalistic critique of miracles occurs in the sixth chapter of the *Tractatus Theologico-Politicus*. The similarity between his and Cicero's critique is hard to miss:

Since nothing is necessarily true save by the divine decree, it quite clearly follows that the universal laws of Nature are merely God's decrees, following from the necessity and perfection of the divine nature. So if anything were to happen in Nature contrary to her universal laws, it would also be necessarily contrary to the decree, intellect, and nature of God. Or if anyone were to maintain that God performs some act contrary to the laws of Nature, he would at the same time have to maintain that God acts contrary to his own nature—than which nothing could be more absurd.[16]

This is Cicero's critique of miracles, but with a twist. The twist Spinoza introduces is that he places it within the context of the Cartesian philosophy. The Cartesian was ever seeking epistemic certainty (i.e., knowledge that was totally secure and free from doubt). Spinoza's naturalistic critique fits snugly with the Cartesian picture of human knowledge, for a nature that works solely by natural laws can be known with certainty, whereas a nature that is arbitrarily interrupted by divine interventions cannot.

Spinoza's naturalistic critique of miracles must not be confused with an epistemological critique of miracles which he also offered. Spinoza's naturalistic critique does not simply say that miracles, as violations of natural law, cannot be *known*. Such would merely be an epistemological critique. Spinoza does offer such an epistemological critique (as does David Hume almost a century later).[17] An epistemological critique of miracles corresponds to what nowadays is called the god-of-the-gaps objection to miracles: Even if there were such a thing as a miracle (i.e., an event within nature not caused according to universal laws of natural causation), how could we ever recognize it? Alternatively, how could we definitively exclude the possibility that an event was after all naturally caused? Spinoza states his epistemological critique as follows:

> Just as men are accustomed to call divine the kind of knowledge that surpasses human understanding, so they call divine, or the work of God, any work whose cause is generally unknown. . . . Therefore unusual works of Nature are termed miracles, or works of God by the common people; and partly from piety, partly for the sake of opposing those who cultivate the natural sciences, they prefer to remain in ignorance of natural causes, and are eager to hear only what is least comprehensible to them.[18]

According to this epistemological critique, to know that a miracle has occurred is to know the truth of a universal negation. Thus for a person to know that an event is a miracle, the person would have to know that no natural laws explain the event. But this seems to require that one explicitly identify every conceivable natural law that might explain the event and then systematically eliminate each of these laws as inadequate for explaining the event. Formulated this way, the task of demonstrating that the event is a miracle becomes impossible for any finite rational agent.

Though he makes this epistemological critique, Spinoza's naturalistic critique cuts much deeper. According to his naturalistic critique, "to maintain that God performs some act contrary to the laws of Nature [is] to maintain that God acts contrary to his own nature—than which nothing could be more absurd." Spinoza's naturalistic critique threatens miracles with self-contradiction—absurdity. Spinoza's epistemological critique, on the other hand, leaves open the possibility that miracles might exist, though it denies that we could ever know them.

Unlike his naturalistic critique, Spinoza's epistemological critique does not overthrow the concept of miracle. Indeed the epistemological critique is easily enough challenged.[19] Moreover, even if left unchallenged, it does not demonstrate that belief in miracles is irrational. It is consistent with an epistemological critique that miracle remains a coherent concept. Perhaps miracles do not elicit faith, and perhaps they cannot be known in a strict scientific sense. But no epistemological critique can show that it is impossible for events within nature to have nonnatural causes. For a putative miracle like the bodily resurrection of Jesus, for instance, an explanation of how this event could have occurred naturally has yet to be given. Since it is always possible that a naturalistic explanation might be forthcoming, Spinoza's epistemological critique at best shows that designating Jesus' bodily resurrection a miracle is potentially falsifiable. What this critique does not show, however, is that this designation is incoherent. For that we need Spinoza's naturalistic critique, which does contend that the very notion of miracle is incoherent.

Spinoza's naturalistic critique of miracles claims that the very idea of a miracle is self-contradictory. Where then does Spinoza locate the contradiction? Spinoza equates an action of God that is "contrary to the laws of Nature" with an act of God "contrary to his own nature." Since for Spinoza God is supremely rational, God acting contrary to his own nature must be excluded as absurd. But since this possibility is for Spinoza logically equivalent to God acting contrary to the laws of nature, it follows that for God to act contrary to the laws of nature must also be absurd. The obvious question now is how to justify this identification of "laws of nature" with "God's nature." To answer this question we need to remember that Spinoza was a monist. According to this view, God and nature are identical. Thus within Spinoza's monism the identification of "laws of Nature" with "God's nature" was immediate.

Schleiermacher, too, wanted to make this identification, but in his case he had a tougher row to hoe. For Schleiermacher, who had to engage a Christian tradition that regarded Spinoza as an enemy, more had to be said about this identification. So long as the identification was warranted, Spinoza's naturalistic critique could be made to stand. What Schleiermacher did in *The Christian Faith* was to lay out Spinoza's naturalistic critique in greater precision and argue for the validity of Spinoza's identification of the "laws of Nature" with "God's nature." We therefore turn next to Schleiermacher's assimilation of Spinoza's naturalistic critique of miracles.

2.3 Schleiermacher's Assimilation of Spinoza
If Christians in Spinoza's day could not condemn him loudly enough, by Schleiermacher's day they could hardly keep from singing Spinoza's praises. Schleiermacher is a case in point. Indeed throughout his life Schleiermacher could hardly contain his enthusiasm for Spinoza. In his early days (1793-1796) Schleiermacher had regarded Spinoza as "in every

respect superior" to Leibniz—no mean feat.[20] In his subsequent *Speeches* (1799) Schleiermacher would write,

> Offer with me reverently a tribute to the manes of the holy . . . Spinoza. The high World-Spirit pervaded him; the Infinite was his beginning and his end; the Universe was his only and his everlasting love. In holy innocence and in deep humility he beheld himself mirrored in the eternal world and perceived how he also was its most worthy mirror. He was full of religion, full of the Holy Spirit. Wherefore, he stands there alone and unequalled.[21]

In his still later *History of Philosophy* (1812) Schleiermacher would refer to Spinoza as the flower and crown of the movement that began with Descartes.[22] In *The Christian Faith* Schleiermacher defines *freedom* in terms identical with Spinoza's (i.e., a being is free if its actions are determined by itself alone).[23]

In his own naturalistic critique of miracles Schleiermacher faithfully follows Spinoza's sixth chapter of the *Tractatus Theologico-Politicus*. But although the logic of their critiques is in the end the same, on the relation of evidence to faith and on the role of miracles in this relation, Schleiermacher's critique is far more illuminating than Spinoza's. Having placed himself within the Christian tradition, Schleiermacher must try to make sense of that tradition in the light of a naturalistic critique of miracles. Unlike Spinoza, who never hides his contempt for miracles, Schleiermacher must try his best to make room for miracles within what he calls the "system of nature."

Granted, Schleiermacher never in the end succeeds in making room for miracles. But his valiant attempts are more instructive than Spinoza's continual invective against the superstitions of "the common people." Having dashed miracles against the altar of nature, Schleiermacher attempts every means possible to resurrect them. If there is anything Spinoza has missed, Schleiermacher will be sure to find it. More significant, by analyzing what it would mean for God to substitute a miracle for an event that otherwise would have occurred by natural causes, Schleiermacher clarifies what is at stake in preserving the traditional understanding of miracle as God intervening in nature.[24]

In *The Christian Faith* Schleiermacher defines *absolute miracles* as events that entail "an absolute suspension of the interrelatedness of nature."[25] Earlier in *The Christian Faith* Schleiermacher had given his own epistemological critique of miracles (similar to Spinoza's), defining miracles as events "in the realm of physical nature which are supposed not to have been caused in a natural manner."[26] In setting the stage for his naturalistic critique of miracles, Schleiermacher therefore needs to tighten his earlier definition of miracles. At issue is what it means for an event not to have been caused naturally.

Schleiermacher sets up the problem as follows: Nature (or the system of nature as he calls it) is an interrelated (or interdependent) nexus of causes and effects. Ordinarily when an event happens, there is a natural cause that explains it. Thus ordinarily when an event E happens, there is a natural cause C that explains E. Let us denote this relation of natural causation between C and E by "C causes E." Consider now what it must mean for an event M to be a miracle in the sense of suspending the causal interrelatedness of nature (i.e., for M to be an absolute miracle). Certainly M must satisfy the following universal negation: there is no natural cause C such that C causes M. This can be expressed more formally by the following condition:

(i) For all natural causes X, it is not the case that X causes M.

This cannot be the whole story, however. For Schleiermacher (as for Spinoza), nature forms a closed causal nexus. It is therefore insufficient to characterize a putative miracle M as simply an isolated event lacking a natural cause. The problem is that in suspending the interrelatedness of nature, the occurrence of a miracle M precludes the occurrence of some other event W that *would have occurred* if the deity had not intervened and replaced W with M in the causal nexus of nature. A miracle thus always involves a *substitution*. Something that would ordinarily have happened must not happen if a miracle is to occur.[27] A cause C was all set to operate to produce W. But instead the deity intervened and produced an event M that is incompatible with W. Formally this relation between C, M and W can be represented as follows:

(ii) C has happened; C causes W; M is incompatible with W; but M happened instead of W.

Schleiermacher's conception of an absolute miracle can now be characterized as follows: an absolute miracle is any event M that satisfies (i) and (ii). Conditions (i) and (ii) taken together unpack what Schleierma-cher means by "an absolute suspension of the interrelatedness of nature." Absolute miracles are not simply events that are inexplicable in terms of natural causes or (equivalently) natural laws. In addition, they are events that usurp the place of the ordinary events that would other-wise have occurred. Absolute miracles have no place in Schleierma-cher's theology. The upshot of Schleiermacher's naturalistic critique of miracles in *The Christian Faith* is that absolute miracles are incoherent and therefore need to be removed from Christian theology.

Schleiermacher's naturalistic critique of miracles in *The Christian Faith* can now be summarized as follows. With Spinoza, Schleiermacher makes the standard rationalist move of making causality a form of entailment. One thing entails another if the thing entailed has to be true provided that thing doing the entailing is true. Alternatively, A entails B means that it is impossible for B to be false if A is true.[28] Once causality is subsumed under entailment, (ii) is no longer simply a physical claim about the actual world but a logical claim that holds across all possible worlds and whose internal coherence is subject to the ordinary rules of logic.

Corresponding to the original condition (ii), one therefore obtains the following logically equivalent reformulation of this condition:

(ii') C; C entails W; not both M and W; but M.

Unlike the original causal version (ii), the logical version (ii') is directly subject to the ordinary rules of logic. By manipulating this logic, one very quickly derives a contradiction from (ii'):

Since M, but not both M and W, therefore not-W. Since C entails W and not-W, therefore by modus tollens not-C. But C. Contradiction.

Those unfamiliar with elementary logic need not worry about the details of this chain of reasoning. The point is that (ii') is self-contradictory, which, so long as causality is a form of entailment, implies that (ii) is self-contradictory; and this means that the concept of a miracle is incoherent.

2.4 Unpacking Schleiermacher's Naturalistic Critique
This is the bare bones of Schleiermacher's naturalistic critique of miracles.

Let us now unpack it. The most helpful way I know of understanding Schleiermacher's critique is by playing it off against the science of his day. Schleiermacher wrote *The Christian Faith* in the 1820s, well after the rise of modern science with Copernicus, Kepler, Galileo and Newton. In identifying the causal relation with the entailment relation, was Schleiermacher making a move mandated by the science of his day? The correct answer to this question is no. Though in Schleiermacher's day Newton remained the premier scientist, Schleiermacher attributed only limited importance to him. Thus in his *History of Philosophy* Schleiermacher remarks, "[The Newtonian philosophy] is full of true discoveries, but still always only from the observation of single functions of nature, and thus a mere aggregate, without any tendency to bring forth a whole."[29]

The science of Schleiermacher's day was too miserly in its philosophical commitments to yield the comprehensive world picture that Schleiermacher and his fellow Romantics desired. Newton and the British empiricists generally, whether devout Christians like Robert Boyle or skeptical libertines like David Hume, would thus have been unwilling to follow Schleiermacher in assimilating natural causes to logical necessity. Their attitude toward natural causes would have been captured, rather, in Newton's "General Scholium" to the second edition of his *Principia*, namely, "*Hypotheses non fingo*" ("I feign no hypotheses").[30] As Pearcey and Thaxton aptly remark, "[Newton] insisted that the concept of force he had introduced was not an ultimate explanation at all—either occult *or* mechanistic. It was merely a postulate used to explain observations. Ultimate explanations, Newton said, should be left out of science. This is the context in which he uttered his famous expression *hypotheses non fingo*."[31]

Given this minimalist view of science, Newton and his disciples had no difficulty retaining a full-fledged notion of miracles wherein a transcendent deity intervened within nature.[32] Even John Locke, Newton's contemporary and the premier philosopher of his day, regarded miracles as having evidential value and being perfectly capable, as he put it, of "procuring belief."[33]

Hume was the only notable exception among the British empiricists, arguing on the basis of a crude inductivism that empirical evidence could never establish a miracle.[34] Hume's critique, like Spinoza's and Schleiermacher's epistemological critiques, focused on our incapacity to know miracles. Now for all the attention that philosophers have heaped on

Hume's critique, it, like all epistemological critiques of miracles, must always remain inconclusive. Humans are ever devising new ways of knowing things. Even within the hard sciences, Hume's inductivism has long since been discarded. The models of rationality that philosophers of science are currently using to describe the nature and development of scientific knowledge do not close the door to miracles.[35] Epistemological critiques must invariably confront G. K. Chesterton's insight that "we do not know enough about the unknown to know that it is unknowable."[36]

Even if an epistemological critique succeeds in weakening our conception of miracle (say by convincing us that miracles are much harder to validate than previously suspected), an epistemological critique can never succeed in overthrowing the concept of miracle. The problem with epistemological critiques is that our capacity or incapacity to know something is never determinative of a thing's status in reality. Mathematicians are quick to appreciate this point. Consider Goldbach's conjecture, a famous open problem in arithmetic that has been on the books for over two centuries now. As philosophers Bradley and Swartz describe this problem,

> Goldbach's Conjecture [asserts that] every even number greater than two is the sum of two primes. . . . Goldbach's Conjecture is easily understood. In fact we understand it well enough to be able to test it on the first few of an infinite number of cases. . . . [But] for all we know, it may turn out to be unprovable by any being having the capacities for knowledge-acquisition which we human beings have. Of course, we do not *now* know whether or not it will eventually succumb to our attempts to prove it. Maybe it will. In this case it will be known ratiocinatively. But then, again, maybe it will not. In that case it may well be one of those propositions whose truth is not known because its truth in *unknowable*. At present we simply do not know which.[37]

The point to appreciate about Bradley and Swartz's remarks is that regardless whether mathematicians ever prove or disprove Goldbach's conjecture, there is a right and a wrong answer to the question, *Is Goldbach's conjecture true?*—the right answer being either yes or no.

Reality and our ability to know reality are always two separate questions. In the case of Goldbach's conjecture, a definite fact of the matter is at stake. Either mathematical reality is so constituted that every even number greater than 2 is decomposable into a sum of two primes, or there is some even number N greater than 2 for which no primes p and q can be found such that $p + q = N$. So, too, in the case of any putative miracle M, one can take the view that a definite fact of the matter is at stake—Is M a miracle or is it not? One's capacity to know whether a given event M constitutes a miracle will then always be a separate question. Perhaps faith needs to be presupposed before we can know that an event M is a miracle.[38] But the question itself whether M is a miracle will continue to have a definite answer—the right answer being either yes or no.

Now it is precisely at this point that Schleiermacher's naturalistic critique seeks to overthrow the concept of miracle. Yes, mathematical reality is so constituted that Goldbach's conjecture is either true or false. But no, physical reality is not so constituted that miracles can meaningfully be affirmed or denied. To use another mathematical analogy, miracles are like dividing by zero and asking what number one gets. Mathematical reality excludes division by zero. One simply cannot divide by zero. The question—What number does one get when one divides the number two by zero?—admits no answer. The question is ill-formed. It is illegitimate. So, too, to ask whether a given event M is a miracle is illegitimate according to Schleiermacher. The very concept of miracle is incoherent. It cannot avoid self-contradiction. This is the upshot of Schleiermacher's naturalistic critique of miracles.

2.5 Critiquing the Naturalistic Critique

Spinoza's and Schleiermacher's naturalistic critiques of miracles have not gone unchallenged. When their critiques are challenged, invariably the fault is located in their choice of metaphysical first principles.[39] The key philosophical difficulty in Spinoza's and Schleiermacher's critiques remains their identification of causality with logical necessity, or what we previously called entailment. Thus F. R. Tennant will write, "[Spinoza] naively assumed the order and connexion of pure ideas to be identical with the order and connexion of things, and *causa* to be identical with *ratio*. Hence it was natural for representatives of the rationalistic school to assert that laws concerning actuality were characterised by logical necessity."[40]

Unfortunately, simply noting that Spinoza and Schleiermacher collapsed causality into logical necessity does not take us very far in critiquing their view of miracles. Tennant is right in saying that Spinoza identified causality with logical necessity. He is not right, however, in saying that Spinoza did this naively. Spinoza and Schleiermacher knew exactly what was at stake in this identification, both philosophically and theologically.

The fundamental thing at stake for them in this identification was whether everything that happens in the world is ordained by God. What happens in the world belongs to the realm of causality. What God ordains belongs to the realm of logical necessity (the idea being that whatever God ordains happens necessarily). Yet unless what happens in the world can be subsumed under what God ordains, the world becomes a place beyond God's control; worse yet, God becomes a truncated deity who can no longer claim such attributes as omniscience and omnipotence without mincing words. Spinoza and Schleiermacher were not atheists, nor were they process theologians. They were hard-core theological determinists whose theology demanded that everything in nature be ordained by God.

The problem of adequately critiquing Schleiermacher's naturalistic critique of miracles therefore consists not simply in recognizing that causality and logical necessity have been collapsed but rather in showing how they can avoid being collapsed if an omnipotent God who ordains everything down to the minutest detail is to be kept in the picture. This is the rub. Until Spinoza's naturalistic critique of miracles took hold, miracles had been construed as providing evidence for such an omnipotent God. To be sure, without an omnipotent God who ordains everything down to the last detail, it is easy enough to avoid collapsing causality and logical necessity.[41] The problem therefore is to avoid this collapsing of causality and logical necessity without getting rid of God. Equivalently the problem is to find a theological determinism that avoids a strict causal determinism.

To see what is at stake in such a theological determinism, consider once again Schleiermacher's definition of miracle. As he defined it, M is a miracle just in case M satisfies the following two conditions:

(i) For all natural causes X, it is not the case that X causes M.
(ii) There is some natural cause C such that C has happened; C causes W; M is incompatible with W; but M happened instead of W.

Suppose now we ascribe to God omnipotence in the sense that anything God ordains comes to pass necessarily. Omnipotence in this sense can be expressed formally by the following condition:

(iii) For all Y (Y totally unrestricted), it is necessarily the case that if God ordains Y, then Y comes to pass.

Whether Schleiermacher's notion of omnipotence is richer than (iii) can for now be disregarded. The point is that in ascribing omnipotence to God, Schleiermacher (and Spinoza) demanded no less than (iii).[42]

Given (ii) and (iii), Schleiermacher's naturalistic critique of miracles may now be characterized as follows: God ordains the system of nature taken as a whole and thus by implication ordains every instance of the causal relation as it connects a given cause to a given effect; hence for any putative miracle M, (iii) underwrites the identification of C causes W with C entails W in (ii); but once this identification is made, (ii) becomes self-contradictory, and the notion of miracle becomes incoherent. The logic in this chain of reasoning is impeccable, with the chain itself constituting a valid argument. If therefore the conclusion of this argument is problematic, one of its premises has to be problematic. But which one?

The problematic premise is that God should have ordained what Schleiermacher calls a *system of nature*. I submit that there is no system of nature. Schleiermacher's system of nature is not what philosophers call the world, that is, the place where humans live, move and have their being. The very conception of a system of nature already presupposes that the world is a self-contained system of natural causes. In other words, Schleiermacher's system of nature presupposes naturalism from the start. The system of nature is therefore not the world, but a metaphysical fiction that Schleiermacher (and Spinoza) has substituted for the world.

The preceding paragraph asserts more than I can justify in the remaining pages of this chapter. Ultimately the status of Schleiermacher's system of nature must be decided on theological grounds, not with the historical and philosophical analyses that I am attempting here. Indeed, as a strictly logical matter, there is no inherent contradiction in God ordaining physical reality to operate strictly in accord with universal laws of natural causation. As strictly a logical possibility, God could have ordained the world to be a system of nature in Schleiermacher's sense.

But this is hardly the only possibility. It is also possible that God ordained the world to be other than a system of nature. If God ordained the world to be a system of nature, then it is necessary for everything that happens in the world to obey universal laws of natural causation. Nevertheless it is another question entirely whether it is necessary for God to have so ordained the world in the first place. The idea that it is necessary for God to have ordained the world as a system of nature is, as we shall now see, unsound.

The problem with requiring God to ordain the world as a system of nature is that it artificially constricts the range of things God may ordain. This artificial constriction of metaphysical options becomes especially evident in Schleiermacher's treatment of prayer. In arguing against the possibility of miracles as "an absolute suspension of the interrelatedness of nature," Schleiermacher notes that a principal reason Christians are unwilling to give up on miracles is because they understand answered prayer in miraculous terms. As Schleiermacher puts it, "Prayer seems really to be heard only when because of it an event happens which would not otherwise have happened: thus there seems to be the suspension of an effect which, according to the interrelatedness of nature should have followed."[43]

Again we have a case of condition (ii) being fulfilled, this time with an answer to prayer substituting for the event that would have happened if the prayer had not been offered. Naturally this understanding of prayer is unacceptable to Schleiermacher: "Prayer and its fulfillment or refusal are only part of the original divine plan, and consequently the idea that otherwise something else might have happened is wholly meaningless."[44]

Schleiermacher is rejecting what is known as "efficacious prayer."[45] By efficacious prayer I mean prayer that makes a difference in the sense that if the prayer had not been offered, things would have turned out differently. Though Schleiermacher's rejection of efficacious prayer follows as a corollary from his naturalistic critique of miracles, there is a problem here that becomes much more evident in the context of prayer than in the context of miracles. The problem centers around the question of fatalism. Though Schleiermacher was a determinist, he was not a fatalist.[46] The rejection of fatalism by philosophically sophisticated determinists goes back at least to the ancient Stoics. As Roy Weatherford remarks in his book on determinism,

> While the Stoics were determinists, they rejected fatalism. Against the "Idle Argument" (When I am ill it is idle to consider calling the physician, for if I am fated to die, the physician cannot prevent it and if I am fated to get well, I have no need of the physician), Chrysippus responded with the notion of "condestinate" events: events that are [destined] to occur only together.

Thus, I am [destined] to get well *as a result of* my calling the physician. The universal causal determinism of the Stoics makes *nothing* idle or pointless—every little thing or event has its role to play in the grand scheme of the Universe [cf. Schleiermacher's system of nature], without which the world would be different and contrary to God's plan.[47]

Schleiermacher's refutation of prayer constitutes an "Idle Argument." Schleiermacher explicitly repudiates conditionals of the form *If I had not prayed, things would be different.* Yet as a nonfatalist Schleiermacher must surely embrace conditionals of the form *If I had not gone to the physician, things would be different,* especially if he is ill and the physician holds the key to his cure. Chrysippus's refutation of the Idle Argument through condestinate events requires that counterfactual conditionals like *If I had not gone to the physician, things would be different* be taken seriously. How then does Schleiermacher justify dismissing counterfactual conditionals like *If I had not prayed, things would be different?* Whence comes the double standard?

The answer clearly depends on how Schleiermacher understands the range of God's ordaining activity. For Schleiermacher (and Spinoza) God ordains precisely one thing, to wit, a system of nature (for Spinoza it is Nature writ large) whose operation is from start to finish determined by universal laws of natural causation. *If I had not gone to the physician, things would be different* is not an idle conditional for Schleiermacher because the physician operates in accord with those universal laws of natural causation that govern the cure of illness. On the other hand, *If I had not prayed, things would be different* is an idle conditional for Schleiermacher because there is no chain of natural causes from, say, Isaac praying that Rebecca bear a child to Rebecca actually conceiving and bearing a child.

We must now confront the obvious question: Why should God be limited to ordaining a system of nature? It seems that there are all sorts of things God could, at least in principle, ordain. God could ordain that prayers offered in faith get answered and make a difference. God could ordain that nature exhibit a certain regularity for a time and thereafter cease to exhibit it. God could ordain a certain event unconditionally (e.g., God's promise to Abraham to make him a great nation). God could ordain another event conditionally (cf. God's promise to bless Israel if Israel keeps the law). In line with Schleiermacher, God could ordain that all things operate according to universal laws of natural causation within a system of nature. Alternatively God could ordain that only some things, and not others, operate according to such natural laws.

Or God could ordain that nothing operates by universal natural laws but instead ordain only individual events (whether conditionally or unconditionally). Thus in the operation of the physical world God would ordain not natural laws but individual events; moreover, any patterns we discover from examining these events would represent flexible regularities—not inviolable uniformities. On this account miracles constitute sharp deviations from these flexible regularities. Yet regardless what happens, whether an event stays within the expected range of statistical variation or explodes off the charts, the event is as much ordained by God in one case as in the other.

Finally, my own metaphysical preference is to view creation as an interrelated set of entities, each endowed by God with certain inherent capacities to interact with other entities. In some cases these inherent capacities can be described by natural laws. Nevertheless, no logical necessity attaches to these laws, nor for that matter to the inherent capacities. On this view God freely bestows capacities and can freely rescind them, not least the capacity to exist. In performing a miracle God overrules the inherent capacities of an entity, endowing the entity with new capacities. There is, for instance, no inherent capacity for a three-day-old corpse to revive spontaneously. Thus in resurrecting Jesus' body, God had to endow it with new capacities.

In the end, therefore, the naturalistic critique of miracles initiated by Spinoza and perfected by Schleiermacher is an exercise in question begging. Essentially Spinoza and Schleiermacher have God lock the door and throw away the key, and then they ask whether God can get back into the room. Since God presumably makes the best locks in the business, even God is not capable of getting back into the room without a key. By ordaining a system of nature, God builds a closed system of natural causes which has no way of accommodating miracles. But does the world truly constitute a system of nature? As a strictly logical possibility, Spinoza and Schleiermacher may be right in asserting that the world constitutes a system of nature—God could conceivably ordain everything to work according to universal laws of natural causation. This assertion, however, must always remain but one of several live metaphysical options. It is not a necessary truth. It is not the only game in town.

2.6 The Significance of the Naturalistic Critique

In concluding this chapter I want to consider the contemporary significance of Spinoza's and Schleiermacher's naturalistic critique of miracles, especially as it relates to design. Though Spinoza and Schleiermacher are no longer household words and though their naturalistic critique is known only to a relative handful, the legacy of their critique has been to establish a certain normative method for conducting serious inquiry. That normative method is appropriately named "methodological naturalism."[48] According to methodological naturalism, the proper way to conduct any serious inquiry is to focus strictly on naturalistic explanations to account for a phenomenon in question (thereby perforce excluding miracles). Methodological naturalism pervades academic discourse (cf. chapter four).

How has Spinoza's and Schleiermacher's naturalistic critique of miracles helped make methodological naturalism normative for serious inquiry? Granted, their critique is flawed in that it purports to demonstrate conclusively that miracles are impossible, but it actually only shows that they are impossible given that nature is conceived as a closed system of natural causes. Their critique therefore leaves as an open metaphysical question whether nature is such a closed system. Certainly this fault in their naturalistic critique constitutes a philosophical mistake and is worth exposing. But is it a serious fault? And if it is a serious fault, why does their critique continue to carry so much weight? More to the point, why does it continue to underwrite methodological naturalism?

To answer this question, we must consider what motivated the naturalistic critique of miracles in the first place. As noted earlier in this chapter, throughout history there have been protests against miracles. Invariably the reason for such protests is the fear that miracles will undo the intelligibility of the world.[49] Whether it be the world of science or the world of religion, a world into which a deity can miraculously intervene is a world ultimately beyond human grasp. Such a world guarantees that the scientist's search for "a theory of everything"[50] (or what in times past was called the holy grail or the philosopher's stone) is doomed to failure.

The positivistic push for comprehensive rational knowledge, however, has been intense these last few centuries. When comprehensive rational knowledge becomes an overriding desideratum, what philosopher of science Dudley Shapere calls an "inviolability thesis" comes into play. An inviolability thesis is an unalterable presupposition that is to be accepted before rational inquiry can even begin. According to Shapere, worldviews that are controlled by an inviolability thesis "have in common the idea that there is something about . . . the knowledge-seeking or knowledge-acquiring enterprise that cannot be rejected or altered in the light of any other beliefs at which we might arrive, but that, on the contrary, must be accepted before we can arrive, or perhaps even seek, such other beliefs."[51] Shapere argues that the history of science shows that inviolability theses are invariably a bad idea. According to Shapere any such theses must themselves have been learned and therefore may legitimately be altered as we learn more (in which case they lose their inviolability).

Spinoza's and Schleiermacher's naturalistic critique of miracles presupposes the following inviolability thesis: The world is a closed system of natural causes operating according to universal natural laws. For both Spinoza and Schleiermacher, this thesis constitutes an unalterable presupposition that must be accepted before the world can become intelligible. The contemporary twist on this inviolability thesis is that it need no longer be a metaphysical claim as it was for Spinoza and Schleiermacher but simply a regulative principle by which we are expected to conduct serious inquiry. Nonetheless its effect is the same—to ensure the intelligibility of the world by restricting inquiry to naturalistic explanations and thus by precluding miracles. Whereas Spinoza and Schleiermacher were metaphysical naturalists, viewing nature as a closed causal system, contemporary thinkers are usually not as explicit in their metaphysical commitments. Where they follow Spinoza and Schleiermacher, however, is in keeping the world intelligible by considering only naturalistic and therefore nonmiraculous causes.

Is intelligibility worth purchasing at the expense of miracles? And what sort of intelligibility are we purchasing anyway if we employ methodological naturalism as a regulative principle for dispensing with miracles? Is there any circumstance in which we might actually understand something better by explaining it in terms of a miracle as opposed to leaving it unexplained or offering a promissory note that at some future date a naturalistic explanation will be found? This chapter is far spent, so this is not the place to begin answering these questions. Given, however, the infrequency with which these questions are raised in our day and the fact that they were answered differently in times past, it is appropriate to start raising them again.

Methodological naturalism is Spinoza's and Schleiermacher's legacy to us. Under the sway of methodological naturalism, evidence remains as disconnected from faith as ever, the concept of miracle remains a non-starter, and only naturalistic explanations that appeal to inviolable natural laws are permissible. Consequently, methodological naturalism leaves no room for a designing intelligence whose action transcends natural laws (whether by performing a miracle or simply by being irreducible to natural laws). But methodological naturalism is supportable only if miracles can be precluded. And as we've seen, the naturalistic critique of miracles by Spinoza and Schleiermacher fails to preclude miracles. It follows that methodological naturalism is insupportable and that it cannot legitimately be used to bar design. The possibility of design is therefore reopened.

3

The Demise of British Natural Theology

3.1 Pauli's Sneer

Physicist Wolfgang Pauli, once when asked to comment on the view of another scientist, referred to it disparagingly as "not even false." Pauli intended an even greater slur than simply calling the view false. A false view, after all, can frequently be salvaged by correcting some aspect of it. And even if a view cannot be salvaged, it may still be instructive for the way it highlights an opposing view. But to call a view "not even false" is to say it is so misconceived that it should not be dignified with a refutation. If a view is "not even false," to refute it is like answering yes or no to the question, "Have you stopped beating your wife lately?" Either answer gets you in trouble, and so the only sensible thing is to sidestep the question and challenge its presuppositions.

There is a problem, however, with referring to a view as "not even false." The problem is that consigning views to this category can degenerate into nothing more than a trick aimed at avoiding the hard work of refutation. It is one thing to call a view "not even false" because it is so ill-conceived as not to be worthy of refutation. It is another to designate it thus because we have become so jaundiced in our own views that we can no longer consider its merits fairly. Views can be relegated to oblivion for no other reason than that our own prejudices and misunderstandings render them ridiculous, rather than for the nobler reason that newer and better ways of thinking have come along to displace them.

Contemporary accounts of British natural theology almost invariably treat natural theology as a foil to Darwin's theory of evolution. Thus natural theology becomes the evil stepchild that from time immemorial has defiled her noble sister biology, and which through Darwin's efforts has finally been banished from the family of science. At the heart of British natural theology were two tenets: (1) that a designer had created the world together with the living forms in it and (2) that there was a good argument to demonstrate that a designer had indeed acted in this capacity (namely, the design argument).[1] Yet as historian and philosopher of biology David Hull notes, "He [Darwin] dismissed it [design] not because it was an incorrect scientific explanation, but because it was not a proper scientific explanation at all."[2] This assessment—that design does not qualify as a proper scientific explanation along with an accompanying sense of gratitude to Darwin for having freed us from so benighted a way of looking at the world—constitutes the received wisdom about nineteenth-century biology.[3] Accordingly natural theology and especially its core idea of design is regarded as "not even false."

An interesting exception, however, is the philosopher of biology Elliott Sober. Sober, mind you, is no friend of natural theology. Nor does he fault historians for giving the laurel to Darwin rather than to the prince of British natural theologians, William Paley. But against the received wisdom that treats British natural theology as not much better than flat-earth cosmology, Sober's reassessment of the design argument strikes a truly different chord:

> Before Darwin's time, some of the best and the brightest in both philosophy and science argued that the adaptedness of organisms can be explained only by the hypothesis that organisms are the product of intelligent design. This line of reasoning—the *design argument*—is worth considering as an object of real intellectual beauty. It was not the fantasy of crackpots but the fruits of creative genius.[4]

Nor is Sober content to say that British natural theology was a good idea in its own day but was then definitively superseded. Sober will even admit that the core idea of British natural theology—design—may still have some life in it: "Perhaps one day, [design] will be formulated in such a way that the auxiliary assumptions it adopts are independently supported. My claim is that no [one] has succeeded in doing this yet."[5]

Sober makes these concessions because of the way he conceives science. Sober's conception of science does not permit him to bar design from science outright. For him there is no way properly to restrict what entities or constructs a scientific theory may employ. The problem with design, therefore, is not whether it introduces a "nonnaturalistic" entity (i.e., a designer) that on a priori grounds can then be barred from scientific discourse. The ontological status of the designer is irrelevant. The point for Sober is that scientific theories always operate in tandem with auxiliary hypotheses. It's the auxiliary hypotheses that bring theories in touch with the world and make them testable.

Design as the view that living systems originated through the agency of an intelligent cause (and this is precisely what the British natural theologians advocated) is thus according to Sober squarely within the realm of science. Alternatively Sober won't admit that there are any good a priori reasons for barring such a theory from science. But what is needed to make design a viable scientific enterprise—to give it teeth and transform it into a robust scientific research program—is a set of auxiliary hypotheses that brings design in touch with experience and enables scientists to engage in fruitful research. Thus for Sober design remains a live possibility.

How then are we to understand the anthropologist Vincent Sarich when in one of his dozen or so debates with the creationist Duane Gish, Sarich remarks that his debate with Gish is redundant because the same debate was conducted a hundred years earlier and, as Sarich puts it, "You guys lost!"? Though Paley's natural theology had lost much of its appeal prior to the publication of Darwin's *Origin of Species,* design as the unifying principle for biology remained largely intact.[6] But with the publication of the *Origin of Species,* this hegemony of design in biology was lost. In the twenty or so years following its publication, the shift from teleology to mechanism in biology became virtually complete. This is not to say that design was utterly banished from people's minds. Design, reconceptualized as God's providence worked out in nature, was still a faith-commitment to which many working scientists subscribed.[7] Nevertheless, in the period between the publication of Darwin's *Origin of Species* in 1859 and his death in 1882, design effectively ceased to enter the content of science. Sarich was therefore right in this respect: the British natural theologians and by implication their modern day successors had effectively been banished from the domain of science. This, I take it, is what Sarich means when he says, "You guys lost!"

In this chapter I want to analyze the banishment of design from science. Certainly there was a multiplicity of relevant factors here. One can legitimately point to everything from the sociological significance of Malthus's views on overpopulation, to advances in geology that challenged the biblical account of creation, to the intrinsic merits of Darwin's theory. Nevertheless I shall focus on what to me constitutes the overriding reason for the demise of British natural theology, transforming it from a legitimate form of scientific inquiry to a form of metaphysical speculation with no empirical content.[8] Here I have in mind an emerging positivist conception of science for which appeals to a God or designer could only stifle scientific inquiry. In particular I shall trace how this emerging positivist conception of science undermined the key regulative principle of British natural theology, to wit, design.

In pursuing this inquiry I want always to keep in mind the following meta-historical question: Must a respectable historical analysis of the demise of British natural theology invariably presuppose the very view of science that was responsible for its demise in the first place? Sober is one of the very few contemporary scholars who even leaves open the possibility that the answer to this question might be no. Most contemporary scholarship, however, follows David Hull, whom I quoted earlier to the effect that natural theology is "not even false." My own view is that dismissing natural theology as "not even false" cannot in the end be sustained and that natural theology contains an empirical core whose fate is far from decided. I shall therefore argue that adopting the positivist view of science that led to the demise of British natural theology is a positive hindrance for the historian who is trying to understand the demise of British natural theology.

3.2 From Contrivance to Natural Law

When Vincent Sarich informs contemporary creationists that their dispute with Darwinism was settled a hundred years ago and then adds triumphantly "You guys lost!" what exactly is he referring to? In the demise of British natural theology, what exactly died? The history of British natural theology is mentioned in texts that range over everything from philosophy of religion to systematic theology to philosophy of science to evolutionary biology to cosmology. Typically, British natural theology is dismissed with an off-handed reference to William Paley's well-known watchmaker. Even those scholars who give it more than short shrift tend to treat it as a historical curiosity—a close cousin perhaps of nineteenth-century phrenology. To take it seriously is the exception. Scientific correctness demands that the central claims made by British natural theology be rejected out of hand.

There is a litany of objections to British natural theology which over time have become so abbreviated that one wonders whether they can be unpacked as cogent arguments. These objections include the following: to identify God with a designer is to engage in an anthropomorphism; design is a metaphor from engineering that is unsuitable for trying to understand life; Hume showed that the design argument is either a failed argument from analogy or a failed argument from induction—a failure in either case; Darwin showed that design is superfluous; design is insupportable in view of the imperfections in nature; to invoke design is to commit a god-of-the-gaps fallacy, substituting an extraordinary explanation where an ordinary explanation will do; science has no place for a designer. The problem with these objections, however, is that once they are analyzed without presupposing a self-defeating conception of design, the objections are hardly as shattering as they first appear.[9]

British natural theology was born of that great flowering of science in Britain at the end of the seventeenth century. Isaac Newton is the chief luminary here. Underlying British natural theology from its inception was the fundamental intuition that the order of the universe is inexplicable apart from a designing intelligence. Now order is a slippery concept. Order can signify marks of intelligence as epitomized in contrivances. But order can also signify the systematic outworking of lawlike regularities.

For instance, the watchmaker analogy for which William Paley is so famous conceives of the order in nature in terms of contrivance. The watchmaker analogy was common coin among eighteenth-century natural theologians. William Derham popularized it in his Boyle Lectures of 1711–1712, and it was known to Robert Boyle even before that.[10]

According to Paley, if we find a watch in a field, the watch's adaptation of parts to telling time ensures that it is the product of an intelligence. So too, the marvelous adaptations of means to ends in organisms ensure that organisms are the product of an intelligence.

Thus from its inception British natural theology conceived of order in terms of *contrivance*. But order can also be conceived in terms of lawlike regularities. The laws of nature, and in particular Newton's laws, could as well be regarded as instances of order in the world. From its inception British natural theology therefore also conceived of order in terms of *natural law*.

These dual notions of contrivance and natural law were to have an uneasy alliance within British natural theology, with natural law in the end swallowing up contrivance. Even in the watchmaker analogy we see the seeds for a conflict between contrivance and natural law. Once a watch is manufactured and set in operation, natural laws govern its behavior. The structure of the watch is a matter of contrivance. But once that structure is in place, the dynamics of the watch are controlled by natural laws. But take this reasoning a step further. The structure of the watch itself is attributable to the dynamics of certain watchmakers, watchmakers busily at work putting their watches together. What is to prevent the dynamics of those watchmakers in turn from being characterized by natural laws?

Short of things just popping into existence, anything that has a history within the nexus of cause and effect presumably operates in accord with natural laws. Now if the putative contrivances of nature could themselves be explained in terms of natural laws, then the only instance of order for which British natural theology would need to invoke a designer is the natural laws themselves. But then the watchmaker analogy falls flat, for natural laws are not themselves contrivances. What's more, it is no longer clear what need there is for a designer since designers by definition design artifacts/contrivances, not abstracted lawlike regularities. A designer who is merely a law-giver always ends up being dispensable, for the laws of nature always have an integrity of their own and can thus just as well be treated as brute facts (as opposed to edicts of a clandestine law-giver).

Here we see the course by which British natural theology died. When during the heyday of British natural theology in the late eighteenth century

William Paley and Thomas Reid fashioned their design arguments in terms of contrivance, their arguments fell on eager ears. By the time the authors of the Bridgewater treatises recycled the same arguments for their readers in the 1830s and "played endlessly on the theme of God's wisdom and goodness deduced from nature,"[11] their arguments fell on deaf ears. By the 1830s the action in natural theology among the British intelligentsia was no longer in contrivance but in natural law. It's therefore not surprising that the eight Bridgewater treatises should quickly be dubbed the "Bilgewater treatises."[12]

Charles Babbage, the Lucasian professor of mathematics at Cambridge,[13] offers an invaluable window into the state of British natural theology in the 1830s. Shortly following the publication of the eight original Bridgewater treatises, Babbage wrote a response to them, which he cheekily entitled the *Ninth Bridgewater Treatise*. The tack Babbage took is revealing. To be sure, Babbage was having some fun tweaking the noses of the Bridgewater authors, especially William Buckland.[14] The thing to note, however, is that Babbage never doubted that the wisdom and goodness of God were revealed in creation. The question in dispute was over how these attributes of God were revealed:

> [*The Ninth Bridgewater Treatise*] presented God as a divine programmer, and Babbage used his hand-cranked calculator to prove the point. He set out to undermine the conservative view of God as a tinkering miracle-monger. He was a divine legislator, far-seeing, not a feudal monarch acting on whim. Out went the notion of "Creative Interference," as Buckland called it; no more *ad hoc* miracles each time a minor mollusc or fossil feline was needed. Such nonsense undermined rational science and sound religion, denying God "the highest attribute of omnipotence," foresight. On Babbage's smart machine any sequence of numbers could be programmed to cut in, however long another series had been running. By analogy, God at Creation had appointed new sets of animals and plants to appear like clockwork throughout history—he had created the laws which produced them, rather than creating them direct. Babbage's God displayed "a degree of power and of knowledge of a far higher order."[15]

It would appear that Babbage was giving his readers more for their natural-theological dollar (or should I say pound sterling) than the authors of the eight Bridgewater treatises. Whereas the designer of the eight Bridgewater treatises is a Chinese acrobat, simultaneously twirling an incredible number of plates poised on sticks, constantly having to intervene to keep those plates from crashing to the ground, the designer of the *Ninth Bridgewater Treatise* is a gray eminence who in working secretly behind the scenes through various inscrutable laws has master-minded the whole show of creation. Surely the latter constitutes a more noble conception of the Creator than the former. And yet there is a fundamental sense in which Babbage, with his newfangled, hyped-up, law-based natural theology, is delivering less than the oldfangled natural theology of Paley. For the programs that the divine programmer has woven into the laws of nature and that produce all the things for which the authors of the eight Bridgewater treatises credited supernatural inter-vention (Buckland's "creative interference") are unknowable.

We can commend the maker of a contrivance because we ourselves are makers of contrivances. We can compare contrivances in terms of their complexity and commend the maker of a contrivance in accord with the difficulties that stand in the way of making the contrivance. Miniaturiza-tion, functional interdependence of parts, elegance, reliability, complexity and redundancy are just a few of the criteria by which we identify and assess the intelligence responsible for a contrivance.

But how shall we even begin to commend a programmer whose pro-grams are entirely beyond our ken? Babbage never claimed to have access to the natural laws qua programs which the Creator employed to produce things like mollusks or felines, much less how natural laws qua programs could give rise to such objects of nature. At best then Babbage's program-mer could be commended for the objects generated by the natural laws qua programs. Babbage's programs could never be known directly but only through the putative outputs of those programs. But a program that is known only by its outputs is no more perspicuous than a designer who acts according to Buckland's "creative interference."

And this is why Babbage's approach to natural theology ultimately failed to carry the day. Babbage, despite being the premier logician of his day, failed to follow the logic of his approach through to the end. At first blush it seems far more sophisticated and clever—and far more worthy of an exalted Creator—to locate design not in contrivances but in natural laws. Moreover, the damage done to natural theology by tak-ing this approach, at least at first, seems minimal. Thus instead of repeated acts of supernatural intervention producing the contrivances of nature, unknown (and perhaps unknowable) natural laws put in operation by the Creator henceforth produce the contrivances of nature.

But in fact the effect of locating design in natural laws is far more radical. The problem is that by locating design in natural laws rather than in the objects of nature, it becomes impossible to form a coherent connection between nature and any putative designer of nature. For natural laws produce their effects by an impersonal, automatic necessity.[16] What to the oldfangled natural theologians like William Paley and Thomas Reid had seemed like contrivances, that is, instances of order exhibiting clear marks of intelligence, now became contrivances only in the derivative sense of being produced by automatic processes that were in turn designed.

But as soon as design is located in natural laws, design becomes an empty metaphor. I know what it is for a watch to be designed. I only know what it is for the *process* of making a watch to be designed in the derivative sense that I know what it is for a watch to be designed. Locating design in natural laws has the effect of reversing this ordinary logic and thereby vitiating design. If I can't ascertain that a thing is designed, I can't ascertain that the process giving rise to the thing is designed. Unless we can infer an intelligent agent from the structure, dynamics and function of *things*, we are not going to infer such an agent from the *processes* that agent supposedly used to bring about those things. If imputing design to things is problematic, then imputing design to the processes that give rise to those things is doubly problematic.

And this is why the oldfangled natural theologians like Reid and Paley always located design in the contrivances of nature. As Thomas Reid put it in the 1780s,

> Whoever maintains that there is no force in the [general rule that from marks of intelligence and wisdom in effects a wise and intelligent cause may be inferred], denies the existence of any intelligent being but himself. He has the same evidence for wisdom and intelligence in God as in a father or brother or friend. He infers it in both from its effects, and these effects he discovers in the one as well as the other.[17]

That there were objects in nature which Paley and Reid could rightly call "contrivances" followed because such objects exhibited *marks* or *indicia* that clearly signaled the activity of an intelligent agent, that is, a designer. In contrast, the newfangled natural theologians, like Babbage, by locating design not in the contrivances of nature but in natural law, stripped design of its force and meaning.

This became particularly evident once Babbage's successors, like Darwin, who were no longer impressed that the inscrutable wisdom of God was being worked out in those natural laws, started trying to make sense of those very natural laws that for Babbage had been instituted by the divine legislator. Try as they might, Darwin and his circle could never find any law that was designed. What they found instead was this: As soon as one begins to understand any natural law that accounts for the appearance of design, it no longer becomes possible to locate design in the law except as a superadded principle devoid of empirical content. Natural laws produce their effects by an impersonal, automatic necessity. Natural laws that can account for contrivance thus explain away contrivance, for they explain their effects without themselves needing explanation.

Of course one can always choose to explain natural laws by recourse to a designer, as Babbage did, but one can explain them equally well as brute facts. Both approaches become empirically equivalent as soon as natural laws are regarded as empirically adequate to account for all the objects of nature. Indeed it's only when natural laws are viewed as incomplete, so that without the activity of an intelligent agent it is not possible to bring about a given object of nature, that natural theology can remain a valid enterprise.

3.3 From Natural Law to Agnosticism

But natural theology did not remain a valid enterprise, succumbing instead to a positivist view of science that emerged in the nineteenth century. Neal Gillespie describes this positivist view of science in terms of several key regulating principles, including the uniformity of nature, the regularity of law and the full sufficiency of physical causes.[18] Gillespie is right as far as he goes in his description of positivism. But what Gillespie omits is that when the emerging positivist science of Darwin's day finally reached maturity in the 1870s, it was to incorporate a full-blown agnosticism that viewed anything beyond physical causes as not only unknown but also unknowable. It was this agnosticism that would ultimately deal the death blow to British natural theology.

Initially this agnosticism was not spelled out. For Babbage it was still a matter of course that God had designed the world, even if God had used more subtle means than Buckland's creative interference. But with Darwin the design of the world and of life in particular was no longer evident. As Gillespie describes it,

> There were, in effect, two Darwins: one had caught the vision of [the new positivistic] method; the other still adhered to the older view that the very possibility of there being such a thing as science was necessarily linked to theism as the source of meaning and rationality in nature. . . . [Darwin] rejected the creationist doctrine of divine intervention or superintendence because it was philosophically incompatible with the tenets of an emerging positive science . . . ; because its acceptance restrained the advance of science by erecting metaphysical and mysterious barriers against inquiry; and because, if true, it made God responsible for the horrors, wastes, and irrationalities of nature, and the order of nature itself a delusion and a mockery. Darwin's own approach to evolution fell short of complete positivism. Because of the theological elements in his thought, he continued to speculate—how seriously is admittedly a question—on the possibility of the creation of the first form of life and was loath to abandon the universe to the full meaninglessness that a completely positive view of the cosmos entailed.[19]

The point to recognize is that whereas Babbage, by employing a computer metaphor, was still willing to locate design in the world, Darwin could no longer make this move with conviction. Of Gillespie's two Darwins, the Darwin qua scientist consistently resisted design. On the other hand, the Darwin qua metaphysician was in a constant muddle over design. Toward the end of his life Darwin would deny design any epistemic force by writing that God's existence is "beyond the scope of man's intellect."[20]

It was therefore entirely appropriate that around this time Darwin's chief apologist, Thomas Huxley, should have coined the words *agnostic* and *agnosticism*. According to the second edition of the *Oxford English Dictionary*, the word *agnostic* was coined by Huxley in 1869, with the word *agnosticism* making its appearance the following year. The occasion for Huxley introducing the term was a party to celebrate the formation of the Metaphysical Society, forerunner to the Aristotelian Society. R. H. Hutton, in a letter dated 1881, notes that Huxley took the word *agnostic* from "St. Paul's mention of the altar to 'the Unknown God'."[21]

There's a deep irony here. In the book of Acts Paul informs the Athenian intellectuals of the Areopagus that the God who is unknown to them and whom they commemorate with their altar to "the Unknown God" is the very God whom Paul will now make clear to them: "For as I passed by, and beheld your devotions, I found an altar with this inscription, TO THE UNKNOWN GOD. Whom therefore ye ignorantly worship, him declare I unto you" (Acts 17:23 KJV). On the other hand, after two millennia of Western thought thoroughly imbued with Paul's teachings about God, Huxley would have his colleagues revert to the unknown God of the Athenians. Insofar as Huxley will retain any God, it is one about whom he has no knowledge, nor indeed can have any knowledge. Thus for Huxley, Paul was presumptuous, claiming too much for his theology.

The primary definition that the second edition of the *Oxford English Dictionary* assigns to the term *agnostic* (and by implication to the "doctrine of the agnostics," i.e., *agnosticism)* is the one originally intended by Huxley: "One who holds that the existence of anything beyond and behind material phenomena is unknown and (so far as can be judged) unknowable, and especially that a First Cause and an unseen world are subjects of which we know nothing." Huxley invented the term *agnostic* as a label for himself to avoid having to affirm or deny God's existence. As Desmond and Moore note, "[Huxley] did not pretend to know whether the world is made of matter, spirit, or whatever. Like 'lunar politics,' the subject was endlessly and pointlessly debateable. Darwin's science stood above such squabbles, dealing with the knowable world. To Huxley Darwinism was 'not only "unsectarian" but . . . altogether "secular".' "[22]

Though agnosticism began as a device for Huxley to avoid the charge of atheism (*atheism* at the time still being a term of reproach), agnosticism soon became a doctrine in its own right. In his discussions of agnosticism John Warwick Montgomery distinguishes soft-boiled agnostics from hard-boiled agnostics.[23] The soft-boiled variety admit that they don't know whether there is a God but are willing to investigate the matter to find out. The hard-boiled variety also admit that they don't know whether there is a God but then immediately contend that such knowledge is impossible to attain. It's clear that Huxley's agnosticism was never a soft-boiled agnosticism, that is, never a synonym for removable ignorance. Indeed the agnosticism that entered science in the 1870s and became a regulating principle for the proper conduct of science was to regard God and design as strictly outside scientific competence.

Huxley's agnosticism might appear to leave an opening for natural theology: Although natural theology doesn't fall within science, it might fall within some other mode of discourse. But of course that was the whole point of British natural theology, that the general revelation of nature, whose study belonged to science, as well as the special revelation of Scripture, whose study belonged to theology, could both provide reliable knowledge about the Creator. The move to agnosticism as a regulative principle for science thus became the death blow for British natural theology. It's not that natural theology was false but that it had entered Pauli's category of being "not even false." It had effectively been severed from science.

The effect of agnosticism was to purge science of anything nonmaterial. The initial positivist impulse to give natural laws their proper due thus quickly turned into the positivist dogma that no aspect of nature stands outside the absolute and total control of natural laws. Babbage wanted to give natural laws their proper due as a means of assigning proper credit to the designer who had instituted those natural laws. The agnosticism of the 1870s dissolved Babbage's problem of properly assigning credit to natural laws on the one hand and the designer on the other. The designer was henceforth wholly dispensable, and science became concerned solely with what was accountable in terms of natural laws. To invoke a designer was no longer scientifically neutral. Rather it was to stifle scientific inquiry, for science properly conceived was about the outworking of natural laws. As a matter of scientific correctness, talk of a designer was properly to be omitted from polite scientific conversation.[24] British natural theology was dead in the water.

3.4 Darwin and His Theory

I have described the demise of British natural theology as occurring in three stages. In its heyday natural theology viewed nature as replete with contrivances directly attributable to God's action in nature (cf. Paley and Reid).[25] Under the positivist impulse to explain natural phenomena by means of natural laws, natural theology next sought to locate divine action in natural laws (cf. Babbage and Lyell).[26] Natural laws, however, proved too thin a soup to support the activity of a designer. Thus a mature positivism, in setting itself the task of explaining natural phenomena without recourse to design, delivered natural theology its death blow.

In this shift from a thriving industry at the turn of the nineteenth century to a moribund enterprise in the 1870s, what was Darwin's role?

When Richard Dawkins, tongue in cheek, remarks that Darwin made it possible to become an intellectually fulfilled atheist,[27] he is not far from the truth. Of course Darwin never admitted to atheism, nor was he consciously trying to convert anyone to atheism.[28] Nevertheless, by means of his theory he, probably more than any other nineteenth-century figure, undermined the notion that God is indispensable for explaining the apparent contrivances in nature. Biology still needed an explanation. The living world, after all, was filled with things that looked contrived. Let the positivists talk all they want about the power of natural laws to generate organisms. In his *Dialogues Concerning Natural Religion* David Hume had argued the same.[29]

Yet even the self-avowed atheist Richard Dawkins will admit that at the end of the eighteenth century he would have found Paley more persuasive than Hume.[30] It was not enough for positivists and prepositivists like Hume and Spinoza to tout the potentialities of natural laws to create living things. Until they could explicitly identify the natural laws that gave rise to the apparent contrivances of nature, the persuasive power of the design arguments advanced by British natural theologians would remain intact.

Napoleon III once remarked that one never really destroys a thing till one has replaced it. Atheists, materialists and naturalists had been offering promissory notes left and right that natural laws were sufficient to explain life. It was Darwin's theory, however, that put paid to these promissory notes. At least this is how Darwin saw his accomplishment. The fact is, however, that even at the height of Darwin's personal popularity in the 1870s and 1880s, when he was known as the sage of Down (his place of residence), there were few strict adherents to his theory. After his death doubts about his theory grew even worse.[31]

According to Darwin's theory, speciation occurs through the joint action of variation and natural selection. Organisms exhibit variations, and nature selects those organisms whose variations confer some advantage upon them. Over time this joint action of variation and selection is said to produce new species. When Darwin's theory appeared, it generally was not accepted in the form he delivered it. Indeed very few of Darwin's contemporaries and immediate successors held that his selectionist mechanism was sufficient to account for speciation. How then does one account for Darwin's amazing popularity and prestige when the very theory on which his fame was supposed to rest was in general not accepted? Darwin's fame stands in marked contrast to the fame of physicists like Isaac Newton and James Maxwell, whose theories, in addition to making them famous, were also taken over *in toto*. Gillespie accounts for this paradox as follows:

> Darwin . . . found scientists becoming more and more positivistic, and made them aware of the implications of this for biology. He made them evolutionists; but, ironically, he could not make them selectionists. As Chauncy Wright noted, "It would seem, at first sight, that Mr. Darwin has won a victory, not for himself but for Lamarck." It is sometimes said that Darwin converted the scientific world to evolution by showing them the process by which it had occurred. Yet the uneasy reservations about natural selection among Darwin's contemporaries and the widespread rejection of it from the 1890s to the 1930s suggest that this is too simple a view of the matter. It was more Darwin's insistence on totally natural explanations than on natural selection that won their adherence.[32]

Gillespie has hit the nail on the head. It was not the precise formulation of Darwin's theory that in the end was responsible for his fame. This is not to say that the details of his theory were unimportant. Indeed, though transmutation (i.e., the evolution of living forms) was in the air since the early 1800s, it generally lacked rigor and was poorly packaged.[33] Darwin was the first to offer a "complete theoretical account for effecting the transmutation of species."[34] He showed how it could be done in purely naturalistic terms. By giving a plausible picture of how mechanization could take command and make life submit to mechanistic explanation, he cleared the ground for the triumphant march of mechanistic explanations in biology. The precise formulation of his theory was therefore not of primary importance. If he did not give us the true theory of life, he at least showed us what the true theory must look like. And he left no doubt that the true theory must be mechanistic.

The question remains, however, if in Darwin's own day his theory was not in general accepted as is, and if to this day biologists dispute the precise naturalistic mechanism that accounts for the origin and development of life, whence came the confidence that there even is a naturalistic mechanism of this sort? Darwinism fits too conveniently with the rising tide of positivism in mid-nineteenth-century Britain. To paraphrase Voltaire, if Darwin didn't exist, the positivists would have had to invent him.

It's therefore fair to ask, Is Darwin's insistence that biology limit its attention to naturalistic mechanisms, like variation and selection, a case of the science driving the metaphysics? That is, Is it that science has solved or, perhaps better yet, dissolved the problems raised by a designer who acts in the world, and has science done this by giving an adequate naturalistic account of everything that was previously attributed to that designer? Or is it rather a case of a naturalistic metaphysics driving science and redefining the nature of science? Darwin's contemporary William Hopkins, for instance, attributed the success of Darwinism to the naturalistic metaphysics bequeathed by positivism: "Views like [Darwin's] rest, in fact, on no demonstrative foundation, but . . . on *a priori* considerations, and on what appears to us a restricted, instead of an enlarged view of the physical causes, operations, and phenomena which constitute what we term Nature."[35] Let us now turn to this criticism of Darwin, analyzing it in relation to the problem of miracles.

3.5 Design and Miracles

In this day when the fact-value distinction has been considerably blurred and when the myth of scientific neutrality has been exploded, to say that Darwinism was driven by a naturalistic metaphysics is to be greeted not so much with outrage as indifference. So what? So what if the naturalistic metaphysics characteristic of Comte's positivism was the impetus for Darwin formulating his theory? It's the theory that's important. It's the theory that must stand or fall on its own merits. Is that theory helping us to understand how life originated and developed? I share this sentiment. But if this sentiment—to improve our understanding of biological origins and development—is really the important thing, then it seems unconscionable to define out of existence alternative explanations that attempt to account for life. And this is precisely what Darwin and his circle did. Not only did they put forward a theory of speciation, but they also insulated that theory within a positivistic cocoon that henceforth would admit only those theories that proposed to account for life in terms of naturalistic mechanisms. Darwin's theory just happened to be the best such naturalistic account available.[36]

It's this artificial constraining of discourse which Phillip Johnson in his critique of Darwinism challenges so strenuously,[37] and which I want now to examine in reference to British natural theology. Specifically I will argue that the dismantling of natural theology at the hands of Darwin and his positivist circle was never successfully carried out but rather was achieved by a subterfuge. This is not to say that natural theology was without faults—Darwin rightly pointed to many faults, especially naive expositions that focused unduly on the benevolence of nature.[38] But at its core natural theology harbored a notion of design which the Darwinian revolution never adequately addressed. If the fundamental question had not been *What is the best empirical account of life that satisfies a naturalistic metaphysics?* but instead *What is the best empirical account of life irrespective of metaphysical commitments?* then design could never have been dismissed as easily as it was.

In repudiating natural theology Darwin and his circle invariably conflated design with miracles. Miracles, especially the biblical accounts of special creation when construed literally, were said to lie outside of science. As Darwin put it, "I would give absolutely nothing for the theory of Natural Selection if it requires miraculous additions at any one stage of descent."[39] After all, what sort of science explains events by attributing them to "miraculous additions"? *Why is such-and-such the case? Because God did it!* What sort of science makes God the stopgap for every pocket of human ignorance? It was this objection, what nowadays is known as the god-of-the-gaps objection to natural theology, that underlay Darwin's critique of natural theology in general and of design in particular. According to this critique, miracles, as extraordinary events caused by a supernatural agent, stand outside the domain of science because the cause of such events is not open to empirical scrutiny.[40] Thus if design presupposes "miraculous additions," then design cannot be a proper subject for scientific investigation.

But—and this is the crucial point—as soon as it is realized that design and miracles are separate issues that are not logically connected, the question of design in biology immediately revives. Among the very few of Darwin's contemporaries who understood this point was, perhaps surprisingly, the Princeton theologian Charles Hodge. With a keen sense for the obvious, Hodge was quick to grasp that the reason Darwin had to propose a naturalistic mechanism to explain life in the first place was because life demanded an explanation.[41] Like a tree in a forest, this point is so obvious as to be easily missed. Even if life was not the contrivance of an artificer, it had the appearance of contrivance, and that appearance needed explaining.[42] Darwin's theory offered one solution to the problem of contrivance in nature, a solution in terms of naturalistic mechanisms. But the approach to life through naturalistic mechanisms was not the only one. Corresponding to the three stages in the demise of British natural theology that I described earlier, Hodge outlined three generic ways of trying to account for apparent contrivance in nature. As he wrote in 1874,

> There are in the animal and vegetable worlds innumerable instances of at least apparent contrivance, which have excited the admiration of men in all ages. There are three ways of accounting for them. The first [looks to an] intelligent agent. . . . In the external world there is always and everywhere indisputable evidence of the activity of two kinds of force: the one physical, the other mental. The physical belongs to matter and is due to the properties with which it has been endowed; the other is the . . . mind of God. To the latter are to be referred all the manifestations of design in nature and the ordering of events in Providence. This doctrine does not ignore the efficiency of second causes; it simply asserts that God overrules and controls them. . . .
>
> The second method of accounting for contrivances in nature admits that they were foreseen and purposed by God, and that He endowed matter with forces which He foresaw and intended should produce such results. But here His agency stops. He never interferes to guide the operation of physical causes. . . .
>
> The third method of accounting for the contrivances manifested in the organs of plants and animals is that which refers them to the blind operation of natural causes. This is the doctrine of the Materialists, and to this doctrine, we are sorry to say, Mr. Darwin . . . has given in his adhesion.[43]

This passage raises a number of interesting questions, but the one I want to focus on principally is this: In Hodge's first method of accounting for contrivance, what role do miracles play in bringing about the "manifestations of design in nature"? The short answer of course is, none whatsoever. Miracles are notably absent from Hodge's discussion. Now there is a good reason why they are absent. Hodge places at his disposal two kinds of causality (or "forces" as he calls them), what may be called physical and intelligent causes. Moreover, for Hodge these causes work in tandem and need not conflict. This is clear from his comment that design "does not ignore the efficiency of second causes." Since intelligent causes are responsible for design in the world, and since these are able to work in tandem with physical causes, the problem of miracles simply does not arise for Hodge. Thus according to Hodge one doesn't need to posit a miracle to infer design.

Hodge is working in the tradition of Paley and Reid. Though both Paley and Reid believed in miracles on scriptural grounds, in their capacity as natural theologians they had no need to invoke miracles.[44] As far as Paley and Reid were concerned, we are able to detect unmistakable marks of intelligent agency in an object without having to tell a story about *how* that object came into being (e.g., by invoking a miracle).[45] In particular for Paley and Reid, detecting design in the productions of nature never meant attributing those productions to miracles.

That detecting design in the productions of nature doesn't require a miracle-working God should have been clear to the nineteenth-century positivists from the history of the subject. The Stoics after all made generous use of design in their cosmologies even though they had no notion of a transcendent, much less a personal, miracle-working God. The Logos that for the Stoics was immanent in the world and brought order and design to the world was not a miracle-worker.[46] On the other hand, the British natural theologians were Christian theists who believed in a miracle-working God. How then does one account for Thomas Reid's free use of ancient sources like the Stoics in his *Lectures on Natural Theology* if design was inextricably linked to miraculous interventions? Consider, for instance, Reid's use of Cicero:

> Cicero in his tract *De Natura Deorum* speaks thus: Can anything done by chance have all the marks of design? If a man throws dies and both turn up aces, if he should throw 400 times, would chance throw up 400 aces? Colors thrown carelessly upon a canvas may come up to appear as a human face, but would they form a picture beautiful as the pagan Venus? A hog grubbing in the earth with his snout may turn up something like the letter A, but would he turn up the words of a complete sentence? Thus in order to show the absurdity of supposing what has the marks of design could arise from chance, [Cicero] gives a variety of examples where the absurdity is palpable.[47]

Reid is clearly arguing that "the marks of design" can be reliably detected, and by implication that their detection does not depend on any prearranged doctrine of miracles.[48]

Positivism, however, had no room for intelligent causes even if such causes could work in harmony with physical causes. Positivism was intent on subsuming everything under natural law—no exceptions. As John Tyndall told the British Association at Belfast the same year that Hodge's book on Darwinism appeared in print, "Science demands the . . . absolute reliance upon law in nature."[49] By the 1870s this sentiment was typical of scientists in Britain. On the other hand, it was precisely the irreducibility of intelligent causes to physical causes and by implication the irreducibility of intelligent causes to the natural laws governing physical causes that had been the cornerstone of British natural theology.

In resisting the reduction of everything to physical causes governed by natural law, natural theologians like Paley and Reid found themselves in good company. Over two millennia earlier Plato had argued for the absurdity of trying to reduce intelligent causes to physical causes. In the *Phaedo* Plato places an argument in the mouth of his hero Socrates in which Socrates argues for the irreducibility of intelligence to anything other than intelligence. Specifically Socrates argues that it is absurd to reduce "the cause of my sitting here in a bent position" to the fact

> that my body is composed of bones and sinews, and that the bones are rigid and separated at the joints, [and that] the sinews are capable of contraction and relaxation, and form an envelope for the bones with the help of the flesh and skin, the latter holding all together, and since the bones move freely in their joints, the sinews by relaxing and contracting enable me somehow to bend my limbs.[50]

To Socrates this reduction represents the height of absurdity, for Socrates's intentions are clearly controlling his physical actions and not vice versa. Socrates is seated, awaiting execution in an Athenian jail, because he has chosen to face his executioners rather than run off to Megara or Boeotia. Intentionality—intelligence—is controlling Socrates' physical actions. This is not to say that the structure and dynamics of Socrates's body parts (i.e., his flesh, skin, bones, limbs, joints and sinews) can be detached from his intentions. Nor is it to say that the structure and dynamics of his body parts violate any natural laws. But the action of those body parts is controlled by Socrates's intentions, and those intentions are not reducible to the natural laws.

Likewise for Hodge and the British natural theologians, to appeal alternately to physical and intelligent causes was to employ two separate modes of explanation. These modes of explanation were distinct, with one not prejudicing the other. In particular in the debate over design in biology, miracles were a red herring since design made sense and was detectable without reference to miracles. The problem with Darwinism for Hodge was not that it eschewed miracles but that by using a selectionist mechanism to explain the origin and development of life, Darwin was making a physical cause do the work of an intelligent cause. Darwin was trying to subsume intelligent causation under physical causation. Admit this point and the whole edifice of British natural theology would come tumbling down. Hodge and the British natural theologians, however, saw no reason to admit this point.

3.6 The Presupposition of Positivism

At the start of this chapter I posed the following question: Must a respectable historical analysis of the demise of British natural theology invariably presuppose the same positivist view of science that was responsible for its demise in the first place? I suppose that simply by posing the question this way I have made it difficult to answer affirmatively. But if I had posed the question differently (Must a respectable historical analysis of the demise of British natural theology invariably reject the prepositivist view of science that left room for intelligent causes, purpose and design?) answering affirmatively would have been too easy. Historians are supposed to be conversant with the progress of science since the time of Darwin, and leaving room for intelligent causes, purpose and design is no longer a proper way to do science. As Jacques Monod remarks in *Chance and Necessity*, "The cornerstone of the scientific method is the postulate that nature is objective. In other words, the *systematic* denial that 'true' knowledge can be got at by interpreting phenomena in terms of final causes—that is to say, of 'purpose.' "[51]

The only way to justify a negative principle like this, however, is to argue that science has uniformly failed to make headway when it has employed the notion of an intelligent cause. And even this argument cannot preclude the possibility that for all its past failures, a concept may yet prove useful in the future. The fact remains, however, that intelligent causes have played, are playing and will continue to play an important role in science. Entire industries, economic and scientific, depend crucially on such notions as intelligence, intentionality and information. Included here are forensic science, intellectual property law, insurance claims investigation, cryptography, random number generation, archaeology and the search for extraterrestrial intelligence (SETI).

What then is needed to accurately reassess the demise of British natural theology? At the very least one must take seriously Hodge's three methods of accounting for contrivance in nature. The usual move in contemporary history and philosophy of science is simply to assume Hodge's third method, namely, that Darwin's selectionist mechanism or some other naturalistic mechanism is adequate to account for the origin and development of life, and thereafter to treat Hodge's first and second methods as wrongheaded attempts from a bygone era to account for life. Hodge's third method is certainly the simplest. If it could provide an adequate account of life, then by all means it should be employed. We don't invoke intelligent causes to explain how rocks get strewn about in an avalanche. And unless we suffer from paranoia, we don't explain tripping on a rug as a malicious plot devised by the rug's owner. Yet as Einstein taught us, "Everything should be made as simple as possible, but not simpler." There are occasions where we cannot avoid intelligent causes (e.g., we need them to account for human artifacts and cannot account for human artifacts strictly in terms of physical causes).

But once intelligent causes are admitted into scientific discourse, the question arises how to make sense of them. Hodge's first and second methods of accounting for contrivances in nature go about this differently. Hodge's second method eliminates the question of miracles by locating design in laws that produce contrivance. In the history of ideas this second method has always constituted an unstable equilibrium. Physics does not preclude a metal sphere from balancing on the point of a dagger; but nudge that dagger ever so slightly and the sphere is sure to tip. The problem with Hodge's second method is that it tends inevitably toward the first or third of Hodge's methods, which in Hodge's scheme constitute the stable equilibria. As soon as one starts to investigate what those laws that produce the contrivances of nature are and seriously entertains the hope of discovering them, design becomes a lost cause, for in the process of becoming known the laws turn out to be nothing more than natural laws describing physical causes. The progression from method two to method three is by far the most common. It mirrors the course of British natural theology from Babbage's divine programmer of the 1830s to Huxley's agnosticism of the 1870s.

The impulse to retain some conception of divine action, however, can override the positivistic push from method two to method three. When this happens, unless there is a clear conception of the difference between intelligent and physical causes and unless attributing an intelligent cause to an effect in nature is made precise—which is to say unless one goes back squarely to Hodge's first method—one is likely to end up in the muddle that B. B. Warfield, the successor to Hodge's chair in theology at Princeton, later found himself in. Committed to "the scientific vision," as Livingstone and Noll put it, "Warfield believed Christians could hold a virtually mechanistic account of nature provided they allowed for at least occasional supernatural intervention and maintained the belief that providence sustains the physical world."[52] This is exactly the worst of both worlds. Contrary to British natural theology, it uses physical causes to do the work of intelligent causes; contrary to positivism, it employs the taboo concept of miracle. Warfield's position leaves hardly anybody happy. And indeed, his views on the connection between faith and science have few advocates these days.

The only way to stay consistently with Hodge's second method is to have the laws or principles that the designer instituted to produce the contrivances of nature remain mysteries. Babbage's view of God as a divine programmer whose programs now and again kick in to produce novel forms is one instance of this that we have already seen. Augustine's conjecture that God implanted hidden seeds in creation which lie dormant until the right time is another.[53] Howard Van Till's recent reworking of this idea of Augustine in which the world was created from the start fully equipped by God with all the capacities needed to bring forth the contrivances of nature is yet another.[54] Babbage's programs, Augustine's seeds and Van Till's creaturely capacities are in each case principles instituted by the designer to produce the contrivances of nature. Yet they remain mysterious. They have no empirical content and are immune to empirical evidence.

And that leaves Hodge's first method. The validity of this method for explaining the contrivances in nature depends on whether the distinction between physical and intelligent causes (what Hodge calls "two kinds of force: the one physical, the other mental") can be reliably drawn. Moreover the reliability of drawing this distinction depends on whether there are marks of intelligence that reliably signal the activity of an intelligent cause. Only if such criteria are in place and have been justified can design have empirical content and thus properly be considered scientific. In the time of Reid and Paley such marks of intelligence were taken as largely self-evident. The criteria employed by British natural theologians for detecting design, however, proved in many instances naive, yielding too many false positives, that is, attributions of design where design was subsequently found to be lacking. For instance, although the adaptedness of organisms to their environments was thought impossible without the aid of an intelligent cause, Darwin's selectionist mechanism accounted for many adaptations of organisms to their environments. Finding a reliable criterion for detecting the activity of intelligent causes has to date constituted the key obstacle facing Hodge's first method. The next two chapters show that such a criterion does in fact now exist.

Part 2
A Theory of Design

4

Naturalism & Its Cure

4.1 Nature and Creation

Turn on the television to watch a nature program and you will be regaled with all the wonderful things nature does. Nature is responsible for the giraffe's neck, the eagle's talons and the angler fish's lure. Nature gives us rain forests, roses and rutabagas. Nature feeds, clothes and entertains us. Nature spans everything from quarks to galaxy clusters. Most significant, we are part of nature. With nature fulfilling so many vital roles, it's fair to ask, What is nature? Definitions abound. Nature is the material or physical world. Nature is the biophysical universe. Nature is the natural order. Nature is the realm of space, time and energy. Nature is that part of reality described by natural laws. Nature is what scientists study—the domain of science.

Each of these definitions is right as far as it goes. Implicit in these definitions, however, is a telling omission. In no instance do we find nature identified with creation. To be sure, in common parlance we often merge the two, referring to nature and creation interchangeably. But creation is always a divine act, whereas nature is a self-contained entity independent of God. God is irrelevant to nature. Nature treats the world as though it were self-sufficient and not in need of a creator. Creation requires a creator, but nature requires no creator. A creator might exist, but one need not exist for the world to be nature. Nature is what the world would be if there were no God.

There is something profoundly unsettling about conceiving of the world as nature, and we are apt to miss it because of the success of modern science. Thus we are likely to view the distinction between creation and nature as purely pragmatic. Whereas the theologian studies creation, the scientist studies nature. The scientist wants to study the order that God has placed in world, but does not want to study God's relation to the world. The scientist therefore ignores questions about God and looks at the world in and for itself, independently of God. In our day this seems perfectly reasonable.

Thus when we read of the French mathematician Laplace being asked by Napoleon where God fit into his cosmological equations, we are amused to learn Laplace's response: "Sire, I have no need of that hypothesis." For the scientist, God is a hypothesis and an unnecessary one at that. There are aspects of the created order that it seems we can understand perfectly well without invoking God. Nothing of any importance seems at stake here. Certainly Laplace has not disproved God. Laplace has merely shown that there are areas of human inquiry where we don't need to explicitly invoke God. So what? In everyday life we get along quite nicely without invoking God at every stroke. As long as scientists are making new discoveries and getting results, why compel them to bring God into the picture?

But this misses the point. No one is asking that God be invoked artificially or arbitrarily. The problem with conceiving of the world as nature is rather this: For nature to be an object of inquiry for the scientist, nature must have an order which the scientist can grasp. If nature were totally without form and order, no science would be possible. A higgledy-piggledy world in which objects fall to the ground one day, levitate the next and occasionally move sideways is an incomprehensible world, and one where scientists are out of a job. Einstein once remarked that the most incomprehensible thing about the world is that it is comprehensible. The world is not a blooming, buzzing confusion but an orderly place which our minds seem ideally suited to understand. This is the mystery confronting the scientist. Why is the world ordered and whence cometh this order?

There are but two options: Either the world derives its order from a source outside itself (à la creation) or it possesses whatever order it has intrinsically, that is, without the order being imparted from outside. So long as the order is coming from outside, we are dealing with a world that is a creation. On the other hand, if the order belongs to the world intrinsically, we are dealing with nature. The question *Whence cometh the order of the world?* is one of the most important questions we can ever ask. Moreover it is inevitable that each of us shall at some point in our lives ask it.

Throughout Scripture the fundamental divide separating humans is between those who can discern God's action in the world and those who are blind to it. Those who can discern God's action in the world that Scripture calls "spiritual"; those who cannot, Scripture calls "natural" or "soulish."[1] For those who cannot discern God's action in the world, the world is a self-contained, self-sufficient, self-explanatory, self-ordering system. Consequently they view themselves as autonomous and the world as independent of God. This severing of the world from God is the essence of idolatry and is in the end always what keeps us from knowing God. Severing the world from God, or alternatively viewing the world as nature, is the essence of humanity's fall.

4.2 The Root of Idolatry
In *For the Life of the World* Alexander Schmemann remarked, "It is not the immorality of the crimes of man that reveal him as a fallen being; it is his 'positive ideal'—religious or secular—and his satisfaction with this ideal."[2] Those who are blind to God's action in the world have one overriding satisfaction: That this world belongs to them and to them alone. Call those who are blind to God's action in the world "naturalists," and call the view that nature is self-contained "naturalism." For the naturalist God plays no role in the world. Religious believers are apt to think that a world without God is a terribly sad place in which no one given the choice would want to live. But to the naturalist it is precisely the presence of God in the world that threatens to undo it.

There is an irony here. Starting with the observation that some things are better understood without invoking God at every turn, we end up with the view that the whole world is best understood without God. How could this happen? We need to understand that it is impossible to be neutral about God's relation to the world. Is God the source and sustenance of the world, or does the world exist in and for itself? It makes a big difference whether the world is a creation or whether it is only nature.

There are very definite advantages to severing the world from God. Thomas Huxley, for instance, found great comfort in not having to account for his sins to a creator. Naturalism does not leave one accountable to a God who condemns sin. Rather, one's accountability is only to the laws of nature. And whereas there are rewards and punishments with God, there are only consequences in nature. Naturalism promises to free humanity from the weight of sin by dissolving the very concept of sin. Sin makes sense so long as an offense against a person has been committed. But we cannot properly sin against nature. It is not proper even to speak of violating the laws of nature since if nature is all there is, then everything we do is constrained by nature's laws. With no possibility of escaping the laws of nature, we cannot violate them. Yes, we pollute the earth and decimate rain forests and cause plants and animals to go extinct. But all of this is in accord with nature's laws, not in violation of them.

Although viewing the world as nature is typically seen as a scientific move, we need to realize that it is a profoundly religious move. Whence comes the order of the world? is a question that admits two answers: creation or nature. Either God imparts order to the world or the order in the world is intrinsic to it. Science cannot demonstrate that the order of the world is intrinsic to it. This is not a scientific question but a metaphysical, yes, even religious question. To see this, it is instructive to examine the earliest Hindu scriptures, the *Rig Veda*. According to Ainslie Embree, a fundamental characteristic of Vedic literature was "the sense of a cosmic order or law pervading the universe."[3] Embree elaborates,

> This cosmic law was not made by the gods, although they are the guardians of it. It is reflected not only in the physical regularity of the night and day and of the seasons but also in the moral order that binds men to each other and to the gods. The word (*rita*) used for this cosmic law becomes a synonym for truth, thus opening up possibilities for the development of wide-ranging philosophical and theological speculations as to the nature of the universe.[4]

Notice that not just scientific laws but morality and truth itself are all brought under *rita*, the cosmic law. This cosmic law is the ground of being, the first principle, the ultimate reference point. It is embedded in nature and undergirds nature. This cosmic law supplants divine creation. There can be no transcendent God within such a framework. The gods of the Vedas are not prior to nature but intrinsic to it. These are gods who control nature as much as they are controlled by it. Indeed, they are inseparable from nature.

Hindu pantheism is perhaps the most developed expression of religious naturalism. In our Western society we are much more accustomed to dealing with what is called scientific naturalism. Ironically, scientific naturalism is just as religious as the overtly religious naturalism of Hinduism. Only with scientific naturalism there is the pretense that science has finally established naturalism once and for all. In fact, science provides no evidence for naturalism one way or the other, though the assumption of naturalism profoundly affects how we do science. Naturalism is always a deep philosophical and religious commitment, as much as any commitment to divine creation.

Naturalism leads irresistibly to idolatry. As we read Scripture today, we often wonder at all the excitement about idols and graven images. Idolatry is uniformly condemned in the Old Testament, and yet we are less horrified than amused at the idol makers who fashion an idol from a piece of rock or wood and bow down before it. It all seems rather ludicrous to us enlightened Westerners. If we speak about idols at all these days, we speak of money, reputation and power. But these are not properly speaking idols. They can become idols, but in themselves they are not idols.

Although in ancient times graven images were the most obvious sign of idolatry, idolatry is not so much a matter of investing any particular object with extraordinary significance. Rather it is a matter of investing the world with a significance it does not deserve. We need to ask ourselves why anyone would want to worship a material object in the first place. The ancients certainly knew as well as we that a carved figure by itself holds no special significance. What is significant about a graven image is not the image itself but what it signifies. Some images in the East, for instance, are hollow on the inside and have a hole so that the reality signified by the image may enter the image and thus become the proper object of worship for the worshiper. Similarly in making a golden calf for the Israelites and claiming that here were Israel's gods that had led them out of Egypt, Aaron was not attributing to this chunk of metal any special power.

The problem is that all our images can signify only other things in creation and not the One who gave creation its being in the first place. A graven image signifies something else in the world, some power, some influence, some favor that the worshiper wants to tap into. The tacit assumption here is that what needs to be tapped into is part of the world, not the God who created the world in the first place. Idolatry is always a denial of the Creator, for it sets the creation above the Creator and thereby transforms creation into nature.

Don't let the polytheism of the ancients fool you. The gods of Aryan culture, whether Greek or Hindu, were never ultimate. We always come upon them *in medias res*. They are never the fount from which all else proceeds. Instead they are themselves subject to fate, to destiny, to cosmic law, to some underlying order that they themselves cannot escape (cf. the Greek *moira* and the Hindu *rita*). By invoking the gods of the ancients, one invokes that aspect of nature which the god personifies and over which the god is supposed to exercise control. These gods are really quite pathetic because nature's fundamental laws can always overrule them. These are gods who mean well, who feel the pain of their followers, who wish them well but who can offer no guarantees and who may even prove faithless.

Contrast this with the God of creation. The God of creation can be loyal and fulfill his promises because the world is subject to him and not he to the world. God is almighty. This means that there is no power above him but that all things are finally subject to him. The Hebrew notion of *ḥeseḏ*, God's lovingkindness, steadfastness and tender mercy, all find their guarantee in God's role as Creator. Only a God who creates and rules the world is a God we can count on. The gods that emerge out of nature, on the other hand, are fickle and not proper objects of worship.

Yet worship them we do. The temptation to worship and serve the creature rather than the Creator is ever present to us. It happens when we lose sight that this is God's world and that nothing happens apart from his consent. Whether through discouragement, self-deception or vice, the temptation is to turn in on ourselves and lose the divine perspective. In its place we find an impersonal world of stark necessities as well as caprice. Our best hope then is to make our peace with this naturalized world, adapt to it so that we can minimize our pain and maximize our pleasure. But ultimately we shall want to leave this world since the pleasures and pains it offers are insubstantial, and the ultimate reality is only the laws that govern nature.

The Bible uses many words and images to characterize idolatry, but the most apt is *foolishness*. What can be more foolish than to elevate what is second best to what is best? It's like preferring the publisher of Shakespeare to Shakespeare himself. It's like preferring golden eggs to the goose that lays the golden eggs. Because the creation is so marvelous, it is easy to understand why we become enamored of it. But as Maximus the Confessor reminds us in his *Four Centuries on Love*, "If the creation is so marvelous, how much more marvelous is the one who created it?"[5] The creation is good and even very good. But it is not best. God is best. In fact, God so far surpasses what is second best that giving anything eminence comparable to God is simply outrageous.

Naturalism is in the air we breathe. It pervades our cultural atmosphere. We see it whenever the mysteries of the faith are ridiculed. We see it whenever a PBS nature program credits nature for some object of wonder instead of God. We see it whenever psychologists claim to have gotten to the root of our problems but forget that we are fallen beings made in God's image. We see it, alas, whenever we forget God and worship the creature more than the Creator.

4.3 Naturalism Within Western Culture

Within Western culture, naturalism has become the default position for all serious inquiry. From biblical studies to law to education to science to the arts, inquiry is allowed to proceed only under the supposition that nature is self-contained. To be sure, this is not to require that we explicitly deny God's existence. God could, after all, have created the world to be self-contained. Nonetheless for the sake of inquiry we are required to pretend that God does not exist and proceed accordingly. Naturalism affirms not so much that God does not exist as that God need not exist. It's not that God is dead so much as that God is absent. And because God is absent, intellectual honesty demands that we get about our work without invoking him. This is the received wisdom.

How then do we defeat naturalism? Naturalism is an ideology. Its key tenet is the self-sufficiency of nature. Within Western culture its most virulent form is known as scientific naturalism. Scientific naturalism locates the self-sufficiency of nature in the natural laws of science. Accordingly scientific naturalism would have us to understand the universe entirely in terms of such laws. Thus in particular, since human beings are a part of the universe, who we are and what we do must ultimately be understood in naturalistic terms. This is not to deny our humanity. But it is to reinterpret our humanity as the consequence of brute material processes that were not consciously aiming at us. Nor is this to deny God. But it is to affirm that if God exists, he was marvelously adept at covering his tracks and giving no evidence that he ever interacted with the world. To be sure, there is no logical contradiction for the scientific naturalist to affirm God's existence, but this can be done only by making God a superfluous rider on top of a self-contained account of the world.

What evidence is there of God interacting with the world? How we answer this question is absolutely crucial to how effective we are going to be in overcoming naturalism (scientific or otherwise). Theists know that naturalism is false. Nature is not self-sufficient. God created nature as well as any laws by which nature operates. Not only has God created the world, but God upholds the world moment by moment. Daniel's words to Belshazzar hold equally for the dyed-in-the-wool naturalist: "Thou hast praised the gods of silver, and gold, of brass, iron, wood, and stone, which see not, nor hear, nor know: and the God in whose hand thy breath is, and whose are all thy ways, hast thou not glorified" (Daniel 5:23 KJV). The world is in God's hand and never leaves his hand. Theists are not deists. God is not an absentee landlord.

That said, the question remains, what evidence has God given of interacting with the world? Because God is intimately involved with the world moment by moment, there is no question that God interacts with the world. Controversy arises, however, once we ask whether God's interaction with the world is *empirically detectable*. It is one thing as a matter of faith to hold that God exists, interacts with and sovereignly rules the world. Alternatively, one may argue on philosophical grounds that the world and its laws are not self-explanatory and therefore point to a transcendent source. But it is another thing entirely to assert that empirical evidence supports God's interaction with the world, rendering God's interaction empirically detectable. Theology and philosophy are perfectly legitimate ways for understanding God's interaction with the world. Nonetheless neither theology nor philosophy can answer the evidential question whether God's interaction with the world is empirically detectable.

To answer this question we must to look to science. The science we look to, however, needs to be unencumbered by naturalistic philosophy. If we prescribe in advance that science must be limited to strictly natural causes, then science will necessarily be incapable of investigating God's interaction with the world. But if we permit science to investigate intelligent causes (as many special sciences already do, e.g., forensic science and artificial intelligence), then God's interaction with the world, insofar as it manifests the characteristic features of intelligent causation, becomes a legitimate domain for scientific investigation.

There's an important contrast to keep in mind here. Science, we are told, studies natural causes, whereas to introduce God is to invoke supernatural causes. This is the wrong contrast. The proper contrast is between *natural causes* on the one hand and *intelligent causes* on the other. Intelligent causes can do things that natural causes cannot. Natural causes can throw scrabble pieces on a board but cannot arrange the pieces to form meaningful words or sentences. To obtain a meaningful arrangement requires an intelligent cause. Whether an intelligent cause operates within or outside nature (i.e., is respectively natural or supernatural) is a separate question entirely from whether an intelligent cause has operated (cf. appendix A.9).

4.4 The Cure: Intelligent Design

This distinction between natural and intelligent causes has underlain the design arguments of past centuries. Throughout the centuries theologians have argued that nature exhibits features that nature itself cannot explain but that instead require an intelligence beyond nature. From church fathers like Minucius Felix and Gregory of Nazianzus (third and fourth centuries) to medieval scholars like Moses Maimonides and Thomas Aquinas (twelfth and thirteenth centuries) to reformed thinkers like Thomas Reid and Charles Hodge (eighteenth and nineteenth centuries), we find theologians making design arguments, arguing from the data of nature to an intelligence that transcends nature.[6]

Design arguments are old hat. Indeed design arguments continue to be a staple of philosophy and religion courses. The most famous of the design arguments is William Paley's watchmaker argument.[7] According to Paley, if we find a watch in a field, the watch's adaptation of means to ends (i.e., the adaptation of its parts to telling time) ensure that it is the product of an intelligence and not simply the result of undirected natural processes. So, too, the marvelous adaptations of means to ends in organisms, whether at the level of whole organisms or at the level of various subsystems (Paley focused especially on the mammalian eye), ensure that organisms are the product of an intelligence.

Though intuitively appealing, design arguments had until recently fallen into disuse. That is now changing. Indeed design is experiencing an explosive resurgence.[8] Scientists are beginning to realize that design can be rigorously formulated as a scientific theory. What has kept design outside the scientific mainstream these last hundred and forty years is the absence of precise methods for distinguishing intelligently caused objects from unintelligently caused ones. For design to be a fruitful scientific theory, scientists have to be sure they can reliably determine whether something is designed. Johannes Kepler, for instance, thought the craters on the moon were intelligently designed by moon dwellers. We now know that the craters were formed naturally. It's this fear of falsely attributing something to design only to have it overturned later that has prevented design from entering science proper. With precise methods for discriminating intelligently from unintelligently caused objects, scientists are now able to avoid Kepler's mistake.

What has emerged is a new program for scientific research known as *intelligent design*. Within biology, intelligent design is a theory of biological origins and development. Its fundamental claim is that intelligent causes are necessary to explain the complex, information-rich structures of biology and that these causes are empirically detectable. To say intelligent causes are empirically detectable is to say there exist well-defined methods that on the basis of observational features of the world are capable of reliably distinguishing intelligent causes from undirected natural causes. Many special sciences have already developed such methods for drawing this distinction—notably forensic science, artificial intelligence (cf. the Turing test), cryptography, archaeology and the search for extraterrestrial intelligence (as in the movie *Contact*).[9]

Whenever these methods detect intelligent causation, the underlying entity they uncover is information. Intelligent design properly formulated is a theory of information. Within such a theory, information becomes a reliable indicator of intelligent causation as well as a proper object for scientific investigation. Intelligent design thereby becomes a theory for detecting and measuring information, explaining its origin and tracing its flow. Intelligent design is therefore not the study of intelligent causes per se but of informational pathways induced by intelligent causes.[10] As a result, intelligent design presupposes neither a creator nor miracles. Intelligent design is theologically minimalist. It detects intelligence without speculating about the nature of the intelligence. Biochemist Michael Behe's "irreducible complexity," mathematician Marcel Schützenberger's "functional complexity" and my own "specified complexity" are alternate routes to the same reality.[11]

It is the empirical detectability of intelligent causes that renders intelligent design a fully scientific theory and distinguishes it from the design arguments of philosophers or what has traditionally been called "natural theology." Natural theology reasons from the data of nature directly to the existence and attributes of God—typically the trinitarian God of Christianity with all the usual perfections. Perhaps the weakest part of Paley's *Natural Theology* is his closing chapter, where he sings the praises of nature's delicate balance and how only a beneficent deity could have arranged so happy a creation.[12] Darwin turned this argument on its head, focusing instead on the brutality of nature and seeing anything but the hand of a beneficent deity.

Intelligent design is at once more modest and more powerful than natural theology. From observable features of the natural world, intelligent design infers to an intelligence responsible for those features. The world contains events, objects and structures that exhaust the explanatory resources of undirected natural causes and that can be adequately explained only by recourse to intelligent causes. This is not an argument from ignorance. Nor is this a matter of personal incredulity. Precisely because of what we know about undirected natural causes and their limitations, science is now in a position to demonstrate design rigorously.[13]

In the past design was a plausible but underdeveloped philosophical intuition. Now it is a robust program of scientific research. Consequently intelligent design is under no obligation to speculate about the nature, moral character or purposes of any designing intelligence it happens to infer. (Here rather is a task for the theologian—to connect the intelligence inferred by the design theorist with the God of Scripture.) Indeed this is one of the great strengths of intelligent design, that it distinguishes design from purpose. We can know that something is designed without knowing the ultimate or even proximate purpose for which it was designed. As Del Ratzsch notes, "The Smithsonian has an entire collection of obviously designed human artifacts, concerning the purposes of which no one has a clue."[14]

What will science look like once intelligent causes are readmitted to full scientific status? The worry is that intelligent design will stultify scientific inquiry. For after determining that something is designed, what remains for the scientist to do? Even if there are reliable methods for deciding when something is designed, and even if those methods tell us that some natural object is designed, so what? Suppose Paley was right about the mammalian eye exhibiting sure marks of intelligent causation. How would this recognition help us understand the eye any better as scientists? Actually it would help quite a bit. For one thing, it would put a stop to all those unsubstantiated just-so stories that evolutionists spin out in trying to account for the eye through a gradual succession of undirected natural causes. By telling us the mammalian eye requires an intelligent cause, intelligent design precludes certain types of scientific explanation. This is a contribution to science, albeit a negative one.

Even so, intelligent design is hardly finished once it answers whether an object was designed. Another question immediately presents itself, namely, *how* was the object produced? Consider a Stradivarius violin. Not only do we know that it is designed, but we also know the designer—Stradivarius. Nevertheless to this day we are unable to answer the "how" question: we no longer know how to manufacture a violin as good as a Stradivarius, much less how Stradivarius himself actually went about making his violins. Lost arts are lost precisely because we are no longer able to answer the "how" question, not because we have lost the ability to detect design. Now the problem of lost arts is the problem of *reverse engineering*. Unlike the ordinary engineer who constructs an object from scratch, the reverse engineer is first given an object (in this case a violin) and then must show how it could have been constructed.

Intelligent design's positive contribution to science is to reverse engineer objects shown to be designed. Indeed the design theorist is a reverse engineer. Unconstrained by naturalism, the design theorist finds plenty of natural objects attributable to design (this is especially true for biological systems). Having determined that certain natural objects are designed, the design theorist next investigates how they were produced. Yet because evidence of how they were produced is typically incomplete (at least for natural objects), the design theorist is left instead with investigating how these objects could have been produced. This is reverse engineering.

In this vein consider again the Stradivarius example. In attempting to reconstruct Stradivarius's art of violin making, the contemporary violin maker does well to learn as much as possible about Stradivarius's actual methods for producing violins. Nonetheless, because the extant account of Stradivarius's methods is incomplete, the contemporary violin maker can do no better than try to reinvent Stradivarius's methods. Without a complete record of Stradivarius's actual methods, one can never be sure of reconstructing his methods exactly. Still, one can legitimately claim to have reinvented Stradivarius's methods if one is able to produce a violin as good as his.

To sum up, intelligent design consists in empirically detecting design and then reverse engineering those objects detected to be designed. The worry that intelligent design stifles scientific inquiry is therefore ill-founded. Indeed, one can argue that many scientists are design theorists already, though in naturalistic clothing. In biology, for instance, very few researchers confine themselves to Miller-Urey type experiments, attempting to generate biological complexity solely through undirected natural processes.[15] No, most researchers studying biological complexity bring all their expertise and technological prowess to bear, especially when trying to reconstruct complex biological systems. As Paul Nelson aptly remarked, scientists ought to line their labs with mirrors to remind themselves that at every point they are in the labs designing and conducting their experiments.[16] Intelligent design is one intelligence determining what another intelligence has done. There is nothing mysterious about this. The only reason it seems mysterious is because naturalism so dominates our intellectual life.

4.5 Not Theistic Evolution
Where does intelligent design fit within the creation-evolution debate? Logically, intelligent design is compatible with everything from utterly discontinuous creation (e.g., God intervening at every conceivable point to create new species) to the most far-ranging evolution (e.g., God seamlessly melding all organisms together into one great tree of life). For intelligent design the primary question is not how organisms came to be (though as

we've just seen, this is a vital question for intelligent design) but whether organisms demonstrate clear, empirically detectable marks of being intelligently caused. In principle an evolutionary process can exhibit such "marks of intelligence" as much as any act of special creation.

That said, intelligent design is incompatible with what typically is meant by "theistic evolution" (or what is also called "creative evolution," "teleological evolution," "evolutionary creation" or most recently "fully gifted creation").[17] Theistic evolution takes the Darwinian picture of the biological world and baptizes it, identifying this picture with the way God created life. When boiled down to its scientific content, however, theistic evolution is no different from atheistic evolution, treating only undirected natural processes in the origin and development of life.[18]

Theistic evolution places theism and evolution in an odd tension. If God purposely created life through Darwinian means, then God's purpose was ostensibly to conceal his purpose in creation. Within theistic evolution, God is a master of stealth who constantly eludes our best efforts to detect him empirically. Yes, the theistic evolutionist believes that the universe is designed. Yet insofar as there is design in the universe, it is design we recognize strictly through the eyes of faith. Accordingly the physical world in itself provides no evidence that life is designed. For all we can tell, our appearance on planet earth is an accident.

Now it may be that God has so arranged the physical world that our native intellect can discover no reliable evidence of him. Yet if this is so, how could we know it? Scripture and church tradition are hardly univocal here. Throughout church history we find Christian thinkers who regard our native intellect as hopelessly inadequate for finding even a scrap of reliable knowledge about God from the physical world, and others who regard our native intellect as able to extract certain limited though still reliable knowledge about God from the physical world. Thus in the early church we find Tertullian inveighing against our native intellect, but Basil the Great and Gregory of Nazianzus defending it. In the Middle Ages we find Occam's occasionalism undermining the powers of our native intellect and Thomas Aquinas raising it to new heights. In the modern era we find Blaise Pascal, Søren Kierkegaard and Karl Barth making the *Deus absconditus* a fundamental plank of their theology, yet Isaac Newton, Thomas Reid and Charles Hodge asserting how wonderfully God is revealed in physical world. The current theological fashion prefers an evolutionary God inaccessible to scientific scrutiny over a designer God whose actions are clearly detectable.

How then do we determine whether God has so arranged the physical world that our native intellect can discover reliable evidence of him? The answer is obvious: Put our native intellect to the task and see whether indeed it produces conclusive evidence of design. Doing so poses no threat to the Christian faith. It challenges neither the cross, the tomb, the resurrection on the third day, the ascension into heaven, the sitting at the right hand of the Father nor the second coming of Christ. Indeed the physical world is silent about the revelation of Christ in Scripture. On the other hand, nothing prevents the physical world from independently testifying to the God revealed in the Scripture.[19] Now intelligent design does just this—it puts our native intellect to work and thereby confirms that a designer of remarkable talents is responsible for the physical world. How this designer connects with the God of Scripture is then for theology to determine.

Intelligent design and theistic evolution therefore differ fundamentally about whether the design of the universe is accessible to our native intellect. Design theorists say yes; theistic evolutionists say no. Why the disagreement? To be sure, there is a scientific disagreement: Design theorists think the scientific evidence favors design whereas theistic evolutionists think it favors Darwin or one of his naturalistic successors. Nonetheless in discounting intelligent design, theistic evolutionists tend also to appeal to philosophical and theological considerations. Pessimism about the powers of the native intellect to transcend the physical world is a dominant theme in certain theological traditions.[20] Often aesthetic criteria for how God should create or interact with the world take precedence (e.g., *A worthy deity wouldn't have done it that way!*).[21] My own view is that it is much more shaky to speculate about what God would have done or what the world might in principle reveal than simply to go to the world and see what it actually does reveal.

If theistic evolution finds no solace from intelligent design, neither does it find solace from the Darwinian establishment. For the Darwinian establishment the "theism" in theistic evolution is superfluous. For the hard-core naturalist, theistic evolution at best includes God as an unnecessary rider in an otherwise purely naturalistic account of life. Thus by Occam's razor, since God is an unnecessary rider in our understanding of the physical world, theistic evolution ought to dispense with all talk of

God outright and get rid of the useless adjective *theistic*. This, at any rate, is the received view within the Darwinian establishment.

It's for failing to take Occam's razor seriously that the Darwinian establishment despises theistic evolution. Not to put too fine a point on it, the Darwinian establishment views theistic evolution as a weak-kneed sycophant that desperately wants the respectability that comes with being a full-blooded Darwinist but refuses to follow the logic of Darwinism through to the end. It takes courage to give up the comforting belief that life on earth has a purpose. It takes courage to live without the consolation of an afterlife. Theistic evolutionists lack the stomach to face the ultimate meaninglessness of life, and it is this failure of courage that makes them contemptible in the eyes of full-blooded Darwinists. (Richard Dawkins is a case in point.)

Unlike full-blooded Darwinists, however, the design theorists' objection to theistic evolution rests not with what the term *theistic* is doing in the phrase "theistic evolution" but rather with what the term *evolution* is doing there. The design theorists' objection to theistic evolution is not in the end that theistic evolution retains God as an unnecessary rider in an otherwise perfectly acceptable scientific theory of life's origin and development. Rather their objection is that the scientific theory which is supposed to undergird theistic evolution, often called the neo-Darwinian synthesis, is itself problematic.

The design theorists' critique of Darwinism begins with Darwinism's failure as an empirically adequate scientific theory, not with its supposed incompatibility with some system of religious belief. This point is vital to keep in mind in assessing intelligent design's contribution to the creation-evolution controversy. Critiques of Darwinism by creationists have tended to conflate science and theology, making it unclear whether Darwinism fails strictly as a scientific theory or whether it must be rejected because it is theologically unacceptable. Design theorists refuse to make this a Bible-science controversy. Their critique of Darwinism is not based on any supposed incompatibility between Christian revelation and Darwinism. Instead they begin their critique by arguing that Darwinism is *on its own terms* a failed scientific research program—that it does not constitute a well-supported scientific theory, that its explanatory power is severely limited and that it fails abysmally when it tries to account for the grand sweep of natural history.

Darwinists will no doubt object to this characterization of their theory. For them Darwinism continues to be a fruitful theory—one whose imminent demise I am greatly exaggerating. Now there's no question that Darwin's mutation-selection mechanism constitutes a fruitful idea for biology, and one whose fruits have yet to be fully plundered. But Darwinism is more than just this mechanism. Darwinism is the totalizing claim that this mechanism accounts for all the diversity of life. The evidence simply does not support this claim. What evidence there is supports limited variation within fixed boundaries, or what typically is called microevolution. Macroevolution—the unlimited plasticity of organisms to diversify across all boundaries—even if true, cannot legitimately be attributed to the mutation-selection mechanism. To do so is to extrapolate the theory beyond its evidential base. This is always a temptation in science—to think that one's theory encompasses a far bigger domain than it actually does. In the heady early days of Newtonian mechanics, physicists thought Newton's laws provided a total account of the constitution and dynamics of the universe. Maxwell, Einstein and Heisenberg each showed that the proper domain of Newtonian mechanics was far more constricted. So, too, the proper domain of the mutation-selection mechanism is far more constricted than most Darwinists would like to admit.[22]

Indeed the following problems have proven utterly intractable not only for the mutation-selection mechanism but also for any other undirected natural process proposed to date: the origin of life, the origin of the genetic code, the origin of multicellular life, the origin of sexuality, the scarcity of transitional forms in the fossil record, the biological big bang that occurred in the Cambrian era, the development of complex organ systems and the development of irreducibly complex molecular machines.[23] These are just a few of the more serious difficulties that confront every theory of evolution that posits only undirected natural processes. It is thus sheer arrogance for Darwinists like Richard Dawkins and Daniel Dennett to charge design theorists with being stupid or wicked or insane for denying the all-sufficiency of undirected natural processes in biology, or to compare challenging Darwinism with arguing for a flat earth.[24]

The strength of the design theorists' critique against Darwinism, however, rests not in the end with their ability to find holes in the theory. To be sure, the holes are there and they create serious difficulties for the theory.

The point, however, at which the design theorists' critique becomes interesting and novel is when they begin raising the following sorts of questions: Why does Darwinism, despite being so inadequately supported as a scientific theory, continue to garner the full support of the academic establishment? What is it that continues to keep Darwinism afloat despite its many glaring faults? Why are alternatives that introduce design ruled out of court by fiat? Why must science explain solely by recourse to undirected natural processes? Who determines the rules of science? Is there a code of scientific correctness which instead of helping lead us into truth, actively prevents us from asking certain questions and thereby coming to the truth?

We are dealing here with something more than a straightforward determination of scientific facts or confirmation of scientific theories. Rather we are dealing with competing worldviews and incompatible metaphysical systems. In the creation-evolution controversy we are dealing with a naturalistic metaphysic that shapes and controls what theories of biological origins are permitted on the playing field in advance of any discussion or weighing of evidence. This metaphysic is so pervasive and powerful that it not only rules alternative views out of court, but it cannot even permit itself to be criticized.[25] The fallibleness and tentativeness that are supposed to be part of science find no place in the naturalistic metaphysic that undergirds Darwinism. It is this metaphysic then that constitutes the main target of the design theorists' critique of Darwinism and to which we turn next.

4.6 The Importance of Definitions

The design theorists' critique of the naturalistic metaphysic that undergirds Darwinism can be reduced to an analysis of three words. They are *creation, evolution* and *science.* Let us start with the words *creation* and *evolution.* Suppose you are on a witness stand and required to respond yes or no to two questions: (1) Do you believe in creation? (2) Do you believe in evolution? Could you respond to these questions with a simple yes or no and still feel satisfied that you had expressed yourself adequately? Probably not. The problem is that the words *creation* and *evolution* both have multiple senses.

For instance, creation can be construed in the narrow sense of a literal six-day creation as presented in Genesis 1 and 2. On the other hand, creation can also be construed in the broad sense of simply asserting that God has created the world, where the question of how God created the world is simply set to one side. Similarly evolution can be construed as a fully naturalistic, purposeless process which by means of natural selection and mutation has produced all living things. On the other hand, evolution can mean nothing more than that organisms have changed over time (leaving the extent of change unspecified). Depending on how one construes the words *creation* and *evolution*, one's answer to the question *Do you believe in creation?* and *Do you believe in evolution?* are likely to show quite a bit of variability.

Now it is the design theorists' contention that the Darwinian establishment, in order to maintain its political, cultural and intellectual authority, consistently engages in a fallacy of equivocation when it uses the terms *creation* and *evolution*. The fallacy of equivocation is the fallacy of speaking out of both sides of your mouth. It is the deliberate confusing of two senses of a term, using the sense that's convenient to promote one's agenda. For instance, when Michael Ruse in one of his defenses of Darwinism writes, "Evolution is a fact, *fact, FACT!*" how is he using the term *evolution?*[26] Is it a fact that organisms have changed over time? There is plenty of evidence to confirm that organisms have experienced limited change over time. Is it a fact that the full panoply of life has evolved through purposeless naturalistic processes? This might be a fact, but whether it is a fact is very much open to debate.

Suppose you don't accept the Darwinian picture of natural history, that is, you don't believe that the vast panoply of life evolved through undirected naturalistic processes. Presumably then you are a creationist. But does this make you a young-earth creationist? Ever since Darwin's *Origin of Species* Darwinists have cast the debate in these terms: Either you're with us, or you're a creationist (by which they mean a young-earth creationist). But of course it doesn't follow, logically or otherwise, that by rejecting fully naturalistic evolution you automatically embrace a literal reading of Genesis 1 and 2. Rejecting fully naturalistic evolution does not entail accepting young-earth creationism. The only thing one can say for certain is that to reject fully naturalistic evolution is to accept some form of creation broadly construed, that is, the belief that God or some intelligent designer is responsible for life. Young-earth creationism certainly falls under this broad construal of creation but is hardly coextensive with it.

Let us now assume we've got our terms straight. No more terminological confusions. No more fallacies of equivocation. No more straw men. From here on in we're going to concentrate on the substance of the creation-evolution debate. Henceforth this debate will be over whether life exhibits nothing more than the outcome of undirected natural processes or whether life exhibits the activity of an intelligent cause—usually called a designer—who in creating life has impressed on it clear marks of intelligence. For simplicity let us refer to the first view as *naturalistic evolution*. As for the second view, we already know it as *intelligent design*. Thus the key question to be resolved in the creation-evolution controversy is deciding which of these views is correct.

How do we resolve this question? The first thing to notice is that naturalistic evolution and intelligent design both make definite assertions of fact. To see this, consider your own personal genealogy. Here you are. You had parents. They in turn had parents. They too had parents. And so on. If we run the video camera back in time, generation upon generation, what do we see? Do we see a continuous chain of natural causes which go from apes to small furry mammals to reptiles to slugs to slime molds to blue-green algae and finally all the way back to a prebiotic soup, with no event in the chain ever signaling the activity of an intelligent cause? Or as we trace back the genealogy, do we find events that clearly signal the activity of an intelligent cause? There exist reliable criteria for inferring the activity of intelligent causes. Does natural history display clear marks of intelligence and thereby warrant a design inference, or does it not? To answer this question one way is to embrace intelligent design; to answer it the other way is to embrace naturalistic evolution.

Now Darwinists are quite clear about rejecting intelligent design and affirming naturalistic evolution. For instance, in *The Meaning of Evolution* George Gaylord Simpson, one of the founders of the neo-Darwinian synthesis, asserted,

> Although many details remain to be worked out, it is already evident that all the objective phenomena of the history of life can be explained by purely naturalistic or, in a proper sense of the sometimes abused word, materialistic factors. They [that is, the objective phenomena of the history of life] are readily explicable on the basis of differential reproduction in populations [that's natural selection], and the mainly random interplay of the known processes of heredity [that's random mutation, the other major element in

the Darwinian picture]. Therefore, man is the result of a purposeless and natural process that did not have him in mind.[27]

Where does Simpson derive his confidence that naturalistic evolution is correct and that intelligent design is incorrect? How can Simpson so easily elide the weaknesses in his theory and then with perfect equanimity assert, "It is already evident that all the objective phenomena of the history of life can be explained by purely naturalistic factors"? And how does Simpson know that when the "many details that remain to be worked out" actually do get worked out, they won't overthrow naturalistic evolution and instead confirm intelligent design? Science is after all a fallible enterprise. Where then does Simpson get his certainty?

To answer this question we need to examine how the Darwinian establishment employs the third word in our trio, namely, *science.* Although design theorists take the question *Which is correct, naturalistic evolution or intelligent design?* as a perfectly legitimate question, it is not treated as a legitimate question by the Darwinian establishment. According to the Darwinian establishment, naturalistic evolution addresses a "scientific" question whereas intelligent design addresses a "religious" question. Thus for the Darwinian establishment intelligent design is a nonstarter. Yes, naturalistic evolution and intelligent design taken together may be mutually exclusive and exhaustive, but naturalistic evolution is the only viable scientific option. Intelligent design must therefore be ruled out of court.

Why is this? The answer is quite simple. Science, according to the Darwinian establishment, by definition excludes everything except the material and the natural. It follows that all talk of purpose, design and intelligence is barred entry from the start. By defining science as a form of inquiry restricted solely to what can be explained in terms of undirected natural processes, the Darwinian establishment has ruled intelligent design outside of science. But suppose now that a design theorist comes along and, like most Americans, thinks intelligent design is correct and naturalistic evolution is incorrect. (According to a 1993 Gallup poll, close to 50 percent of Americans are creationists of a stricter sort, thinking that God specially created human beings; another 40 percent believe in some form of God-guided evolution; and only 10 percent are full-blooded Darwinists. It's this 10 percent, however, that controls the academy.)[28] The design theorist's first inclination might be to say, "No big deal. Intelligent design is at least as good an answer to biological origins as naturalistic evolution. Science just happens to be limited in the questions it can pose and the answers it can give." Any such concession is deadly and turns science into the stooge of naturalistic philosophy.

The problem is this. As Phillip Johnson rightly observes, science is the only universally valid form of knowledge within our culture. This is not to say that scientific knowledge is true or infallible. But within our culture, whatever is purportedly the best scientific account of a given phenomenon demands our immediate and unconditional assent. This is regarded as a matter of intellectual honesty. Thus to consciously resist what is currently the best scientific theory in a given area is, in the words of Richard Dawkins, to be either ignorant, stupid, insane or wicked.[29] Thankfully Richard Dawkins is more explicit than most of his colleagues in making this point and therefore does us the service of not papering over the contempt with which the Darwinian establishment regards those who question its naturalistic bias.

It bears repeating: the only universally valid form of knowledge within our culture is science. Within late-twentieth-century Western society neither religion, philosophy, literature, music, art makes any such cognitive claim. Religion in particular is seen as making no universal claims that are obligatory across the board. The contrast with science here is stark. Science has given us technology—computers that work as much here as they do in the Third World. Science has cured our diseases. Whether we are black, red, yellow or white, the same antibiotics cure the same infections. It's therefore clear why relegating intelligent design to any realm other than science (like religion) ensures that naturalistic evolution will remain the only intellectually respectable option for the explanation of life.

But there's a problem here. Intelligent design and naturalistic evolution both inquire into definite matters of fact. Naturalistic evolution and intelligent design are real possibilities. Moreover, as mutually exclusive and exhaustive possibilities, one of these positions has to be correct. Now the Darwinian establishment so defines science that naturalistic evolution alone can constitute a legitimate scientific answer to the question *How did life originate and develop?* Nonetheless, when Stephen Jay Gould, Michael Ruse, Richard Dawkins, George Gaylord Simpson and their disciples assert that naturalistic evolution is true, they purport that naturalistic evolution is the conclusion of a scientific argument based on empirical evidence. But it is nothing of the sort. The empirical evidence is in fact weak, and the conclusion follows necessarily as a strict logical deduction once science is as a matter of definition restricted to undirected natural processes. Naturalistic evolution is therefore built directly into a naturalistic construal of science.

Logicians have names for this—"circular reasoning" and "begging the question" being the best known. The view that science must be restricted solely to undirected natural processes also has a name. It is called *methodological naturalism*. So long as methodological naturalism sets the ground rules for how the game of science is to be played, intelligent design has no chance of success. Phillip Johnson makes this point eloquently. So does Alvin Plantinga.[30] In his discussion of methodological naturalism Plantinga notes that if one accepts methodological naturalism then naturalistic evolution is the only game in town.

Okay, since naturalistic evolution is so poorly supported empirically and since intelligent design is having such a hard time passing for science, what's wrong with a simple profession of ignorance? In response to the question *How did life originate and develop?* what's wrong with simply saying, *We don't know?* (Such a profession of ignorance, by the way, was the reason Michael Denton's book *Evolution: A Theory in Crisis* was panned by the Darwinian establishment.)[31] As philosophers of science Thomas Kuhn and Larry Laudan have pointed out, for scientific paradigms to shift, there has to be a new paradigm in place ready to be shifted into.[32] You can't shift into a vacuum. If you're going to reject a reigning paradigm, you have to have a new improved paradigm with which to replace it. Naturalistic evolution is the reigning paradigm. But what alternative is there to naturalistic evolution? Logically the only alternative is intelligent design. But intelligent design, we're told, isn't part of science.

There's a simple way out of this impasse: *dump methodological naturalism*. We need to realize that methodological naturalism is the functional equivalent of a full-blown metaphysical naturalism. Metaphysical naturalism asserts that nature is self-sufficient. Methodological naturalism asks us for the sake of science to pretend that nature is self-sufficient. But once science is taken as the only universally valid form of knowledge within a culture, it follows that methodological and metaphysical naturalism become functionally equivalent. What needs to be done, therefore, is to break the grip of naturalism in both guises, methodological and metaphysical. And this happens once we realize that it was not empirical evidence but the power of a metaphysical worldview that was all along urging us to adopt methodological naturalism in the first place.

4.7 A New Generation of Scholars

Naturalism is the intellectual pathology of our age. It artificially constricts the life of the mind and shuts down inquiry into the transcendent. All the nineteenth-century doctors of modernity were infected with it, notably, Darwin, Marx, Freud and Nietzsche. The fundamental tenet of naturalism in the West (or what is typically known as scientific naturalism) is the sufficiency of undirected natural causes to account for all of reality. The only way naturalism can be false is if reality is in fact a much richer place than naturalism allows. Specifically reality must include intelligent causes that neither reduce to nor emerge out of undirected natural causes. Moreover the only way to refute naturalism is to show that intelligent causes are empirically detectable. In short, if we're going to show that naturalism is false, we need to locate observable features of the world that demonstrate design.

Naturalism is the disease. Intelligent design is the cure. Intelligent design is a two-pronged approach for eradicating naturalism. On the one hand, intelligent design presents a scientific and philosophical critique of naturalism. Here the scientific critique identifies the empirical inadequacies of naturalistic evolutionary theories (both cosmic and biological), whereas the philosophical critique demonstrates how naturalism is a metaphysical ideology with no empirical backing. The other prong of intelligent design is a positive scientific research program. As a positive research program, intelligent design is the scientific discipline that systematically investigates the effects of intelligent causes. The precise sense in which intelligent design constitutes a scientific discipline will become clear in the next two chapters.

Where does intelligent design stand currently? Through the work of Phillip Johnson, Charles Thaxton, Walter Bradley and Michael Denton, the scientific and philosophical critiques of naturalism are now well in hand. To be sure, naturalists continue to resist these critiques. Nevertheless the tide has turned. The naturalistic dream of turning science into applied materialist philosophy is no longer tenable. Through the work of

Michael Behe, Jonathan Wells, Stephen Meyer, Paul Nelson, mine and others, intelligent design has taken some significant first steps. Intelligent design is a fledgling science. Even so, intelligent design is a fledgling of enormous promise. Many books and articles are in the pipeline. I predict that in the next several years intelligent design will be sufficiently developed to deserve funding from the National Science Foundation. Whether it actually receives such funding will depend not on the merits of intelligent design but on the political forces controlling research moneys.

Virtually every discipline and endeavor is presently under a naturalistic pall. To lift that pall will require a new generation of scholars and professionals who explicitly reject naturalism and consciously seek to understand the design that God has placed in the world. The possibilities for transforming the intellectual life of our culture are immense. Daniel Dennett speaks of Darwinism as a "universal acid" that has fundamentally transformed every aspect of Western culture.[33] Dennett is right. Darwin gave us a creation story, one in which God was absent and undirected natural processes did all the work. That creation story has held sway for over a hundred years. It is now on the way out. When it goes, so will all the edifices that have been built on its foundation. But what will be built in its place? And who will do the building? Intelligent design is a golden opportunity for a new generation of theistic scholars. In *The End of Christendom* Malcolm Muggeridge wrote, "I myself am convinced that the theory of evolution, especially the extent to which it's been applied, will be one of the great jokes in the history books in the future. Posterity will marvel that so very flimsy and dubious an hypothesis could be accepted with the incredible credulity that it has."[34] Muggeridge's posterity is today's generation.

5

Reinstating Design Within Science

5.1 Design's Departure from Science

Should design be permitted back into science generally and biology in particular? Scientists bristle at the very thought. For scientists who are atheists, design is an accident of natural history. Indeed, with no divine architect to start creation on its course, any designing agents, including ourselves, must result from a long evolutionary process that itself was not designed. For the atheist, design occurs at the end of an undesigned natural process and cannot be prior to it.

What about scientists who are not atheists? Many scientists who are theists agree with their atheist colleagues that design should be excluded from science. It's not that they agree that the universe isn't designed. As theists they believe whole-heartedly that the universe is designed—and not just by any designer but by the God of some particular religious creed. Nevertheless, as a matter of scientific integrity they believe science is best served by excluding design. The worry always is that invoking design will stifle scientific inquiry, substituting a supernatural cause where scientists should be seeking an ordinary natural cause.

Against this received view, I want to argue that design should be read-mitted to full scientific status. To make this argument, let me begin by briefly reviewing why design was removed from science in the first place. Design, in the form of Aristotle's formal and final causes, had, after all, once occupied a perfectly legitimate role within natural philosophy, or what we now call science. With the rise of modern science, however, these causes fell into disrepute.

We can see how this happened by considering Francis Bacon. Bacon, a contemporary of Galileo and Kepler, though himself not a scientist, was a terrific propagandist for science. Bacon concerned himself much about the proper conduct of science, providing detailed canons for experimental observation, recording of data and inferences from data. What interests us here, however, is what he did with Aristotle's four causes. For Aristotle, to understand any phenomenon properly one had to understand its four causes, namely its material, efficient, formal and final cause.[1]

A standard example philosophers use to illustrate Aristotle's four causes is a statue—say Michelangelo's David. The material cause is what it's made of—marble. The efficient cause is the immediate activity that produced the statue—Michelangelo's actual chipping away at a marble slab with hammer and chisel. The formal cause is its structure—it's a representation of David and not some random chunk of marble. And the final cause is its purpose—presumably to beautify some Florentine palace.

Although much more can be said about Aristotle's four causes than is evident from this illustration, two points are relevant to this discussion. First, Aristotle gave equal weight to all four causes. In particular Aristotle would have regarded any inquiry that omitted one of his causes as fundamentally deficient. Second, Bacon adamantly opposed including formal and final causes within science (see his *Advancement of Learning*).[2] For Bacon, formal and final causes belong to metaphysics, not to science. Science, according to Bacon, needs to limit itself to material and efficient causes, thereby freeing science from the sterility that inevitably results when science and metaphysics are conflated. This was Bacon's line, and he argued it forcefully.

We see Bacon's line championed in our own day by atheists and theists alike. In *Chance and Necessity* biologist and Nobel laureate Jacques Monod argued that chance and necessity alone suffice to account for every aspect of the universe. Now whatever else we might want to say about chance and necessity, they provide at best a reductive account of Aristotle's formal causes and leave no room whatever for Aristotle's final causes. Indeed, Monod explicitly denies any place for purpose within science.[3]

Monod was an outspoken atheist. Nevertheless, as outspoken a theist as Stanley Jaki will agree with Monod about the nature of science. Jaki is as theologically conservative a historian of science and Catholic priest as one is likely to find. Yet in his published work he explicitly states that purpose is a purely metaphysical notion and cannot legitimately be included within science. Jaki's exclusion of purpose and, more generally, design from science has practical implications. For instance, it leads him to regard Michael Behe's project of inferring biological design from irreducibly complex biochemical systems as misguided.[4]

Now I don't want to give the impression that I'm advocating a return to Aristotle's theory of causation. There are problems with Aristotle's theory, and it needed to be replaced. My concern, however, is with what replaced it. By limiting scientific inquiry to material and efficient causes, Bacon fed into a mechanistic understanding of the universe that was soon to dominate science.

To be sure, mechanism has its advantages. Back in the seventeenth century the French playwright Molière ridiculed Aristotelians for explaining the medicinal properties of opium in terms of its "dormitive power." Appealing to a final cause like "dormitive power" is of course totally unenlightening. Much better is to know the chemical properties of opium and how those properties take advantage of certain nerve centers in the brain. Mechanistic explanations that describe how something works without speculating about its ultimate meaning or purpose seemed a much safer course for science, and one that promised to and in fact did yield much fruit.

Mechanism is still with us, though not the deterministic form that dominated from Newton to the quantum revolution. In our own day scientists take as their preferred mode of scientific explanation a combination of deterministic laws and chance processes. Chance and necessity, to use Monod's phrase, set the boundaries of scientific explanation, and woe to anyone who would reintroduce a sterile and moribund teleology into science.

5.2 Why Reinstate Design?
Faced with a discredited Aristotelian science, a marvelously successful modern science and an entrenched opposition within the scientific commu-

nity against design, why should anyone want to reintroduce design into science? The short answer is that chance and necessity have proven too thin an explanatory soup on which to nourish a robust science. In fact, by dogmatically excluding design from science, scientists are themselves stifling scientific inquiry. To a generation suckled at naturalism's teat, this will no doubt seem counterintuitive. Nevertheless the case for reintroducing design within science becomes compelling as soon as we attend to certain relevant facts.

The first glimmers that excluding design artificially restricts science come from admissions by scientists opposed to design. The arch-Darwinist Richard Dawkins begins his book *The Blind Watchmaker* by stating, "Biology is the study of complicated things that give the appearance of having been designed for a purpose."[5] Statements like this echo throughout the biological literature. In *What Mad Pursuit* Francis Crick, Nobel laureate and codiscoverer of the structure of DNA, writes, "Biologists must constantly keep in mind that what they see was not designed, but rather evolved."[6]

Granted, the biological community thinks it has accounted for the apparent design in nature apart from any actual design (typically through the Darwinian mechanism of mutation and selection). The point to appreciate, however, is that in accounting for the apparent design in nature, biologists regard themselves as having made a successful *scientific* argument against actual design. But scientific refutation is a double-edged sword. Claims that are refuted scientifically *may* be wrong, but they are not *necessarily* wrong. For a claim to be scientifically falsifiable, it must have the possibility of being true.

To see this, consider what would happen if microscopic examination revealed that every cell was inscribed with the phrase "Made by Yahweh." Of course cells don't have "Made by Yahweh" inscribed on them, but that's not the point. The point is that we wouldn't know this unless we actually looked at cells under the microscope. Design always remains a live option in biology. A priori prohibitions against design are easily countered, especially in an age of diversity and multiculturalism where it is all too easy to ask, Who sets the rules for science? Nonetheless, once we admit that design cannot be excluded from science on first principles, a weightier question remains: Why should we want to reinstate design within science?

To answer this question, let us turn it around and ask instead, Why shouldn't we want to reinstate design within science? What's wrong with explaining something as designed by an intelligent agent? Certainly there are many everyday occurrences which we explain by appealing to design. Moreover in our workaday lives it is absolutely crucial to distinguish accident from design. We demand answers to such questions as, Did she fall or was she pushed? Did someone die accidentally or commit suicide? Was this song conceived independently or was it plagiarized? Did someone just get lucky on the stock market or was there insider trading?

Not only do we demand answers to such questions, but entire industries are devoted to drawing the distinction between accident and design. Here we can include forensic science, intellectual property law, insurance claims investigation, cryptography and random number generation—to name but a few. Science itself needs to draw this distinction to keep itself honest. In a January 1998 issue of *Science,* a Medline web search uncovered a "paper published in *Zentralblatt für Gynäkologie* in 1991 [containing] text that is almost identical to text from a paper published in 1979 in the *Journal of Maxillofacial Surgery.*"[7] Plagiarism and data falsification are far more common in science than we would like to admit. What keeps these abuses in check is our ability to detect them.

If design is so readily detectable outside science and if its detectability is one of the key factors keeping scientists honest, why should design be barred from the content of science? With reference to biology, why should we have to constantly remind ourselves that biology studies things that only appear to be designed but that in fact are not designed? Isn't it at least conceivable that there could be good positive reasons for thinking biological systems are in fact designed?

The biological community's response to these questions has been to resist design at all costs. The worry is that for natural objects (unlike human artifacts) the distinction between design and nondesign cannot be reliably drawn. Consider, for instance, the following remark by Darwin in the concluding chapter of his *Origin of Species:*

> Several eminent naturalists have of late published their belief that a multitude of reputed species in each genus are not real species; but that other species are real, that is, have been independently created. . . . Nevertheless they do not pretend that they can define, or even conjecture, which are the created forms of life, and which are those produced by secondary laws.

They admit variation as a *vera causa* in one case, they arbitrarily reject it in another, without assigning any distinction in the two cases.[8]

It's this worry of falsely attributing something to design (here identified with creation) only to have it overturned later that has prevented design from entering science proper.

This worry, though perhaps justified in the past, is no longer tenable. There does in fact exist a rigorous criterion for distinguishing intelligently caused objects from unintelligently caused ones. Many special sciences already use this criterion, though in a pretheoretic form (e.g., forensic science, artificial intelligence, cryptography, archaeology and the search for extraterrestrial intelligence [SETI]). The great breakthrough of the intelligent design movement has been to isolate and make precise this criterion. Michael Behe's criterion of irreducible complexity for establishing the design of biochemical systems is a special case of this general criterion for detecting design.[9]

Yet before examining this criterion, I want briefly to clarify the word *design*. I'm using *design* in three distinct senses. First, I use it to denote the scientific theory that distinguishes intelligent agency from natural causes, a theory that increasingly is being referred to as *design theory* or *intelligent design* (ID). Second, I use *design* to denote what it is about intelligently produced objects that enables us to tell that they are intelligently produced and not simply the result of natural causes. When intelligent agents act, they leave behind a characteristic trademark or signature. The scholastics used to refer to the "vestiges in creation."[10] The Latin *vestigium* means footprint. It was thought that God, though not directly present to our senses, had nonetheless left his "footprints" throughout creation. Hugh Ross has referred to the "fingerprint of God."[11] It is *design* in this sense—as a trademark, signature, vestige or fingerprint—that this criterion for discriminating intelligently from unintelligently caused objects is meant to identify. Lastly, I use *design* to denote intelligent agency itself. Thus to say that something is designed is to say that an intelligent agent caused it. But note, to say that an intelligent agent caused something is not to prescribe how an intelligent agent caused it. In particular, design in this last sense is separate from miracle.

5.3 The Complexity-Specification Criterion
What does this criterion for detecting design look like? Although a detailed explanation and justification of this criterion is fairly technical,[12]

the basic idea is straightforward and easily illustrated. Consider how the radio astronomers in the movie *Contact* detected an extraterrestrial intelligence. This movie, based on a novel by Carl Sagan, was an enjoyable piece of propaganda for the SETI research program—the search for extraterrestrial intelligence. To make the movie interesting, the SETI researchers in *Contact* actually did find an extraterrestrial intelligence. (The *non*fictional SETI program has yet to be so lucky.)

How then did the researchers in *Contact* convince themselves that they had found an extraterrestrial intelligence? To increase their chances of finding an extraterrestrial intelligence, SETI researchers monitor millions of radio signals from outer space. Many natural objects in space produce radio waves (e.g., pulsars). Looking for signs of design among all these naturally produced radio signals is like looking for a needle in a haystack. To sift through the haystack, SETI researchers run the signals they monitor through computers programmed with pattern-matchers. So long as a signal doesn't match one of the preset patterns, it will pass through the pattern-matching sieve (and that even if it has an intelligent source). On the other hand, if it does match one of these patterns, then depending on the pattern matched, the SETI researchers may have cause for celebration.

The SETI researchers in *Contact* did find a signal worthy of celebration—the signal in figure 5.1. They received this signal as a sequence of 1126 beats and pauses, where 1s correspond to beats and 0s to pauses. This sequence represents the prime numbers from 2 to 101, where a given prime number is represented by the corresponding number of beats (i.e., 1s) and the individual prime numbers are separated by pauses (i.e., 0s). The SETI researchers in *Contact* took this signal as decisive confirmation of an extraterrestrial intelligence.

What characteristic about this signal implicates design? Whenever we infer design, we must establish three things: *contingency, complexity* and *specification*. Contingency ensures that the object in question is not the result of an automatic and therefore unintelligent process that had no choice in its production. Complexity ensures that the object is not so simple that it can readily be explained by chance. Finally, specification ensures that the object exhibits the type of pattern characteristic of intelligence. Let us examine these three requirements more closely.

In practice, to establish the contingency of an object, event or structure, one must establish that it is compatible with the regularities

```
11011101111101111111011111111111101111111111111101111111
11111111110111111111111111111110111111111111111111111111
01111111111111111111111111111111101111111111111111111111
11111111011111111111111111111111111111111111111101111111
11111111111111111111111111111111110111111111111111111111
11111111111111111111111101111111111111111111111111111111
11111111111111111110111111111111111111111111111111111111
11111111111111111101111111111111111111111111111111111111
11111111111111111111111110111111111111111111111111111111
11111111111111111111111111111111111111111110111111111111
11111111111111111111111111111111111111111111111111111111
11110111111111111111111111111111111111111111111111111111
11111111111111111111110111111111111111111111111111111111
11111111111111111111111111111111111111111111111111110111
11111111111111111111111111111111111111111111111111111111
11111111111111111111111110111111111111111111111111111111
11111111111111111111111111111111111111111111111111111111
11111111011111111111111111111111111111111111111111111111
11111111111111111111111111111111111111111111111111111101
11111111111111111111111111111111111111111111111111111111
11111111111111111111111111111111111111111111111111111
```

Figure 5.1. SETI signal

involved in its production but that these regularities also permit any number of alternatives to it. Typically these regularities are conceived as natural laws or algorithms. By being compatible with but not required by the regularities involved in its production, an object, event or structure becomes irreducible to any underlying physical necessity. Michael Polanyi and Timothy Lenoir have both described this method of establishing contingency.[13] The method applies quite generally: the position of scrabble pieces on a game board is irreducible to the natural laws governing the motion of scrabble pieces; the configuration of ink on a sheet of paper is irreducible to the physics and chemistry of paper and ink; the sequencing of DNA bases is irreducible to the bonding affinities between the bases; and so on. In the case at hand, the sequence of 0s and 1s to form a sequence of prime numbers is irreducible to the laws of physics that govern the transmission of radio signals. We therefore regard the sequence as contingent.

To see next why complexity is crucial for inferring design, consider the following sequence of bits:

110111011111

These are the first twelve bits in the previous sequence representing the prime numbers 2, 3 and 5 respectively. Now it is a sure bet that no SETI researcher, if confronted with this twelve-bit sequence, is going to contact the science editor at the *New York Times,* hold a press conference and announce that an extraterrestrial intelligence has been discovered. No headline is going to read, "Aliens Master First Three Prime Numbers!"

The problem is that this sequence is much too short (and thus too simple) to establish that an extraterrestrial intelligence with knowledge of prime numbers produced it. A randomly beating radio source might by chance just happen to output this sequence. A sequence of 1,126 bits representing the prime numbers from 2 to 101, however, is a different story. Here the sequence is sufficiently long (and therefore sufficiently complex) that only an extraterrestrial intelligence could have produced it.

Complexity as I am describing it here is a form of probability. Later in this chapter I will require a more general conception of complexity to unpack the logic of design inferences. But for now complexity as a form of probability is all we need. To see the connection between complexity and probability, consider a combination lock. The more possible combinations of the lock, the more complex the mechanism and correspondingly the more improbable that the mechanism can be opened by chance. Complexity and probability therefore vary inversely: the greater the complexity, the smaller the probability. Thus to determine whether something is sufficiently complex to warrant a design inference is to determine whether it has sufficiently small probability.

Even so, complexity (or improbability) isn't enough to eliminate chance and establish design. If I flip a coin 1,000 times, I'll participate in a highly complex (i.e., highly improbable) event. Indeed, the sequence I end up flipping will be one in a trillion trillion trillion . . . (where the ellipsis needs twenty-two more *trillions*). This sequence of coin tosses won't, however, trigger a design inference. Though complex, this sequence won't exhibit a suitable pattern. Contrast this with the previous sequence representing the prime numbers from 2 to 101. Not only is this sequence complex, but it also embodies a suitable pattern. The SETI researcher who in the movie *Contact* discovered this sequence put it this way: "This isn't noise; this has structure."

What is a *suitable* pattern for inferring design? Not just any pattern will do. Some patterns can legitimately be employed to infer design whereas others cannot. The intuition underlying the distinction between patterns that alternately succeed or fail to implicate design is, however, easily motivated. Consider the case of an archer. Suppose an archer stands fifty meters from a large wall with bow and arrow in hand. The wall, let us say, is sufficiently large that the archer cannot help but hit it. Now suppose each time the archer shoots an arrow at the wall, the archer paints a target around the arrow so that the arrow sits squarely in the bull's-eye. What can be concluded from this scenario? Absolutely nothing about the archer's ability as an archer. Yes, a pattern is being matched, but it is a pattern fixed only after the arrow has been shot. The pattern is thus purely ad hoc.

But suppose instead the archer paints a fixed target on the wall and then shoots at it. Suppose the archer shoots a hundred arrows and each time hits a perfect bull's-eye. What can be concluded from this second scenario? We are obligated to infer that here is a world-class archer, one whose shots cannot legitimately be referred to luck but rather must be referred to the archer's skill and mastery. Skill and mastery are of course instances of design.

The archer example introduces three elements that are essential for inferring design:

1. a reference class of possible events (the arrow hitting the wall at some unspecified place)

2. a pattern that restricts the reference class of possible events (a target on the wall)

3. the precise event that has occurred (the arrow hitting the wall at some precise location)

In a design inference the reference class, the pattern and the event are linked, with the pattern mediating between event and reference class and helping to decide whether the event is due to chance or design. Note that in determining whether an event is sufficiently improbable or complex to implicate design, the relevant improbability is not that of the precise event that occurred but that of the target/pattern. Indeed, the bigger the target, the easier it is to hit it by chance and thus apart from design.

The type of pattern where an archer fixes a target first and then shoots at it is common to statistics, where it is known as setting a *rejection region* prior to an experiment. In statistics, if the outcome of an experiment falls within a rejection region, the chance hypothesis supposedly responsible for the outcome is rejected. The reason for setting a rejection region prior to an experiment is to forestall what statisticians call "data snooping" or "cherry picking." Just about any data set will contain strange and improbable patterns if we look hard enough. By forcing experimenters to set their rejection regions prior to an experiment, the statistician protects the experiment from spurious patterns that could just as well result from chance.

Now a little reflection makes clear that a pattern need not be given prior to an event to eliminate chance and implicate design. Consider the following cipher text:

```
nfuijolt ju jt mjlf b xfbtfm
```

Initially this looks like a random sequence of letters and spaces—initially you lack any pattern for rejecting chance and inferring design.

But suppose next that someone comes along and tells you to treat this sequence as a Caesar cipher, in which each letter has shifted one notch down the alphabet. The deciphered sequence then reads,

```
methinks it is like a weasel
```

Even though the pattern (in this case, the decrypted text) is given after the fact, it still is the right sort of pattern for eliminating chance and inferring design. In contrast to statistics, which always identifies its patterns before an experiment is performed, cryptanalysis must discover its patterns after the fact. In both instances, however, the patterns are suitable for inferring design.

Patterns thus divide into two types, those that in the presence of complexity warrant a design inference and those that despite the presence of complexity do not warrant a design inference. The first type of pattern I call a *specification,* the second a *fabrication.* Specifications are the non-ad hoc patterns that can legitimately be used to eliminate chance and warrant a design inference. In contrast, fabrications are the ad hoc patterns that cannot legitimately be used to warrant a design inference. This distinction between specifications and fabrications can be made with full statistical rigor.[14]

To sum up, the complexity-specification criterion detects design by establishing three things: contingency, complexity and specification. When called to explain an event, object or structure, we have a decision to make—are we going to attribute it to *necessity, chance* or *design?* According to the complexity-specification criterion, to answer this question is to answer three simpler questions: Is it contingent? Is it complex? Is it specified? Consequently the complexity-specification criterion can be represented as a flowchart with three decision nodes. I call this flowchart the explanatory filter (see figure 5.2).[15]

5.4 Specification

Because specification[16] is so central to inferring design, I need to elaborate it. For a pattern to count as a specification, the important thing is not when it was identified but whether in a certain well-defined sense it is *independent* of the event it describes. Drawing a target around an arrow already embedded in a wall is not independent of the arrow's trajectory. Consequently such a target/pattern cannot be used to attribute the arrow's trajectory to design. Patterns that are specifications cannot simply be read off the events whose design is in question. Rather, to count as specifications, patterns must be suitably independent of events. I refer to this relation of independence as *detachability* and say that a pattern is *detachable* just in case it satisfies that relation.

Detachability can be understood as asking the following question: Given an event whose design is in question and a pattern describing it, would we be able to construct that pattern if we had no knowledge which event occurred? Here is the idea. An event has occurred. A pattern describing the event is given. The event is one from a range of possible events. If all we knew was the range of possible events without any specifics about which event actually occurred, could we still construct the pattern describing the event? If so, the pattern is detachable from the event.

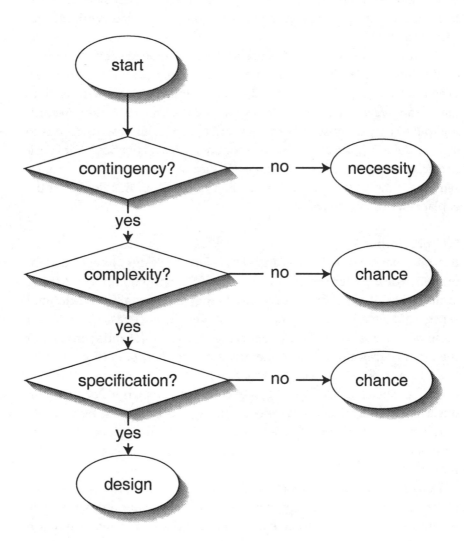

Figure 5.2. The explanatory filter

THTTTHHTHHTTTTTHTHTTHHHTT
HTHHHTHHHTTTTTTTHTTHTTTHH
THTTTHTHTHHTTHHHHTTTHTTHH
THTHTHHHHTTHHTHHHHTHHHHTT

E

Figure 5.3. Event E

To see what's at stake, we will use the example that finally clarified for me what transforms a pattern simpliciter into a pattern qua specification. Consider, therefore, the event E (in figure 5.3), an event that to all appearances was obtained by flipping a fair coin 100 times.

Is E the product of chance or not? A standard trick of statistics professors with an introductory statistics class is to divide the class in two, having students in one half of the class each flip a coin 100 times, writing down the sequence of heads and tails on a slip of paper and having students in the other half each generate purely with their minds a "random looking" string of coin tosses that mimics the tossing of a coin 100 times, also writing down the sequence of heads and tails on a slip of paper. When the students hand in their lists of sequences, the professor must sort them into two piles, those generated by flipping a fair coin and those concocted in the students' heads. To the amazement of the students, the statistics professor is typically able to sort the papers with 100 percent accuracy.

There's no mystery here. The statistics professor simply looks for a repetition of six or seven heads or tails in a row to distinguish the truly random from the pseudo-random sequences. In 100 coin flips, one is quite likely to see six or seven such repetitions. On the other hand, people concocting pseudo-random sequences with their minds tend to alternate between heads and tails too frequently. Whereas with a truly random sequence of coin tosses there is a 50 percent chance that one toss will differ from the next, as a matter of human psychology people expect that one toss will differ from the next around 70 percent of the time.

How then will our statistics professor fare when confronted with E? Will E be attributed to chance or to the musings of someone trying to mimic chance? According to the professor's crude randomness checker, E would be assigned to the pile of sequences presumed to be truly random, for E contains a repetition of seven tails in a row. Everything that at first

```
0100011011000001010011100
1011101110000000100100011
0100010101100111100010011
0101011110011011110111100                                    D
```

Figure 5.4. Pattern D

blush would lead us to regard E as truly random checks out. There are exactly 50 alternations between heads and tails (as opposed to the 70 that would be expected from humans trying to mimic chance). What's more, the relative frequencies of heads and tails check out: there were 49 heads and 51 tails. Thus it's not as though the coin supposedly responsible for generating E was heavily biased in favor of one side versus the other.

Suppose, however, that our statistics professor suspects she is not up against a neophyte statistics student but instead a fellow statistician who is trying to put one over on her. To help organize her problem, study it more carefully and enter it into a computer, she will find it convenient to let strings of 0s and 1s represent the outcomes of coin flips, with 1 corresponding to heads and 0 to tails. In that case the following pattern D (figure 5.4) will correspond to the event E. Now the mere fact that the event E conforms to the pattern D is no reason to think that E did not occur by chance. As things stand, the pattern D has simply been read off the event E.

But D need not have been read off of E. Indeed, D could have been constructed without recourse to E. To see this, let us rewrite D (see figure 5.5). By viewing D this way, anyone with the least exposure to binary arithmetic immediately recognizes that D was constructed simply by writing binary numbers in ascending order, starting with the one-digit binary numbers (i.e., 0 and 1), proceeding then to the two-digit binary numbers (i.e., 00, 01, 10 and 11) and continuing on until 100 digits were recorded. It's therefore intuitively clear that D does not describe a truly random event (i.e., an event gotten by tossing a fair coin) but rather a pseudo-random event, concocted by doing a little binary arithmetic.

Although it's now intuitively clear why chance cannot properly explain E, we need to consider more closely why this mode of explanation fails here. We started with a putative chance event E, supposedly gotten by flipping a fair coin 100 times. Since heads and tails each have

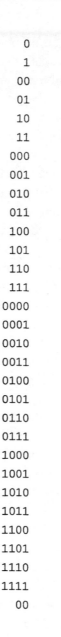

```
                    0
                    1
                   00
                   01
                   10
                   11
                  000
                  001
                  010
                  011
                  100
                  101
                  110
                  111
                 0000
                 0001
                 0010
                 0011
                 0100
                 0101
                 0110
                 0111
                 1000
                 1001
                 1010
                 1011
                 1100
                 1101
                 1110
                 1111
                   00                              D
```

Figure 5.5. Pattern D rewritten

probability ½, and since this probability gets multiplied for each flip of the coin, it follows that the probability of E is 2^{-100}, or approximately 10^{-30}. In addition, we constructed a pattern D to which E conforms. Initially D proved insufficient to eliminate chance as the explanation of E since in its construction D was simply read off of E. Rather, to eliminate chance we had also to recognize that D could have been constructed quite easily by performing some simple arithmetic operations with binary numbers. Thus to eliminate chance we needed to employ additional *side information,* which in this case consisted of our knowledge of binary arithmetic. This side information detached the pattern D from the event E and thereby rendered D a specification.

For side information to detach a pattern from an event, it must satisfy two conditions, a *conditional independence condition* and a *tractability condition.* According to the conditional independence condition, the side information must be conditionally independent of the event E. Conditional independence is a well-defined notion from probability theory. It means that the probability of E doesn't change once the side information is taken into account. Conditional independence is the standard probabilistic way of unpacking epistemic independence. Two things are epistemically independent if knowledge about one thing (in this case the side information) does not affect knowledge about the other (in this case the occurrence of E). This is certainly the case here since our knowledge of binary arithmetic does not affect the probabilities we assign to coin tosses.

The second condition, the tractability condition, requires that the side information enable us to construct the pattern D to which E conforms. This is evidently the case here as well since our knowledge of binary arithmetic enables us to arrange binary numbers in ascending order and thereby construct the pattern D. But what exactly is this *ability to construct a pattern on the basis of side information*? Perhaps the most slippery words in philosophy are *can, able* and *enable.* Fortunately, just as there is a precise theory for characterizing the epistemic independence between an event and side information—namely, probability theory—so, too, there is a precise theory for characterizing the ability to construct a pattern on the basis of side information—namely, *complexity theory.*

Complexity theory, conceived now quite generally and not merely as a form of probability, assesses the difficulty of tasks given the resources available for accomplishing those tasks.[17] As a generalization of computational complexity theory, complexity theory ranks tasks according to difficulty and then determines which tasks are sufficiently manageable to be doable or tractable. For instance, given current technology we find sending a person to the moon tractable, but sending a person to the nearest galaxy intractable. In the tractability condition the task to be accomplished is the construction of a pattern and the resources for accomplishing that task is side information. Thus for the tractability condition to be satisfied, side information must provide the resources necessary for constructing the pattern in question. All of this admits a precise complexity-theoretic formulation and makes definite what I called *the ability to construct a pattern on the basis of side information.*[18]

Taken jointly, the tractability and conditional independence conditions mean that side information enables us to construct the pattern to which an event conforms, yet without recourse to the actual event. This is the crucial insight. Because the side information is conditionally and therefore epistemically independent of the event, any pattern constructed from this side information is obtained without recourse to the event. In this way any pattern that is constructed from such side information avoids the charge of being ad hoc. These then are the detachable patterns. These are the specifications.

5.5 False Negatives and False Positives

As with any criterion, we need to make sure that the judgments of the complexity-specification criterion agree with reality. Consider medical tests. Any medical test is a criterion. A perfectly reliable medical test would detect a disease whenever it is present and fail to detect the disease whenever it is absent. Unfortunately, no medical test is perfectly reliable, and so the best we can do is keep the proportion of false positives and false negatives as low as possible.

All criteria, and not just medical tests, face the problem of false positives and false negatives. A criterion attempts to classify individuals with respect to a target group (in the case of medical tests, those who have a certain disease). When the criterion places in the target group an individual who should not be there, it commits a false positive. Alternatively, when the criterion fails to place in the target group an individual who should be there, it commits a false negative.

Take medical tests again. A medical test checks whether an individual has a certain disease. The target group comprises all those individuals who actually have the disease. When the medical test classifies an individual who doesn't have the disease with those who do, it commits a false positive. When the medical test classifies an individual who does have the disease with those who do not, it commits a false negative.

Let us now apply these observations to the complexity-specification criterion. This criterion purports to detect design. Is it a reliable criterion? The target group for this criterion comprises all things intelligently caused. How accurate is this criterion at correctly assigning things to this target group and correctly omitting things from it? The things we are trying to explain have causal stories. In some of those causal stories intelligent causation is indispensable, whereas in others it is dispensable. An inkblot can be explained without appealing to intelligent causation; ink arranged to form meaningful text cannot. When the complexity-specification criterion assigns something to the target group, can we be confident that it actually is intelligently caused? If not, we have a problem with false positives. On the other hand, when this criterion fails to assign something to the target group, can we be confident that no intelligent cause underlies it? If not, we have a problem with false negatives.

Consider first the problem of false negatives. When the complexity-specification criterion fails to detect design in a thing, can we be sure no intelligent cause underlies it? The answer is no. For determining that something is not designed, this criterion is not reliable. False negatives are a problem for it. This problem of false negatives, however, is endemic to detecting intelligent causes.

One difficulty is that intelligent causes can mimic necessity and chance, thereby rendering their actions indistinguishable from such unintelligent causes. A bottle of ink may fall off a cupboard and spill onto a sheet of paper. Alternatively a human agent may deliberately take a bottle of ink and pour it over a sheet of paper. The resulting inkblot may look identical in both instances, but the one case results by chance, the other by design.

Another difficulty is that detecting intelligent causes requires background knowledge on our part. It takes an intelligent cause to know an intelligent cause. But if we don't know enough, we'll miss it. Consider a spy listening in on a communication channel whose messages are encrypted. Unless the spy knows how to break the cryptosystem used by the parties on whom he is eavesdropping, any messages passing the communication channel will be unintelligible and might in fact be meaningless.

The problem of false negatives therefore arises either when an intelligent agent has acted (whether consciously or unconsciously) to conceal one's actions or when an intelligent agent in trying to detect design has insufficient background knowledge to determine whether design actually is present. Detectives face this problem all the time. A detective confronted with a murder needs first to determine whether a murder has indeed been committed. If the murderer was clever and made it appear that the victim died by accident, then the detective will mistake the murder for an accident. So, too, if the detective is stupid and misses certain obvious clues, the detective will mistake the murder for an accident. In mistaking a murder for an accident the detective commits a false negative. Contrast this, however, with a detective facing a murderer intent on revenge and who wants to leave no doubt that the victim was intended to die. In that case the problem of false negatives is unlikely to arise (though we can imagine an incredibly stupid detective, like Chief Inspector Clouseau, mistaking a rather obvious murder for an accident).

Intelligent causes can do things that unintelligent causes cannot and can make their actions evident. When for whatever reason an intelligent cause fails to make its actions evident, we may miss it. But when an intelligent cause succeeds in making its actions evident, we take notice. This is why false negatives do not invalidate the complexity-specification criterion. This criterion is fully capable of detecting intelligent causes intent on making their presence evident. Masters of stealth intent on concealing their actions may successfully evade the criterion. But masters of self-promotion intent on making sure their intellectual property gets properly attributed find in the complexity-specification criterion a ready friend.

This brings us to the problem of false positives. Even though specified complexity is not a reliable criterion for *eliminating* design, it is, I shall argue, a reliable criterion for *detecting* design. The complexity-specification criterion is a net. Things that are designed will occasionally slip past the net. We would prefer that the net catch more than it does, omitting nothing due to design. But given the ability of design to mimic unintelligent causes and the possibility of our own ignorance passing over things that are designed, this problem cannot be fixed. Nevertheless we want to be very sure that whatever the net does catch includes only what we intend it to catch—things that are designed. Only things that are designed had better end up in the net. If this is the case, we can have confidence that whatever the complexity-specification criterion attributes to design is indeed designed. On the other hand, if things end up in the net that are not designed, the criterion will be worthless.

I want then to argue that specified complexity is a reliable criterion for detecting design. Alternatively I want to argue that the complexity-specification criterion successfully avoids false positives. Thus whenever this criterion attributes design, it does so correctly. Let us now see why this is the case. I offer two arguments. The first is a straightforward inductive argument: In every instance where the complexity-specification criterion attributes design and where the underlying causal story is known, it turns out design actually is present; therefore design actually is present whenever the complexity-specification criterion attributes design. The conclusion of this argument is a straightforward inductive generalization. It has the same logical status as concluding that all ravens are black given that all ravens observed to date have been found to be black.

The naturalist is likely to object at this point, claiming that the only things we can know to be designed are artifacts manufactured by intelligent beings that are in turn the product of blind evolutionary processes (e.g., humans). Hence to use the complexity-specification criterion to extrapolate design beyond such artifacts is illegitimate. This argument doesn't work. It is circular reasoning to invoke naturalism to underwrite an evolutionary account of intelligence and then in turn to employ this account of intelligence to insulate naturalism from critique. Naturalism is a metaphysical position, not a scientific theory based on evidence. Any account of intelligence it entails is therefore suspect and needs to be subjected to independent checks. The complexity-specification criterion provides one such check.

If we dismiss, as we ought, the naturalist's evolutionary account of intelligence, a more serious objection remains. I am arguing inductively that the complexity-specification criterion is a reliable criterion for detecting design. The conclusion of this argument is that whenever the criterion attributes design, design actually is present. The premise of this argument is that whenever the criterion attributes design and the underlying causal story can be verified, design actually is present. Now even though the conclusion follows as an inductive generalization from the premise, the premise itself seems false. There are a lot of coincidences out there that seem best explained without invoking design. Consider, for instance, the Shoemaker-Levy comet. The Shoemaker-Levy comet crashed into Jupiter exactly twenty-five years to the day after the Apollo 11 moon landing. What are we to make of this coincidence? Do we really want to explain it in terms of design? What if we submitted this coincidence to the complexity-specification criterion and out popped design? Our intuitions strongly suggest that the comet's trajectory and NASA's space program were operating independently, and that at best this coincidence should be referred to chance—certainly not design.

This objection is readily met. The fact is that the complexity-specification criterion does not yield design all that easily, especially if the complexities are kept high (or correspondingly, the probabilities are kept small). It is simply not the case that unusual and striking coincidences automatically trigger design. Martin Gardner is no doubt correct when he notes, "The number of events in which you participate for a month, or even a week, is so huge that the probability of noticing a startling correlation is quite high, especially if you keep a sharp outlook."[19] The implication he means to draw, however, is incorrect, namely, that therefore startling correlations/coincidences may uniformly be relegated to chance. Yes, the fact that the Shoemaker-Levy comet crashed into Jupiter exactly twenty-five years to the day after the Apollo 11 moon landing is a coincidence best referred to chance. But the fact that Mary Baker Eddy's writings on Christian Science bear a remarkable resemblance to Phineas Parkhurst Quimby's writings on mental healing is a coincidence that cannot be explained by chance and is properly explained by positing Quimby as a source for Eddy.[20]

The complexity-specification criterion is robust and easily resists counterexamples of the Shoemaker-Levy variety. Assuming, for instance, that the Apollo 11 moon landing serves as a specification for the crash of Shoemaker-Levy into Jupiter (a generous concession at that), that the comet could have crashed at any time within a period of a year and that the comet crashed to the very second precisely twenty-five years after the moon landing, a straightforward probability calculation indicates that the probability of this coincidence is no smaller than 10^{-8}. This simply isn't all that small a probability (i.e., high complexity), especially when considered in relation to all the events astronomers are observing in the solar system. Certainly this probability is nowhere near the universal probability bound of 10^{-150} that I propose in *The Design Inference*.[21] I have yet to see a convincing application of the complexity-specification criterion in which coincidences better explained by chance get attributed to design. I challenge anyone to exhibit a specified event of probability less than my universal probability bound for which intelligent causation can be convincingly ruled out.

5.6 Why the Criterion Works

My second argument for showing that specified complexity reliably detects design considers the nature of intelligent agency and specifically what it is about intelligent agents that makes them detectable. Even though induction confirms that specified complexity is a reliable criterion for detecting design, induction does not explain why this criterion works. To see why the complexity-specification criterion is exactly the right instrument for detecting design, we need to understand what it is about intelligent agents that makes them detectable in the first place. The principal characteristic of intelligent agency is choice. Even the etymology of the word *intelligent* makes this clear. *Intelligent* derives from two Latin words, the preposition *inter*, meaning between, and the verb *lego*, meaning to choose or select. Thus according to its etymology, intelligence consists in *choosing between*. For an intelligent agent to act is therefore to choose from a range of competing possibilities.

This is true not just of humans but also of animals as well as of extraterrestrial intelligences. A rat navigating a maze must choose whether to go right or left at various points in the maze. When SETI researchers attempt to discover intelligence in the extraterrestrial radio transmissions they are monitoring, they assume an extraterrestrial intelligence could have chosen any number of possible radio transmissions and then attempt to match the transmissions they observe with certain patterns as opposed to others. Whenever a human being utters meaningful speech, a choice is made from a range of possible sound-combinations that might have been uttered. Intelligent agency always entails discrimination, choosing certain things, ruling out others.

Given this characterization of intelligent agency, the crucial question is how to recognize it. Intelligent agents act by making a choice. How then do we recognize that an intelligent agent has made a choice? A bottle of ink spills accidentally onto a sheet of paper; someone takes a fountain pen and writes a message on a sheet of paper. In both instances ink is applied to paper. In both instances one among an almost infinite set of possibilities is realized. In both instances a contingency is actualized and others are ruled out. Yet in one instance we ascribe agency, in the other chance.

What is the relevant difference? Not only do we need to observe that a contingency was actualized, but we ourselves need also to be able to specify that contingency. The contingency must conform to an independently given pattern, and we must be able independently to construct that pattern. A random ink blot is unspecified; a message written with ink on paper is specified. To be sure, the exact message recorded may not be specified. But orthographic, syntactic and semantic constraints will nonetheless specify it.

Actualizing one among several competing possibilities, ruling out the rest and specifying the one that was actualized encapsulates how we recognize intelligent agency, or equivalently, how we detect design. Experimental psychologists who study animal learning and behavior have known this all along. To learn a task an animal must acquire the ability to actualize behaviors suitable for the task as well as the ability to rule out behaviors unsuitable for the task. Moreover, for a psychologist to recognize that an animal has learned a task, it is necessary not only to observe the animal making the appropriate discrimination but also to specify the discrimination.

Thus to recognize whether a rat has successfully learned how to traverse a maze, a psychologist must first specify which sequence of right and left turns conducts the rat out of the maze. No doubt a rat randomly wandering a maze also discriminates a sequence of right and left turns. But by randomly wandering the maze, the rat gives no indication that it can discriminate the appropriate sequence of right and left turns for exiting the maze. Consequently the psychologist studying the rat will have no reason to think the rat has learned how to traverse the maze.

Only if the rat executes the sequence of right and left turns specified by the psychologist will the psychologist recognize that the rat has learned how to traverse the maze. Now it is precisely these learned behaviors that we regard as intelligent in animals. Hence it is no surprise that the same scheme for recognizing animal learning recurs for recognizing intelligent agency generally: actualizing one among several competing possibilities, ruling out the others and specifying the one actualized.

Note that complexity is implicit here as well. To see this, consider again a rat traversing a maze, but now take a very simple maze in which two right turns conduct the rat out of the maze. How will a psychologist studying the rat determine whether it has learned to exit the maze? Just putting the rat in the maze will not be enough. Because the maze is so simple, the rat could by chance just happen to take two right turns and thereby exit the maze. The psychologist will therefore be uncertain whether the rat actually learned to exit this maze, or whether the rat just got lucky.

But contrast this with a complicated maze in which a rat must take just the right sequence of left and right turns to exit the maze. Suppose that the rat must take one hundred appropriate right and left turns and that any mistake will prevent the rat from exiting the maze. A psychologist who observes the rat taking no erroneous turns and in short order exiting the maze will be convinced that the rat has indeed learned how to exit the maze and that this was not dumb luck.

This general scheme for recognizing intelligent agency is but a thinly disguised form of the complexity-specification criterion. In general, to recognize intelligent agency we must observe an actualization of one among several competing possibilities, note which possibilities were ruled out and then be able to specify the possibility that was actualized. What's more, the competing possibilities that were ruled out must be live possibilities and sufficiently numerous so that specifying the possibility that was actualized cannot be attributed to chance. In terms of complexity this is just another way of saying that the range of possibilities is complex. In terms of probability this is just another way of saying that the possibility that was actualized has small probability.

All the elements in this general scheme for recognizing intelligent agency (i.e., actualizing, ruling out and specifying) find their counterpart in the complexity-specification criterion. It follows that this criterion formalizes what we have been doing right along when we recognize intelligent agency. The complexity-specification criterion pinpoints how we detect design.

5.7 Irreducible Complexity
Design is present in biology. Perhaps the most compelling evidence for design in biology comes from biochemistry. In a February 1998 issue of *Cell*, Bruce Alberts, president of the National Academy of Sciences, remarked,

> The entire cell can be viewed as a factory that contains an elaborate network of interlocking assembly lines, each of which is composed of large protein machines. . . . Why do we call the large protein assemblies that underlie cell function *machines*? Precisely because, like the machines invented by

humans to deal efficiently with the macroscopic world, these protein assemblies contain highly coordinated moving parts.[22]

Even so, Alberts sides with the majority of biologists in regarding the cell's marvelous complexity as only apparently designed. The Lehigh University biochemist Michael Behe disagrees. In *Darwin's Black Box* Behe presents a powerful argument for actual design in the cell. Central to his argument is his notion of *irreducible complexity*. A system is irreducibly complex if it consists of several interrelated parts so that removing even one part completely destroys the system's function. As an example of irreducible complexity Behe offers the mousetrap. A mousetrap consists of a platform, a hammer, a spring, a catch and a holding bar. Remove any one of these five components and it is impossible to construct a functional mousetrap.[23]

Irreducible complexity needs to be contrasted with *cumulative complexity*. A system is cumulatively complex if the components of the system can be arranged sequentially so that the successive removal of components never leads to the complete loss of function. An example of a cumulatively complex system is a city. It is possible successively to remove people and services from a city until one is down to a tiny village—all without losing the sense of community, which in this case constitutes function.

From this characterization of cumulative complexity, it is clear that the Darwinian mechanism of selection and mutation can readily account for cumulative complexity. Indeed the gradual accrual of complexity via selection mirrors the retention of function as components are successively removed from a cumulatively complex system.

But what about irreducible complexity? Can the Darwinian mechanism account for irreducible complexity? Certainly if selection acts with reference to a goal, it can produce irreducible complexity. Take Behe's mousetrap. Given the goal of constructing a mousetrap, one can specify a goal-directed selection process that in turn selects a platform, a hammer, a spring, a catch and a holding bar, and at the end puts all these components together to form a functional mousetrap. Given a pre-specified goal, selection has no difficulty producing irreducibly complex systems.

But the selection operating in biology is Darwinian natural selection. And this form of selection operates without goals, has neither plan nor purpose and is wholly undirected. The great appeal of Darwin's selection mechanism was, after all, that it would eliminate teleology from biology. Yet by making selection an undirected process, Darwin drastically abridged the type of complexity biological systems could manifest. Henceforth biological systems could manifest only cumulative complexity, not irreducible complexity.

Why is this? As Behe explains in *Darwin's Black Box,*

> An irreducibly complex system cannot be produced . . . by slight, successive modifications of a precursor system, because any precursor to an irreducibly complex system that is missing a part is by definition nonfunctional. . . . Since natural selection can only choose systems that are already working, then if a biological system cannot be produced gradually it would have to arise as an integrated unit, in one fell swoop, for natural selection to have anything to act on.[24]

For an irreducibly complex system, function is attained only when all components of the system are in place simultaneously. It follows that natural selection, if it is going to produce an irreducibly complex system, has to produce it all at once or not at all. This would not be a problem if the systems in question were simple. But they're not. The irreducibly complex biochemical systems Behe considers are protein machines consisting of numerous distinct proteins, each indispensable for function and together beyond what natural selection can muster in a single generation.

One such irreducibly complex biochemical system that Behe considers is the bacterial flagellum. The flagellum is a whiplike rotary motor that enables a bacterium to navigate through its environment. The flagellum includes an acid-powered rotary engine, a stator, O-rings, bushings and a drive shaft. The intricate machinery of this molecular motor requires approximately fifty proteins. Yet the absence of any one of these proteins results in the complete loss of motor function.[25]

The irreducible complexity of such biochemical systems counts powerfully against the Darwinian mechanism and indeed against any naturalistic evolutionary mechanism proposed to date. Moreover, because irreducible complexity occurs at the biochemical level, there is no more fundamental level of biological analysis to which the irreducible complexity of biochemical systems can be referred and at which a Darwinian analysis in terms of selection and mutation can still hope for success.

Undergirding biochemistry is ordinary chemistry and physics, neither of which can account for biological information. Also, whether a biochemical system is irreducibly complex is a fully empirical question: individually knocking out each protein constituting a biochemical system will determine whether function is lost. If it is, we are dealing with an irreducibly complex system. Protein knock-out experiments of this sort are routine in biology.[26]

The connection between Behe's notion of irreducible complexity and my complexity-specification criterion is now straightforward. The irreducibly complex systems Behe considers require numerous components specifically adapted to each other and each necessary for function. On any formal complexity-theoretic analysis, they are complex in the sense required by the complexity-specification criterion. Moreover, in virtue of their function, these systems embody patterns independent of the actual living systems. Hence these systems are also specified in the sense required by the complexity-specification criterion.

Biological specification always denotes function. An organism is a functional system comprising many functional subsystems. The functionality of organisms can be cashed out in any number of ways. Arno Wouters cashes it out globally in terms of the *viability* of whole organisms.[27] Michael Behe cashes it out in terms of the *minimal function* of biochemical systems.[28] Even the staunch Darwinist Richard Dawkins will admit that life is specified functionally, cashing out functionality in terms of the *reproduction* of genes. Thus in *The Blind Watchmaker* Dawkins will write, "Complicated things have some quality, specifiable in advance, that is highly unlikely to have been acquired by random chance alone. In the case of living things the quality that is specified in advance is . . . the ability to propagate genes in reproduction."[29]

5.8 So What?

There exists a reliable criterion for detecting design. This criterion detects design strictly from observational features of the world. Moreover it belongs to probability and complexity theory, not to metaphysics and theology. And although it cannot achieve logical demonstration, it does achieve statistical justification so compelling as to demand assent. This criterion is relevant to biology. When applied to the complex, information-rich structures of biology, it detects design. In particular the complexity-specification criterion shows that Michael Behe's irreducibly complex biochemical systems are designed.

What are we to make of these developments? Many scientists remain unconvinced. So what if we have a reliable criterion for detecting design, and so what if that criterion tells us that biological systems are designed? How is looking at a biological system and inferring it's designed any better than shrugging our shoulders and saying God did it? The fear is that design cannot help but stifle scientific inquiry.

Design is not a science-stopper. Indeed design can foster inquiry where traditional evolutionary approaches obstruct it. Consider the term "junk DNA." Implicit in this term is the view that because the genome of an organism has been cobbled together through a long, undirected evolutionary process, the genome is a patchwork of which only limited portions are essential to the organism. Thus on an evolutionary view we expect a lot of useless DNA. If, on the other hand, organisms are designed, we expect DNA as much as possible to exhibit function. And indeed the most recent findings suggest that designating DNA as "junk" merely cloaks our current lack of knowledge about function. For instance, in a 1997 issue of the *Journal of Theoretical Biology,* John Bodnar and his colleagues describe how "non-coding DNA in eukaryotic genomes encodes a language which programs organismal growth and development."[30] Design encourages scientists to look for function where evolution discourages it.

Or consider vestigial organs that later are found to have a function after all. Evolutionary biology texts often cite the human coccyx as a "vestigial structure" that hearkens back to vertebrate ancestors with tails. Yet if one looks at a recent edition of *Gray's Anatomy,* one finds that the coccyx is a crucial point of contact with muscles that attach to the pelvic floor. Now anatomy is nothing other than an exercise in design, studying the large-scale design plans/blueprints for bodies. Thus here again we find design encouraging scientists to look for function where evolution discourages it. Examples where the phrase "vestigial structure" merely cloaks our current lack of knowledge about function can be multiplied. The human appendix, formerly thought to be vestigial, is now known to be a functioning component of the immune system.[31]

Reinstating design within science can only enrich science. All the tried and true tools of science remain intact. But design also adds new tools to the scientist's explanatory tool chest. Moreover design raises a whole new set of research questions. Once we know that something is designed, we will want to know how it was produced, to what extent the design is optimal and what is its purpose. Note that we can detect design without knowing what something was designed for. There is a room at the Smithsonian filled with obviously designed objects for which no one has a clue about their purpose.[32]

Design also implies constraints. An object that is designed functions within certain design constraints. Transgress those constraints and the object functions poorly or breaks. Moreover we can discover those constraints empirically by seeing what does and doesn't work. This simple insight has tremendous implications not just for science but also for ethics. If humans are in fact designed, then we can expect psychosocial constraints to be hardwired into us. Transgress those constraints and we personally as well as our society will suffer. There's plenty of empirical evidence to suggest that many of the attitudes and behaviors our society promotes undermine human flourishing. Design promises to reinvigorate that ethical stream running from Aristotle through Aquinas known as natural law.[33]

By reinstating design within science, we do much more than simply critique scientific reductionism. Scientific reductionism holds that everything is reducible to scientific categories. Scientific reductionism is self-refuting and easily seen to be self-refuting. The existence of the world, the laws by which the world operates, the intelligibility of the world and the unreasonable effectiveness of mathematics for comprehending the world are just a few of the questions that science raises but is incapable of answering.

Simply critiquing scientific reductionism, however, is not enough. Critiquing scientific reductionism does nothing to change science—and it is science that must change. By eschewing design, science has for too long operated with an inadequate set of conceptual categories. This has led to a constricted vision of reality, skewing how science understands not just the world but also ourselves. Evolutionary psychology, which justifies everything from infanticide to adultery, is just one symptom of this inadequate conception of science.[34] Barring design from science distorts science, making it a mouthpiece for materialism instead of a search for truth.

Martin Heidegger remarked in *Being and Time*, "A science's level of development is determined by the extent to which it is *capable* of a crisis in its basic concepts."[35] The basic concepts with which science has operated these last several hundred years are no longer adequate, certainly not in an information age, certainly not in an age where design is empirically detectable. Science faces a crisis of basic concepts. The way out of this crisis is to expand science to include design. To reinstate design within science is to liberate science, freeing it from restrictions that were always arbitrary and now have become intolerable.

6

Intelligent Design as a Theory of Information

6.1 Complex Specified Information

In *Steps Towards Life* Manfred Eigen states what he takes as the central problem facing origins-of-life research: "Our task is to find an algorithm, a natural law that leads to the origin of information."[1] Eigen is only half right. To determine how life began, it is indeed necessary to understand the origin of information. Neither algorithms nor natural laws, however, are capable of producing information. The great myth of modern evolutionary biology is that information can be gotten on the cheap without recourse to intelligence. In this chapter I want to dispel this myth, but to do so I will need to give an account of information.

No one disputes that there is such a thing as information. As Keith Devlin remarks, "Our very lives depend upon it, upon its gathering, storage, manipulation, transmission, security, and so on. Huge amounts of money change hands in exchange for information. People talk about it all the time. Lives are lost in its pursuit. Vast commercial empires are created in order to manufacture equipment to handle it."[2] But what exactly is information?

To answer this question, let us start with what mathematicians mean by information. The mathematical theory of information focuses on the transmission of signals across a communication channel. What enables these signals to convey information is that they admit multiple alternate possibilities—in other words, they are contingent. As Robert Stalnaker remarks: "Content requires contingency. To learn something, to acquire information, is to rule out possibilities. To understand the information conveyed in a communication is to know what possibilities would be excluded by its truth."[3] A communication channel capable of transmitting only one signal cannot convey information. To convey information a communication channel must allow a multiplicity of distinct possible signals, any one of which might be sent.

Fred Dretske elaborates: "Information theory identifies the amount of information associated with, or generated by, the occurrence of an event (or the realization of a state of affairs) with the reduction in uncertainty, the elimination of possibilities, represented by that event or state of affairs."[4] To measure information, however, it is not enough to count the number of possibilities that were eliminated and offer this number as the relevant measure of information. The problem is that a simple enumeration of eliminated possibilities tells us nothing about how those possibilities were individuated in the first place.

Consider, for instance, the following individuation of poker hands:

(i) a royal flush
(ii) everything else

To learn that something other than a royal flush was dealt (i.e., possibility (ii)) is clearly to acquire less information than to learn that a royal flush was dealt (i.e., possibility (i)). A royal flush is highly specific. We've actually learned something when we discover that a royal flush was dealt. On the other hand, we've hardly learned a thing when we discover that a royal flush wasn't dealt. Most poker hands are not royal flushes, and we expect not to be dealt them. Nonetheless, if our measure of information is simply an enumeration of eliminated possibilities, the same numerical value must be assigned in both instances since in both instances a single possibility is eliminated.

It follows, therefore, that how we measure information needs to be independent of whatever procedure we use to individuate the possibilities under consideration. The way to do this is not simply to count possibilities but to assign probabilities to these possibilities. For a thoroughly shuffled deck of cards, the probability of being dealt a royal flush—possibility (i)—is approximately .000002 whereas the probability of being dealt anything other than a royal flush—possibility (ii)—is approximately .999998. Probabilities by themselves, however, are not information measures. Although probabilities distinguish possibilities according to the information they contain, probabilities are an inconvenient way to measure information.

There are two reasons for this. First, the scaling and directionality of the numbers assigned by probabilities needs to be recalibrated. We are clearly acquiring more information when we learn someone was dealt a royal flush than when we learn someone wasn't dealt a royal flush. And yet the probability of being dealt a royal flush (i.e., .000002) is minuscule compared to the probability of being dealt something other than a royal flush (i.e., .999998). Smaller probabilities signify more information, not less.

The second reason probabilities are inconvenient for measuring information is that they are multiplicative rather than additive. If we learn that Alice was dealt a royal flush playing poker at Caesar's Palace and that Bob was dealt a royal flush playing poker at the Mirage, the probability that both Alice and Bob were dealt royal flushes is the product of the individual probabilities. Nonetheless it is convenient for information to be measured additively so that the measure of information assigned to Alice and Bob jointly being dealt royal flushes equals the measure of information assigned to Alice being dealt a royal flush plus the measure of information assigned to Bob being dealt a royal flush.

Now there is a straightforward mathematical way to transform probabilities that circumvents both these difficulties, and that is to apply a negative logarithm to the probabilities. Applying a negative logarithm assigns more information to less probability and, because the logarithm of a product is the sum of the logarithms, transforms multiplicative probability measures into additive information measures.

What's more, in deference to communication theorists, it is customary to use the logarithm to the base 2. The rationale for this choice of logarithmic base is as follows: The most convenient way for communication theorists to measure information is in bits. Any message sent across a communication channel can be viewed as a string of 0s and 1s. For instance, the ASCII code[5] uses strings of eight 0s and 1s to represent the characters on a typewriter, with whole words and sentences in turn represented as strings of such character strings. Similarly all communication may be reduced to the transmission of sequences of 0s and 1s.

Given this reduction, the obvious way for communication theorists to measure information is in number of bits transmitted across a communication channel. And since the negative logarithm to the base 2 of a probability corresponds to the average number of bits needed to identify an event of that probability, the logarithm to the base 2 is the canonical logarithm for communication theorists. Thus we define the measure of information in an event of probability p as $-\log_2 p$.[6]

To see that this information measure is additive, return to the example of Alice being dealt a royal flush playing poker at Caesar's Palace and Bob being dealt a royal flush playing poker at the Mirage. Let's call the first event A and the second B. Since randomly dealt poker hands are probabilistically independent, the probability of A and B taken jointly equals the product of the probabilities of A and B taken individually. Symbolically, $P(A\&B) = P(A) \times P(B)$. Given our logarithmic definition of information, we therefore define the amount of information in an arbitrary event E as $I(E) =_{def} -\log_2 P(E)$. It then follows that $P(A\&B) = P(A) \times P(B)$ if and only if $I(A\&B) = I(A) + I(B)$ (because the logarithm of the product equals the sum of the logarithms). In the example of Alice and Bob, $P(A) = P(B) = .000002$, $I(A) = I(B) = 19$ and $I(A\&B) = I(A) + I(B) = 19 + 19 = 38$. Thus the amount of information inherent in Alice and Bob jointly obtaining royal flushes is 38 bits.

Since lots of events are probabilistically independent, information measures exhibit lots of additivity. But since lots of events are also correlated, information measures exhibit lots of nonadditivity as well. In the case of Alice and Bob, Alice being dealt a royal flush is probabilistically independent of Bob being dealt a royal flush, and so the amount of information in Alice and Bob both being dealt royal flushes equals the sum of the individual amounts of information.

But consider now a different example. Alice and Bob together toss a coin five times. Alice observes the first four tosses but is distracted and so misses the fifth toss. On the other hand, Bob misses the first toss but observes the last four tosses. Let's say the actual sequence of tosses is 11001 (1 = heads, 0 = tails). Thus Alice observes 1100* and Bob observes *1001. Let A denote the first observation, B the second. It follows that the amount of information in A&B is the amount of information in the completed sequence 11001, namely, 5 bits. On the other hand, the amount of information in A alone is the amount of information in the incomplete sequence 1100*, namely, 4 bits. Similarly the amount of information in B alone is the amount of information in the incomplete sequence *1001, also 4 bits. This time information doesn't add up: $5 = I(A\&B) \neq I(A) + I(B) = 4 + 4 = 8$.

Here A and B are correlated. Alice knows all but the last bit of information in the completed sequence 11001. Thus when Bob gives her the incomplete sequence *1001, all Alice really learns is the last bit in this sequence. Similarly, Bob knows all but the first bit of information in the completed sequence 11001. Thus when Alice gives him the incomplete sequence 1100*, all Bob really learns is the first bit in this sequence. What appears to be four bits of information actually ends up being only one bit of information once Alice and Bob factor in their prior information. We need, therefore, to introduce the idea of conditional information. $I(B|A)$, denotes the conditional information of B given A and signifies the amount of information in Bob's observation once Alice's observation is taken into account. This, as we just saw, is 1 bit. It follows that $5 = I(A\&B) = I(A) + I(B|A) = 4 + 1$.

$I(B|A)$, like $I(A\&B)$, $I(A)$ and $I(B)$, can be represented as the negative logarithm to the base 2 of a probability; only this time the probability under the logarithm is a conditional as opposed to an unconditional probability. By definition $I(B|A) =_{def} -\log_2 P(B|A)$, where $P(B|A)$ is the conditional probability of B given A. But since $P(B|A)$ is by definition the quotient $P(A\&B)/P(A)$, and since the logarithm of a quotient is the difference of the logarithms, $\log_2 P(B|A) = \log_2 P(A\&B) - \log_2 P(A)$, and so $-\log_2 P(B|A) = -\log_2 P(A\&B) + \log_2 P(A)$, which is just $I(B|A) = I(A\&B) - I(A)$. This last equation is equivalent to

(*) $$I(A\&B) = I(A) + I(B|A)$$

Since the information measure I is always nonnegative, this formula implies that $I(A\&B) \geq I(A)$ for all A and B. Formula (*) holds with full generality, reducing to $I(A\&B) = I(A) + I(B)$ when A and B are probabilistically independent (in which case $P(B|A) = P(B)$ and thus $I(B|A) = I(B)$).

Formula (*) asserts that the information in both A and B jointly is the information in A plus the information in B that is not in A. Its point, therefore, is to spell out how much additional information B contributes to A. As such this formula places tight constraints on the generation of new information. Does, for instance, a computer program (call it A) by outputting some data (call the data B) generate new information? Computer programs are fully deterministic, and so B is fully determined by A. It follows that $P(B|A) = 1$ and thus $I(B|A) = 0$ (the logarithm of 1 is always 0). From formula (*) it therefore follows that $I(A\&B) = I(A)$ and therefore that the amount of information in A and B jointly is no more than the amount of information in A by itself. This is an instance of what Peter Medawar calls the law of conservation of information.[7]

For an example in the same spirit consider that there is no more information in two copies of Shakespeare's *Hamlet* than in a single copy. This is of course patently obvious, and any formal account of information had better agree. To see that our formal account does indeed agree, let A denote the printing of the first copy of *Hamlet* and B the printing of the second copy. Once A is given, B is entirely determined. Indeed the correlation between A and B is perfect.

Probabilistically this is expressed by saying the conditional probability of B given A is 1, namely, $P(B|A) = 1$. In information-theoretic terms this is to say that $I(B|A) = 0$. As a result $I(B|A)$ drops out of formula (*), and so $I(A\&B) = I(A)$. Our information-theoretic formalism therefore agrees with our intuition that two copies of *Hamlet* contain no more information than a single copy.

As a purely formal object, the information measure described here is a complexity measure.[8] Complexity measures arise whenever we assign numbers to degrees of complication. A set of possibilities will often admit varying degrees of complication, ranging from extremely simple to extremely complicated. Complexity measures assign nonnegative numbers to these possibilities so that 0 corresponds to the most simple and ∞ to the most complicated. For instance, computational complexity is always measured in terms of either time (i.e., number of computational steps) or space (i.e., size of memory, usually measured in bits or bytes) or some combination of the two. The more difficult a computational problem, the more time and space are required to run the algorithm that solves the problem.

For information measures, degree of complication is measured in bits. Given an event A of probability $P(A)$, $I(A) = -\log_2 P(A)$ measures the number of bits associated with the probability **P**(A). We therefore speak of the "complexity of information" and say that the complexity of information increases as **I**(A) increases (or correspondingly, as **P**(A) decreases). We also speak of "simple" and "complex" information according to whether **I**(A) signifies few or many bits of information.

This information-theoretic account of complexity is entirely consistent with the account of complexity given in chapter five. Likewise, the account of specification given in chapter five carries over to information (information is transmitted through events, and these can be specified or unspecified). It follows that information can be both complex and specified. Information that is both complex and specified will be called *complex specified information,* or CSI for short. CSI is what all the fuss over information has been about in recent years, not just in biology but in science generally.

It is CSI that for Manfred Eigen constitutes the great mystery of life's origin, and one he hopes eventually to unravel in terms of algorithms and natural laws.[9] It is CSI that Michael Behe has uncovered with his irreducibly complex biochemical machines.[10] It is CSI that for cosmologists underlies the fine-tuning of the universe and that the various anthropic principles attempt to understand.[11] It is CSI that David Bohm's quantum potentials are extracting when they scour the microworld for what Bohm calls "active information."[12] It is CSI that enables Maxwell's demon to outsmart a thermodynamic system tending toward thermal equilibrium.[13] It is CSI that for Roy Frieden unifies the whole of physics.[14] It is CSI on which David Chalmers hopes to base a comprehensive theory of human consciousness.[15] It is CSI that within the Kolmogorov-Chaitin theory of algorithmic information identifies the highly compressible, nonrandom strings of digits.[16] How CSI gets from an organism's environment into an organism's genome is one of the long-standing questions addressed by the Santa Fe Institute.

Nor is CSI confined to science. CSI is indispensable in our everyday lives. The sixteen-digit number on your VISA card is an example of CSI. The complexity of this number ensures that a would-be thief cannot randomly pick a number and have it turn out to be a valid VISA number. What's more, the specification of this number ensures that it is your number, and not anyone else's. Even your phone number constitutes CSI. As with the VISA number, the complexity ensures that this number won't be dialed randomly (at least not too often), and the specification ensures that this number is yours and yours only. All the numbers on our bills, credit slips and purchase orders represent CSI. CSI makes the world go round.

The connection between design and information theory is therefore straightforward: To infer design by means of the complexity-specification criterion (see section 5.3) is equivalent to detecting complex specified information. All the elements in the complexity-specification criterion that lead us to infer design find their counterpart in the detection of complex specified information. For an event to satisfy the complexity-specification criterion, it must first of all be contingent. But contingency, as we've seen, is the chief characteristic of information. What's more, for a contingent event to be complex and specified is precisely what it means for that event to express complex specified information (CSI). It follows that the complexity-specification criterion attributes design just in case it detects CSI. Here then is the connection between design and information. Design and CSI are, as mathematicians would say, isomorphic.

6.2 Generating Information via Law

With this characterization of CSI in hand I want to return to Manfred Eigen's central problem—the origin of CSI. Where does CSI come from, and where is it incapable of coming from? According to Eigen, CSI comes from algorithms and natural laws.[17] As he put it, "Our task is to find an algorithm, a natural law that leads to the origin of [complex specified] information."[18] The only question for Eigen is which algorithms and natural laws explain the origin of CSI. The logically prior question of whether algorithms and natural laws are even in principle capable of explaining the origin of CSI is one he ignores. And yet it is a question that undermines Eigen's entire project. Algorithms and natural laws are in principle incapable of explaining the origin of information. To be sure, algorithms and natural laws can explain the flow of information. Indeed, algorithms and natural laws are ideally suited for transmitting already existing information. What they cannot do, however, is originate information.[19]

A mathematical argument is required to demonstrate that algorithms and natural laws cannot originate information. Within mathematics, algorithms and natural laws are functions, that is, relations between two sets which to every member in one set (called the domain) associates one and only one member in the other set (called the range). Typically we say that the function *maps* an element in the domain to its associated element in the range. Functions are fully deterministic: given an element in the domain, a function maps it to a unique element in the range.

Functions meet us at every turn in our lives. There's a function that maps every U.S. citizen to his or her social security number. The reason this is a function is because everyone's social security number is unique (at least for those citizens currently living). There are also functions that map each of us uniquely to our fathers and mothers (each of us has only one father and only one mother). On the other hand, the relation between parents and children is nonfunctional: a given father or mother may have more than one offspring.

Algorithms and natural laws are also functions. For algorithms the domain comprises input data, and the range comprises output data. For natural laws the domain comprises initial and boundary conditions, and the range comprises physical states at subsequent times t. Now suppose we had some CSI j and a function (i.e., an algorithm or natural law) f that, à la Manfred Eigen, led to the origin of j. That would mean some element in the domain of f, call it i, when acted on by f, yielded the output j. Mathematicians represent this relationship by writing $f(i) = j$. But this functional relationship hardly explains the origin of j. One problem has been solved by creating another, for now the origin of i must be explained.

Worse yet, the newly created problem is no easier than the one we started with. Functional relationships at best preserve what information is already there, or else degrade it—they never add to it. Thus however much information resides in j will be contained in any i that via the function f maps onto j. What's more, if j is specified, then the inverse image under the function f will also be specified (the inverse image of j under f are all the elements in its domain that f associates with j). In particular, since i maps onto j via f, i is in this inverse image. In short, if j constitutes complex specified information and f is a function that maps i onto j, then i constitutes specified information at least as complex as j.

Thus instead of explaining the origin of CSI, algorithms and natural laws shift the problem elsewhere—in fact, to a place where the origin of CSI will be at least as difficult to explain as before. Formula (*) of section 6.1 bears this out. Since i fully determines j with respect to f, $I(j \mid i) = 0$. Thus applying formula (*) to i and j yields $I(i\&j) = I(i)$. It follows that j contains no information that was not already contained in i.

Functions only make the information problem worse. Suppose you look at the U.S. Statistical Abstract and find that the average income of a U.S. citizen is so-much-and-so-much. How did this item of information originate? Well, the census bureau had to contact all the U.S. citizens, record their individual incomes, add the incomes together and divide by the number of U.S. citizens. To take an average is to apply a function—given the input data (all the individual U.S. incomes), the output data is uniquely determined. But more significant, to take an average is also to compress data. The information inherent in the record of all individual incomes far exceeds the information inherent in their average. Taking an average is a statistical technique for compressing data. In an information age, information inundates us. To assist the information seeker, information providers will therefore often compress information.

There is one subtlety we need now to consider. I have just argued that when a function acts to yield information, what the function acts upon has at least as much information as what the function yields. This argument, however, treats functions as mere conduits of information and does not take seriously the possibility that functions might add information. I gave the example of taking an average whereby data is compressed and information is lost. But consider the function that maps library call numbers to their corresponding books. Clearly there is less information in the call numbers than in the books. Here we have a function that is adding information. Moreover it is adding information because the information is embedded in the function itself.

Although this observation seems to undermine my previous argument (i.e., that the output of a function can contain no more information than its input), in fact it leaves the argument virtually unchanged. The point is that instead of the function f now merely serving as a conduit mapping information i to information j, the information in f must now itself be taken into account. The way to do this is to employ the universal composition function U, which to an ordered information-function pair (i,f) assigns the information obtained by applying f to i—in this case j. Thus $U(i,f) = f(i) = j$.

Now unlike f, which may well incorporate information, U, the universal composition function, incorporates no information of its own but is merely a conduit for information. By simply taking ordered pairs and treating the second element as a function applied to the first, U introduces no information of its own. Note that in the case of algorithms U is a universal Turing machine.[20]

The form of the original argument is therefore unchanged: the information j arises by applying U (cf. f in the original argument) to the information (i,f) (cf. i in the original argument). Just as in computer science the distinction between data and programs is not hard and fast, so the distinction between functions and information is not hard and fast. We can therefore treat the ordered pair (i,f) as information which, via the universal composition function, maps to the information j. Clearly the information inherent in (i,f) exceeds that in j. Formula (*) of section 6.1 confirms this as well. Like a bulge under a rug, the information problem can be shifted around, but it does not go away.

This argument, by employing the universal composition function, is perfectly general. In particular it answers the attempt by complexity theorists to account for the origin of information in terms of dynamical systems.[21] Complexity theorists, especially the Santa Fe Institute group, continue to hope that information can be gotten on the cheap. "Look at all those amazing fractal patterns," we are told. "The incredibly intricate Mandelbrot set is generated by so modest a function as $h(z) = z^2 + c$." To state the matter this way, however, is misleading. The function $h(z) = z^2 + c$ is simple enough, and even simpler to write down. And granted, it is the crucial element in constructing a graphic depiction of the Mandelbrot set (see figure 6.1). But that is the point: It is the graphic depiction of the Mandelbrot set that has to be explained, not its existence as an abstract mathematical object. And this graphic depiction has to be constructed.[22]

Pixels on a computer screen have to be assigned coordinates representing complex numbers (i.e., numbers of the form $a+ib$ where a and b are real numbers and i is the square root of -1). The function $h(z) = z^2 + c$ has to be iterated with respect to those coordinates. The trajectory of those iterations needs to be tracked to see if the trajectory stays locally bounded or heads off toward infinity. Given these trajectories, a color has to be assigned to the pixel—black if the trajectory stays locally bounded, white if it heads off to infinity. All of this must be programmed. All of this is information far exceeding the information inherent in simply writing down "$h(z) = z^2 + c$."

The function $h(z) = z^2 + c$ is never the function that produces the pretty graphic depictions of the Mandelbrot set that we see in books on fractals.

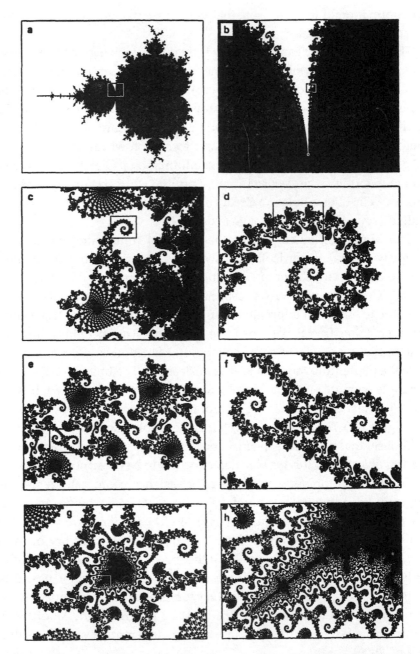

Figure 6.1. Zoom into the Mandelbrot set. Taken from Heinz-Otto Peitgen, Harmut Jürgens and Dietmar Saupe, *Chaos and Fractals: New Frontiers of Science* (New York: Springer-Verlag, 1992), p. 856. Used by permission.

Any function that produces a graphic depiction of the Mandelbrot set will be a complicated algorithm employing a complicated set of input data. Any such algorithm f applied to a data set i can be conjoined as an ordered pair (i,f) and then evaluated by the universal composition function U to produce a graphic depiction of the Mandelbrot set j. But by itself the function $h(z) = z^2 + c$ is too information-poor to produce this graphic depiction of the Mandelbrot set j. Once we examine the precise informational antecedents to j, the illusion that we have generated information for nothing disappears.

What mathematicians call functions and what scientists prefer to call laws cannot explain the origin of CSI. The problem is that laws are deterministic and thus cannot yield contingency, without which there can be no information. The problem with laws is that they invariably yield only a single live possibility. Take a computer algorithm that performs addition. Let us say the algorithm has a correctness proof so that it performs its additions correctly. Given the input data $2 + 2$, can the algorithm output anything other than 4? Computer algorithms are wholly deterministic. They allow for no contingency and thus can generate no information. At best, therefore, laws shift information around, or lose it, as when data gets compressed. What laws cannot do is produce contingency; and without contingency they cannot generate information, to say nothing of complex specified information.[23]

6.3 Generating Information via Chance

If not by means of laws, how then does contingency—and hence information—arise? Two and only two answers are possible here. Either the contingency is a blind purposeless contingency, which is chance; or it is a guided, purposeful contingency, which is intelligent causation. We shall return to intelligent causation in due course, but for now let us examine whether chance is capable of generating CSI. First notice that pure chance, entirely unsupplemented and left to its own devices, is incapable of generating CSI. Chance can generate complex unspecified information, and chance can generate noncomplex specified information. What chance cannot generate is information that is both complex and specified.

To see this, consider a typist at a keyboard. By randomly typing a long sequence of letters, the typist will generate complex unspecified information: the precise sequence of letters typed will constitute a highly improbable unspecified event, yielding complex unspecified information (recall that high probability corresponds to low complexity whereas low probability—i.e., high improbability—corresponds to high complexity). Alternatively the typist, even if typing randomly, might by chance type the short sequence of letters *t-h-e*, thereby generating non-complex specified information: typing *t-h-e* constitutes a specified high-probability event, instancing noncomplex specified information. What random typing cannot do is produce an extended meaningful text, thereby generating information that is both complex and specified.

Why can't this happen by chance? According to the complexity-specification criterion of chapter five, once the improbabilities (i.e., complexities) become too vast and the specifications too tight, chance is eliminated and design is implicated. Just where the probabilistic cutoff is can be debated, but that there is a probabilistic cutoff beyond which chance becomes an unacceptable explanation is clear. The universe will experience heat death before random typing at a keyboard produces a Shakespearean sonnet. The French mathematician Emile Borel proposed 10^{-50} as a universal probability bound below which chance could definitely be precluded—that is, any specified event as improbable as this could not be attributed to chance.[24]

Borel based his universal probability bound on cosmological considerations, looking to the opportunities for repeating and observing events throughout cosmic history. Borel's 10^{-50} probability bound translates to 166 bits of information. In *The Design Inference* I justify a more stringent universal probability bound of 10^{-150} based on the number of elementary particles in the observable universe, the duration of the observable universe until its heat death and the Planck time.[25] A probability bound of 10^{-150} translates to 500 bits of information. Accordingly, specified information of complexity greater than 500 bits cannot reasonably be attributed to chance. This 500-bit ceiling on the amount of specified complexity attributable to chance constitutes a *universal complexity bound* for CSI. If we now define CSI as any specified information whose complexity exceeds 500 bits of information, it follows immediately that chance cannot generate CSI. Henceforth we take the "C" in "CSI" to denote at least 500 bits of information.

Biologists by and large do not dispute that chance cannot generate CSI. Most biologists reject pure chance as an adequate explanation of CSI.

Besides flying in the face of every canon of statistical reasoning, pure chance is scientifically unsatisfying as an explanation of CSI. To explain CSI in terms of pure chance is no more instructive than pleading ignorance or proclaiming CSI a mystery. It is one thing to explain the occurrence of heads on a single coin toss by appealing to chance. It is quite another, as Bernd-Olaf Küppers points out, to take the view that "the specific sequence of the nucleotides in the DNA molecule of the first organism came about by a purely random process in the early history of the earth."[26] CSI cries out for explanation, and pure chance won't do it. Richard Dawkins makes this point eloquently:

> We can accept a certain amount of luck in our explanations, but not too much. . . . In our theory of how we came to exist, we are allowed to postulate a certain ration of luck. This ration has, as its upper limit, the number of eligible planets in the universe. . . . We [therefore] have at our disposal, if we want to use it, odds of 1 in 100 billion billion as an upper limit (or 1 in however many available planets we think there are) to spend in our theory of the origin of life. This is the maximum amount of luck we are allowed to postulate in our theory. Suppose we want to suggest, for instance, that life began when both DNA and its protein-based replication machinery spontaneously chanced to come into existence. We can allow ourselves the luxury of such an extravagant theory, provided that the odds against this coincidence occurring on a planet do not exceed 100 billion billion to one.[27]

Dawkins is right. We can allow our scientific theorizing only so much luck. After that we degenerate into handwaving and mystery. A probability bound of 10^{-150}, or a corresponding complexity bound of 500 bits of information, sets a conservative limit on the amount of luck we can allow ourselves (certainly more conservative than the one Dawkins proposes here). Such a limitation on luck is crucial to the integrity of science. If we allow ourselves too many "wildcard" bits of information, we can explain anything. (With as little as five dollars and twenty wildcard bits of information anyone can walk up to a roulette table in Las Vegas and leave a millionaire.)

6.4 Generating Information via Law and Chance

We can summarize our findings to this point: (1) Chance generates contingency, but not complex specified information. (2) Laws (i.e., Eigen's algorithms and natural laws, or what in section 6.2 we called functions) generate neither contingency nor information, much less complex specified information. (3) Laws at best transmit already present information or else lose it. Given these findings, it seems intuitively obvious that no chance-law combination is going to generate information either. After all, laws can transmit only the CSI they are given, and whatever chance gives to a law is not CSI. Ergo, chance and laws working in tandem cannot generate information. This intuition is exactly right, and I will provide a theoretical justification for it shortly.

Nevertheless the sense that laws can sift chance and thereby generate CSI is deep-seated in the scientific community. This is especially true of trial-and-error problem solving, where trial (an instance of law) sifts error (an instance of chance). Once considered a crude method of problem solving, trial-and-error has so risen in the estimation of scientists that it is now regarded as the fount of wisdom. Probabilistic algorithms like neural nets and genetic algorithms all hinge on trial-and-error. So, too, the Darwinian mechanism of mutation and natural selection is a trial-and-error combination in which mutation supplies the error and selection the trial.

The theoretical justification for why chance and law working in tandem cannot generate information is virtually the same as the theoretical justification given in section 6.2 for why laws by themselves cannot generate information. But instead of considering a deterministic function $f(i)$ in one variable, we need to consider a nondeterministic function $f(i,\omega)$ in two variables where the first variable signifies the object on which the function acts, and the second signifies the randomizing component (i.e., the chance variable). We then define the universal composition function U that inputs the object-chance-function ordered triple (i,ω,f) and outputs $f(i,\omega) = j$, that is, $U(i,\omega,f) = f(i,\omega) = j$. As in the deterministic case, the universal composition function U incorporates no information of its own but is merely a conduit for information. The formalism just described for combining chance and law is perfectly general. In mathematics f is known as a *stochastic process*.[28] Stochastic processes can model everything from Darwin's mutation-selection mechanism to the probabilistic algorithms of computer science (e.g., neural nets and genetic algorithms).

Now suppose we have some CSI j and a nondeterministic function f (i.e., a chance-law combination, or what we just called a stochastic process) that, à la Manfred Eigen, leads to the origin of j. The origin of j can then be broken into two stages. In the first stage a chance outcome ω

occurs. Once ω occurs and is fixed, the function f becomes deterministic, that is, f becomes a function in one variable: $f(\cdot,\omega) = f_\omega(\cdot)$, ω now being treated as a fixed parameter of the function f. This is the standard probabilistic move for transforming stochastic processes into *random functions,* which once the random element ω is fixed become what are called *sample paths.* (Stochastic processes and random functions are mathematically equivalent.)[29] In the second stage the parameterized deterministic function $f_\omega(\cdot)$ (i.e., sample path) gets applied to some element in its domain, call it i, yielding the item of interest, the CSI j.

From this two-stage analysis it becomes clear that no CSI is generated in the production of j. The first stage involves only chance and therefore, as was shown in section 6.3, cannot generate CSI. The second stage involves no chance but only a deterministic function and therefore, as was shown in section 6.2, cannot generate CSI either. Thus at no point in the transition from ω to $f_\omega(\cdot)$ to $f_\omega(i) = j$ is CSI generated. Whatever CSI is inherent in j was already inherent in the nondeterministic function f together with the nonrandom element in the domain of f, namely, i. This argument holds for Darwin's mutation-selection mechanism, for genetic algorithms and indeed for any other chance-law combination. Just as chance or law left to themselves individually cannot purchase CSI, so their joint action cannot purchase CSI either.

It follows that neither genetic algorithms nor mutation and selection are capable of generating CSI. This may seem counterintuitive since both of these mechanisms are routinely touted as originating novel information. It is true, for instance, that genetic algorithms can solve interesting problems in everything from economics to protein folding to jet engine design.[30] Nonetheless programmers have to carefully adapt genetic algorithms to the problems at hand (thereby introducing plenty of novel CSI at the hands of the programmers). Moreover genetic algorithms are hardly all-purpose problem solvers. The "no free lunch" (NFL) theorems of David Wolpert and William Macready place severe restrictions on the type of problems genetic algorithms can solve.[31] Likewise, as we saw in section 5.7, mutation and selection face severe restrictions in generating biological complexity. There is no magic that enables such mechanisms to generate CSI. Indeed the only known source for generating CSI is intelligence.

The argument that law and chance together cannot generate CSI holds with perfect generality. $f(i,\omega) = j$ is a stochastic process. Stochastic processes provide the most general mathematical means for modeling the joint action of law and chance.[32] In fact by zeroing out the randomizing component ω, stochastic processes can also model pure law. Moreover, by zeroing out the nonrandom component i, stochastic processes can also model pure chance. Stochastic processes are capable of modeling law, chance or any combination of the two.

6.5 The Law of Conservation of Information

Since natural causes are precisely those characterized by chance, law or a combination of the two, the broad conclusion of the last section may be restated as follows: *Natural causes are incapable of generating CSI.* I call this result the law of conservation of information, or LCI for short. The phrase "law of conservation of information" is not new. In *The Limits of Science* Peter Medawar used it to describe the weaker claim that deterministic laws cannot produce novel information (cf. section 6.2).[33] Medawar's version is nonstochastic and thus excludes both chance and the joint action of law and chance. Because natural causes comprise law, chance and their combination, the formulation of LCI given here is more general and powerful than Medawar's.

LCI has profound implications for science. Among its immediate corollaries are the following: (1) The CSI in a closed system of natural causes remains constant or decreases. (2) CSI cannot be generated spontaneously, originate endogenously or organize itself (as these terms are used in origins-of-life research). (3) The CSI in a closed system of natural causes either has been in the system eternally or was at some point added exogenously (implying that the system, though now closed, was not always closed). (4) In particular any closed system of natural causes that is also of finite duration received whatever CSI it contains before it became a closed system.

The first corollary can be understood in terms of data storage and retrieval. Data constitute a form of CSI. Ideally data would stay unaltered over time. Nonetheless, entropy being the corrupting force that it is, data tend to degrade and need constantly to be restored. Over time magnetic tapes deteriorate, pages yellow, print fades and books disintegrate. Information may be eternal, but the physical media that house information are subject to natural causes and are thoroughly ephemeral. The first corollary acknowledges this fact.

The second and third corollaries assert that CSI cannot be explained in terms other than itself. CSI cannot be reduced to self-organizational properties of matter, for these would just be natural causes, and LCI discounts natural causes as adequate for generating CSI. Given an instance of CSI, these corollaries allow but two possibilities: either the CSI was always present or it was inserted. Intelligent design theorists differ about which of these possibilities obtains for the universe taken as a whole. On the one hand are those like Michael Denton and, to a lesser extent, Michael Behe, who see all the CSI of the universe present at its start.[34] On the other hand are those like Stephen Meyer, Paul Nelson and myself who see CSI emerging in discrete steps, with no evident informational precursors, and thus through discrete insertions over time.[35] This debate is not new— German teleomechanists and British natural theologians engaged in much the same debate, with the Germans arguing that teleology was intrinsic to the world, the British arguing that it was extrinsic.[36] However this debate gets resolved, CSI is an empirically detectable entity that transcends natural causes.

The fourth and final corollary shows that scientific explanation is not identical with reductive explanation. This corollary is especially relevant to science. Richard Dawkins, Daniel Dennett and many scientists and philosophers are convinced that proper scientific explanations must be reductive, moving from the complex to the simple.[37] The law of conservation of information, however, shows that CSI cannot be explained reductively. To explain an instance of CSI requires at least as much CSI as we started with. A pencil-making machine is more complicated than the pencils it makes. A clock factory is more complicated than the clocks it produces. An author is more complicated than the books he or she writes.

To explain CSI is to fill one hole by digging another. With CSI the information problem never goes away. We've known this since elementary school. The telephone game, where one person whispers information to the next person who whispers it to the next, etc., illustrates how information degrades over time. The players of this game are links in a chain. With each transmission of information from one link to the next, there is the potential for losing information. Ideally each person would repeat exactly the information given by the preceding person in the chain and thus preserve the information given at the start of the chain. In general, however, that doesn't happen. In fact the fun of the telephone game is to see how information degrades as it passes from the first to the last person in the chain.

The telephone game has more serious analogues. Consider the textual transmission of ancient manuscripts. A textual critic's task is to recover as much of the original text of an ancient manuscript as possible. Almost always the original text is unavailable. Instead the textual critic confronts multiple variant texts, each with a long genealogy tracing back to the original text. Fifty generations of copies may separate a given manuscript from the original text. The original text is copied in the first generation, then that copy is itself copied, then that second copy is in turn copied and so on fifty times before we get to the manuscript in our possession. We assume that most of the copyists were trying to preserve the text faithfully. Even so, they were bound to introduce errors now and then. Worse yet are the naughty copyists who use copying as a pretext for inserting their pet ideas into a text. The textual critic must therefore identify errors introduced by careless copying as well as errors stemming from a copyist's personal agenda. This can be enormously difficult. Even so, there is always a fixed reference point: Because the copyist presupposes an original text as the source from which all the variant manuscripts ultimately derive, the original text constitutes the initial CSI on which the textual transmission of the text depends.[38]

In both the telephone game and the transmission of texts, an intelligent cause rather than a natural cause transmits information. Is that a problem here given that the law of conservation of information applies, strictly speaking, only to natural causes? Although this law is concerned solely with placing limits on natural and not intelligent causes, it still applies. Intelligent causes can mimic natural causes, and that is what they are doing here. In both the telephone game and in the transmission of ancient texts, the persons transmitting information are supposed to repeat what they have been given. Repetition is an automatic process for which natural causes are ideally suited and for which intelligent causes are not required.

We can see this more clearly by considering successive photocopies of a black-and-white photograph. Natural causes govern a photocopy machine's operation. Take, therefore, a black-and-white photograph, photocopy it, then photocopy that copy and keep doing this fifty times. The successive photocopies will show increasing degradation of the original photograph (i.e., the initial information). Depending on the quality of the photocopy machine and the resolution of the original photograph, the original photograph may be unrecognizable by the fiftieth photocopy. If the two previous examples were merely suggestive of the law of conservation of information, the photocopy example illustrates this law exactly.

The most interesting application of the law of conservation of information is the reproduction of organisms. Since reproduction proceeds by natural causes, there is no question that the law applies. In reproduction one organism transmits its CSI to the next generation. For most evolutionary biologists, however, this is not the end of the story. Most evolutionists would argue that the Darwinian mechanism of mutation and selection introduces novel CSI into an organism, supplementing the CSI of the parent(s) with CSI from the environment. Accordingly the genetic contribution from the parent(s) and the Darwinian contribution through mutation and selection together constitute the CSI of an organism.

Because I'll take up this claim in the next section, I won't dwell on it here. Nevertheless it is important to understand a feature of CSI that will count decisively against generating CSI from the environment via mutation and selection. The crucial feature of CSI is that it is *holistic*. Although *holism* and *holistic* have become buzzwords in our culture, in reference to CSI these terms have a well-defined meaning. To say that CSI is holistic means that individual items of information (be they simple, complex, specified or even complex specified) cannot simply be added together and thereby form a new item of complex specified information. In technical philosophical jargon *CSI is not the mereological sum of its constituent items of information.*

CSI holism is a case of the whole being greater than the sum of its parts. CSI requires not only having the right collection of parts but also having the parts in proper relation. Consider, for instance, the set {A, IS, IT, LIKE, WEASEL, METHINKS}. All the items of information here are specified (they represent known words in the English language). Of these, METHINKS is the most complex, having 8 letters. For sequences of capital letters and spaces (27 possibilities at each position), the complexity of METHINKS comes to $-\log_2 1/27^8 = 38$ bits of information. Now contrast the set {A, IS, IT, LIKE, WEASEL, METHINKS} with the sentence METHINKS IT IS LIKE A WEASEL. This sentence not only includes all the items of information that appear in the set but also arranges them in a grammatical sequence with semantic content. Unlike the set, for which only the individual words are specified, here the entire sentence is specified. Moreover because the sentence is a sequence of 28 letters and spaces, its complexity comes to $-\log_2 1/27^{28} = 133$ bits of information, far exceeding the complexity of any item in the set.

CSI holism is built directly into the definition of CSI. The independently given specifications that turn complex information into complex specified information are self-contained. The specification that identifies METHINKS IT IS LIKE A WEASEL as a line from *Hamlet* and the specification that identifies IN THE BEGINNING GOD CREATED THE HEAVENS AND THE EARTH as a line from the book of Genesis do not form a joint specification for the juxtaposed lines METHINKS IT IS LIKE A WEASEL IN THE BEGINNING GOD CREATED THE HEAVENS AND THE EARTH. CSI is a top-down, not a bottom-up concept. CSI does not emerge by merely aggregating component parts. CSI is not obtained by arbitrarily stitching items of information together. Only if a specification for the whole is given can parts be suitably arranged to form CSI.

This fact severely limits the ability of selection and mutation to produce CSI. Because the Darwinian mechanism of mutation and selection is nonteleological, it cannot specify in advance the adaptations it will produce. Selection and mutation operate with no memory of the past or knowledge of the future—there's only the present organism with its ability to survive and reproduce given its environment. Consequently whatever CSI mutation and selection generate must be generated in a single generation. To suppose otherwise is to think that mutation and selection can sustain a specification over multiple generations until the adaptation that was specified comes to fruition. But this is teleology, and teleology is utterly inconsistent with the Darwinian mechanism. For mutation and selection to solve the information problem, they must do it in a single generation. Let us now see whether mutation and selection are up to the task.

6.6 Applying the Theory to Evolutionary Biology

Thus far I've sketched a theory of complex specified information and concluded with a general law characterizing the origin and flow of complex specified information—the law of conservation of information. I want next to apply this theory to evolutionary biology. First off let's note that so far nothing in this theory contradicts a purely naturalistic account of evolution. All that has been shown so far is that CSI is not a free lunch in the sense that natural causes cannot generate CSI. Nevertheless natural causes can take already existing CSI and shift it around; and since there is nothing to prevent CSI from being abundant in the universe, there is nothing to prevent natural causes from taking already existing CSI and expressing it in biological systems. With Hubert Yockey we could therefore treat CSI and life as "axiomatic" and leave it at that.[39] Equivalently we could say CSI is a "brute fact" or a "frozen accident." Like the principle of rationality that according to the ancient Stoics pervaded the universe, we could simply treat CSI as a given.

Although this move can be justified philosophically, it is scientifically unsatisfying. As scientists we want to know how the CSI that supposedly is so abundant in the universe was first introduced into the organisms we see around us. In reference to the origin of life we want to know the informational pathway that takes the CSI inherent in a lifeless universe and translates it into the first organism. In reference to the development of life we want to know the informational pathway that takes the CSI inherent in an already existing organism plus its environment and translates that CSI into a new organism of still greater complexity. Even if the origin of CSI admits no scientific explanation, its flow surely does. How then does CSI flow into and out of biological systems?

The answer to this question, at least in broad terms, is clear: The CSI inherent in an organism consists of the CSI acquired at birth together with whatever CSI it acquires during the course of its life. The CSI acquired at birth derives from *inheritance with modification* (i.e., the CSI inherent in the parent(s) as well as any modifications of this CSI by chance). The CSI acquired after birth consists of *selection* (i.e., the environmental pressure that selects some organisms to reproduce and eliminates others before they can reproduce) along with *infusion* (i.e., the direct introduction of novel information from outside the organism).

Note that *modification,* as used here, is more general than *mutation.* Mutations are random genetic errors that get passed from one generation to the next. Not all randomly induced changes between generations, however, are errors. In sexual reproduction, for instance, genetic information from both parents combines randomly, yet in a well-defined random process that's functionally specified by the organism. Modification signifies not only chance errors but also chance processes specifically under the direction of an organism.

The Darwinian mechanism admits selection and inheritance with modification but proscribes infusion. Not all evolutionary mechanisms, however, take this line. The Lamarckian mechanism, for instance, focuses mainly on infusion. For Lamarck, characteristics acquired by an organism in the course of its life could be passed on to its offspring. These acquired characteristics arise from interaction with the environment. In passing these characteristics to their offspring, organisms therefore transmit information from the environment to the next generation.

Certainly infusion as Lamarck conceived it has largely been discredited. It's been found, for instance, that an organism's genes, which get passed to the next generation, do not change in response to acquired characteristics. Even so, there is good scientific evidence for non-Lamarckian infusion in which CSI from one organism gets transferred to another. For instance, it is well established that bacteria exchange plasmids (i.e., circular pieces of genetic information) as a way of developing antibiotic resistance.[40] More speculative is Lynn Margulis's idea of symbiosis, where one organism assimilates another to form a more complex organism.[41] In both these instances, one organism co-opts information from another.

Inheritance with modification, selection and infusion—these three account for the CSI inherent in biological systems. Together they comprise all the sources of CSI in biology. I want therefore to examine more closely how these three sources contribute to the CSI of an organism. First consider inheritance with modification. According to Franklin Harold, "There are many generalizations in biology but precious few universal laws; and of these, the least controversial may well be that like begets like. Offspring resemble their parents in form as well as function: roses and rabbits, yeast and *Escherichia coli* display the same forms, generation after generation, within a narrow range of variations."[42]

From fertilization through to the adult phenotype, organisms follow well-defined developmental pathways.[43] These pathways are organism-specific and invariant, and supply organisms with all the structures and functions they inherit from their parents.[44] Inheritance is the developmental pathway by which already existing information is transferred from parent organisms to their children. Inheritance is thus merely a conduit for already existing information.

Because organisms do not merely repeat the information inherent in their parents but also modify it through chance, the CSI organisms acquire at birth derives not just from inheritance but also from modification. By modification I mean all the instances where chance enters an organism's developmental pathway and modifies its CSI. Modification includes—to name but a few—point mutations, base deletions, genetic crossover, transpositions and recombination generally.[45] Thus while inheritance is merely a conduit for already existing information, modification is the operation of chance on the information passing through that conduit. Given the law of conservation of information, it follows that inheritance with modification by itself is incapable of explaining the increased complexity of CSI that organisms have exhibited in the course of natural history. Inheritance with modification needs therefore to be supplemented.

The most obvious candidate here is, of course, selection. Selection presupposes inheritance with modification, but instead of merely shifting around already existing information, selection also introduces new information. By seizing on advantageous modifications, selection is able to introduce new information into a population. The majority view in biology—known as the neo-Darwinian synthesis—is that selection and inheritance with modification together are adequate to account for all the CSI inherent in organisms. As a parsimonious account of the origin and development of life, this view has much to commend it. Nonetheless this view places undue restrictions on the flow of biological information, restrictions that biological systems routinely violate.

Michael Behe's irreducibly complex biochemical systems are a case in point. As we saw in section 5.7, irreducibly complex biochemical systems require numerous components specifically adapted to each other and each necessary for function. Such systems are both complex and specified, and therefore exhibit CSI. Consider now an organism that possesses an irreducibly complex biochemical system—for definiteness let's say it is a bacterial flagellum (i.e., the bi-directional outboard motor of a bacterium that propels it through solution). On a Darwinian view that organism evolved via selection and inheritance with modification from an organism without a flagellum. The flagellum is a complex protein machine requiring over forty proteins each necessary for function. For the Darwinian mechanism to produce the flagellum, chance modifications have to generate those various proteins and then selection must preserve them.

But how is selection to accomplish this? Selection is nonteleological, so it cannot cumulate proteins, holding them in reserve until with the passing of many generations they're finally available to form a complete flagellum. The environment contains no blueprint of the flagellum which selection can extract and then transmit to an organism to form a flagellum. No, selection can only build on partial function, gradually improving function that already exists. But a flagellum without its full complement of protein parts doesn't function at all. Consequently if selection and inheritance with modification are going to produce the flagellum, they have to do it in one generation.

But the CSI of a flagellum far exceeds 500 bits. What's more, selection, if operating for only one generation, merely kills off organisms that lack some feature (in this case the flagellum). Selection operating for only one generation does not produce novelty—all the novelty is produced by random modification acting on inheritance. Whatever CSI the environment may hold, selection is therefore incapable of transmitting it in a single generation. Similarly, since selection is nonteleological, it can't transmit environmental CSI over multiple generations either. It follows that inheritance with modification has to produce a flagellum in a single generation. But this is infeasible. This is asking law and chance to produce over 500 bits of CSI. This would violate the law of conservation of information.

If the joint action of selection and inheritance with modification is unable to account for the CSI in biological systems (and specifically for the irreducible complexity of certain biochemical systems like the bacterial flagellum), there remains but one source for the CSI in biological systems—infusion, that is, the direct introduction of novel information from outside the biological system. In principle there is nothing problematic or controversial about infusion. To innovate a given informational structure an organism has informational needs, and these needs can be supplied from outside the organism, either indirectly through selection (whose efficacy, as we've just seen, is quite limited) or directly by the insertion of ready-to-go information into the organism. The latter is, of course, infusion.

Although at this level of generality infusion is unproblematic, it quickly becomes problematic once we start tracing backwards the informational pathways of infused information. Consider for instance what is perhaps the best scientifically confirmed instance of infusion in biology, namely, plasmid exchange among bacteria to develop antibiotic resistance.[46] Plasmids are small circular pieces of DNA that can easily be exchanged among bacteria of the same species and are capable of conferring antibiotic resistance. When one bacterium releases a plasmid and another absorbs it, information is infused from one into the other. By itself this is unproblematic. Problems begin, however, when we ask, where did the bacterium that released the plasmid in turn derive it? There is a regress here, and this regress always terminates in something non-organismal. We can't just keep explaining plasmid infusion into a bacterium by plasmid release from another bacterium. Eventually as we trace the informational pathway back, we must tell a different kind of story. If, for instance, the plasmid is cumulatively complex, then it could have arisen through selection and inheritance with modification (cf. section 5.7). But if it is irreducibly complex, whence could it have arisen?

It will be helpful here to distinguish between *biotic* and *abiotic* infusion and correspondingly between *endogenous* and *exogenous* information. Biotic infusion is the infusion of information from one organism to another; abiotic infusion is the infusion of information from other than an organism. Correspondingly, endogenous information comprises biotically infused information (and thus information already present within biological systems); exogenous information comprises abiotically infused information (and thus information external to biological systems). Now regardless whether plasmids are irreducibly complex (the relevant analysis has yet to be performed), the fact remains that there exist irreducibly complex biochemical systems.[47] What's more, even though biotic infusion may explain how a particular instance of an irreducibly complex biochemical system came to exist in a given organism, it cannot explain how such a system arose in the first place. Because organisms have a finite trajectory back in time, biotic infusion must ultimately give way to abiotic infusion, and endogenous information must ultimately derive from exogenous information.

6.7 Reconceptualizing Evolutionary Biology

The abiotic infusion of exogenous information is the great mystery confronting modern evolutionary biology. It is the mystery posed by Manfred Eigen at the beginning of this chapter. Why is it a mystery? Not because the abiotic infusion of exogenous information is inherently spooky or unscientific but because evolutionary biology has failed to grasp the relevance and centrality of information to its task. The task of evolutionary biology is to explain the origin and development of life. The key feature of life is the presence of complex specified information—CSI. Caught up in the Darwinian mechanism of selection and inheritance with modification, evolutionary biology has failed to appreciate the informational hurdles organisms need to jump in the course of natural history.[48] To jump those hurdles organisms require information. What's more, a significant part of that information is exogenous and must originally have been infused abiotically.

In closing this chapter I want briefly to consider what evolutionary biology would look like if information were taken as its central and unifying concept. First off, let us be clear that the Darwinian mechanism of selection and inheritance with modification will continue to occupy a significant place in evolutionary theory. Nevertheless its complete and utter dominance in evolutionary theory—that selection and inheritance with modification together account for the full diversity of life—will have to be relinquished. As a mechanism for conserving, adapting and honing already existing biological structures, the Darwinian mechanism is ideally suited. But as a mechanism for innovating irreducibly complex biological structures, it utterly lacks the informational resources. As for biotic infusion, its role within an information-theoretic framework must always remain limited, for even though it can account for how organisms trade already existing biological information, it can never get at the root question of how that information came to exist in the first place.

Not surprisingly, therefore, the key task an information-theoretic approach to evolutionary biology faces is to make sense of abiotically infused CSI. Abiotically infused CSI is information exogenous to an organism but which nonetheless gets transmitted to and assimilated by the organism. Two obvious questions now arise: (1) How is abiotically infused CSI transmitted to an organism? and (2) Where does this information reside prior to being transmitted? If this information is clearly represented in some empirically accessible nonbiological physical system, and if there is a clear informational pathway from that system to the organism, and if that informational pathway can be shown suitable for transmitting this information to the organism so that the organism properly assimilates it, only then will these two questions receive an empirically adequate naturalistic answer.

But note that this naturalistic answer, far from eliminating the information question, simply pushes it one step further back, for how did the CSI that was abiotically infused into an organism first get into a prior nonbiological physical system? Because of the law of conservation of information, whenever we inquire into the source of complex specified information, we never resolve the information problem but only intensify it. This is not to say that such inquiries are unilluminating or unscientific (contra Dawkins and Dennett, who think that the only valid explanations in evolutionary biology are reductive, explaining the more complex in terms of the simpler—see section 6.5 and appendix A.4). We learn an important fact about a pencil when we learn that a certain pencil-making machine made it. Nonetheless the information in the pencil-making machine exceeds the information in the pencil. The law of conservation of information guarantees that as we trace informational pathways backwards, we have more information to explain than we started with.

Where then do the informational pathways of life terminate as we trace them backwards? The possibilities are limited. One possibility is that we get nowhere, unable even to begin tracing backwards the information in a biological system. Thus we may discover an irreducibly complex biological system but be unable to trace it back to any abiotic source of exogenous information.[49] Another possibility is that we can trace the information in a biological system back to an abiotic source of exogenous information but then can't trace it back any further. Graham Cairns-Smith, for instance, has a clay-template theory for the origin of life in which self-replicating clays form templates for carbon-based life.[50] The Cairns-Smith theory is clearly an abiotic infusion theory, with exogenous information represented in (abiotic) clays providing templates for carbon-based life. What the Cairns-Smith theory does not treat is how the exogenous information that was transmitted to carbon-based life from clay templates got into those clay templates in the first place. Needless to say, the Cairns-Smith theory is highly speculative.

Still another possibility is that we can trace the information in a biological system all the way back to the initial conditions of the Big Bang.[51] Though this approach appeals to our naturalistic sensibilities, it remains scientifically sterile until a definite informational pathway can be traced back to the Big Bang. Finally, there is the creationist alternative, which traces the information in a biological system to the direct intervention of God.[52] Though this approach appeals to our theistic sensibilities, it remains scientifically sterile until an in-principle argument is offered showing that information inherent in a biological system could not have been contained in any nonbiological physical precursor (and even then it's not clear what action God took to produce biological information).

In tracing back the informational pathways of life, evolutionary biology does well to avoid speculation and to follow only those informational pathways that can be rigorously traced. To take an analogy, I can rigorously trace the informational pathway that issued in my copy of *King Lear* through the various extant editions of the play spanning the last four centuries. On the other hand, I cannot even begin to trace the informational pathway that issued in some isolated first-century papyrus fragment found in the Egyptian desert. Any story behind this fragment is lost and cannot be reconstructed. Likewise, evolutionary biology may trace an informational pathway back to an abiotic source of exogenous information. On the other hand, it may remain stuck at a given irreducibly complex biological structure, forever unable to trace it back to an abiotic source of exogenous information.

To sum up, evolutionary biology needs to be reconceptualized in information-theoretic terms. An evolutionary biology thoroughly cognizant of information theory is one whose chief task is to trace informational pathways. In tracing these pathways evolutionary biology must place a premium on rigor. Detailed informational pathways need to be explicitly exhibited—the just-so stories of Richard Dawkins will not do. Moreover, unlike the nebulous informational pathways sketched by Stuart Kauffman, Christopher Langton and others at the Santa Fe Institute, informational pathways need to conform to biological reality, not to the virtual reality residing in a computer.[53] Finally, empirical evidence—and not metaphysical prejudice or aesthetic preference—must decide whether an informational pathway exists at all. For instance, the Darwinian preference to cash out taxonomy in terms of genealogy must not be taken as evidence for common descent. To establish common descent requires showing that certain informational pathways connect all organisms.[54]

Within this reconceptualization of evolutionary biology, many of the low-level facts of current evolutionary biology will stay put. What's more, information theory is sufficiently flexible to accommodate the mechanisms of evolutionary change proposed to date. Nonetheless their adequacy will have to be evaluated in terms of the information-theoretic constraints to which they are subject. Thus, for instance, the Darwinian mechanism will have to be reformulated information-theoretically as the selection and inheritance with modification of information. At the same time the claim that this mechanism can account for the full diversity of life will have to be rejected given, among other things, its inability to produce irreducibly complex biochemical systems. Many old questions will remain. Many new questions will arise. But some old questions will have to be discarded. In particular all reductionist attempts to explain information in terms of something other than information will have to go by the board. Information is sui generis. Only information begets information.

Part 3

Bridging Science
& Theology

7

Science & Theology in Mutual Support

7.1 Two Windows on Reality

Intelligent design is a scientific theory with theological implications. The relation between science and theology is therefore relevant to intelligent design. Science makes claims about the world. Theology makes claims about the world. How do the claims of science and theology relate? At least four answers to this question are possible: (1) they don't relate at all; (2) they adopt different perspectives; (3) they conflict; (4) they support each other. Though not exhaustive, these are the most interesting possibilities and the ones that have received the most attention in the literature.

To see what's at stake in these possibilities, consider the following analogy. We can imagine theology and science as two windows on reality. To say that theology and science don't relate at all is then to say that the windows face completely opposite directions and view completely different scenes. For instance, one window might face north and the other south. If there is a busy industrial complex to the north and a gentle, bucolic scene to the south, then these windows will give very different pictures of reality.

Alternatively, the windows may face the same scene but adopt such radically different perspectives that what one window tells us is not meaningfully in conversation with what the other tells us. Imagine two airplanes flying near a mountain. Looking out the window, the pilot in one airplane sees the mountain as pink whereas the pilot in the other sees it as gray. It's the same mountain in both instances, but because the planes are in different locations, the way the light reflects off the mountain causes one pilot to see pink, the other to see gray. Even the shape of the mountain may look very different to the two pilots if they are flying on different sides of the mountain. Thus when the pilots meet after their flight and describe their view of the mountain, they may wonder if they're even talking about the same mountain.

Another possibility is that both windows are looking out at the same scene from pretty much the same vantage, but this time one of the windows is distorted. We can imagine one window as perfectly even and clear but the other as warped, having varying degrees of thickness and enclosing numerous air bubbles. Thus whereas one window gives an accurate representation of reality, the other systematically distorts it. For instance, when we look through the window that's even and clear, we see (correctly) that one post is taller than the other; but when we look through the window that's warped and unclear, the shorter post may seem taller.

The final possibility is that the windows face the same scene and do so from perspectives, which, though not identical, are not so disparate that we can't meaningfully relate what we are seeing from both windows. Alternatively, what we learn from both windows can in many cases be meaningfully related. Thus we may again imagine two airplanes flying over the same mountain, but this time the airplanes are flying at such a high altitude that even though they're on different sides of the mountain, the pilot in one plane sees things that the other pilot also sees. Thus when the pilots meet for coffee afterward, they will agree about certain features of the mountain, even though other features may be uniquely associated with their distinctive flight paths.

This windows analogy describes our principal options for relating science and theology. Science and theology are windows onto reality. How does what we learn from one window relate to what we learn from the other? It all depends on where the windows are placed and on the quality of the glass.

If the windows are facing completely opposite directions, there can be no meaningful relation. This is the *compartmentalization model* of the relation between science and theology.[1] On this view science and theology are airtight compartments whose domains never overlap. The usual line here is that science studies the natural world, but theology studies morals and faith. Stephen Jay Gould is a great proponent of this view. So is the National Academy of Sciences.

Close to this view is the *complementarity model*. Unlike the compartmentalization model, the complementarity model admits that science and theology can address the same aspects of reality. Nevertheless when they do, the perspectives of science and theology differ so radically that what science tells us and what theology tells us cannot be correlated within a single coherent discourse. According to the complementarity model, theology and science speak to the same reality but in languages so different that no translation between the two, not even a partial translation, is possible. To be sure, both are necessary to give a complete account of reality. But it is a completeness of aggregation, not integration. Science does its thing. Theology does its thing. It's not for science to tell theology how to do its thing or vice versa. They are conceptually independent even if they depend on the same underlying reality. The American Scientific Affiliation has been the great proving ground for this view.[2]

Complementarity and compartmentalization maintain peace between science and theology. The *conflict model* does not. According to the conflict model, science and theology can't both be right—one or the other distorts our picture of reality. These days science is usually regarded as providing the undistorted view of reality. In an age that regards science as preeminent, theology therefore ends up the loser. For instance, when the workers in France after World War II were asked why they rejected Christian theology, it wasn't, as the socialist vanguard wanted to think, because the church didn't embrace socialism or wouldn't commiserate with the plight of the workers. No, it was because the workers thought that science had disproven the Bible, and Genesis in particular. Rationalists, skeptics, atheists and debunkers are the great purveyors of the conflict model. They regard theology, faith, religion and superstition as one cloth.[3]

The compartmentalization and complementarity models arose historically in reaction to the conflict model. Compartmentalization and complementarity are insulating strategies, designed to protect theology from the assaults of science. The compartmentalization model redraws the boundaries of theology so that it cannot conflict with science. The complementarity model reconceptualizes the nature of theological discourse so that again theology cannot conflict with science. In either case, these models avoid conflict, but at the cost of removing theology from any productive conversation with science.

None of these three models is adequate. Each of them captures an important truth but then totalizes it in a way that is not helpful for understanding the relation between science and theology. Compartmentalization rightly notes that there are areas in which science and theology don't overlap. For instance, science has nothing to say about the doctrine of the Trinity, nor does theology have anything to say about the bonding affinities between carbon and hydrogen. But to say that there is no overlap whatsoever misses the boat.

Likewise, complementarity rightly notes that theological discourse is different from scientific discourse. Theology gets its data from Scripture, science from nature. Nature may therefore testify to God in ways quite distinct from Scripture. The fault of the complementarity model, however, is that it makes theological and scientific discourse so radically discontinuous that the two cannot communicate substantively. For instance, it is not possible within the complementarity model for a theological claim about creation, say, to challenge a scientific claim about inflationary cosmology. Complementarity straightjackets science and theology so that they can't hurt each other. It enforces peace but at the cost of sterility.

Nor is the conflict model without its legitimate insights. Galileo, after all, was right, and the Catholic cardinals were wrong. As Charles Hodge notes in his systematic theology:

> Theologians are not infallible in the interpretation of Scripture. It may, therefore, happen in the future, as it has in the past, that interpretations of the Bible, long confidently received, must be modified or abandoned, to bring revelation into harmony with what God teaches in his works. This change of view as to the true meaning of the Bible may be a painful trial to the Church, but it does not in the least impair the authority of the Scriptures. They remain infallible; we are merely convicted of having mistaken their meaning.[4]

Conflict, however, is not a one-way street. Science can get things wrong as well. Thus it's possible for theology to be vindicated at the expense of science. Fred Hoyle's steady-state theory of the 1950s was explicitly formulated to bolster an infinite and eternal universe and thereby undercut the Christian doctrine of *creatio ex nihilo*. But with the discovery of the cosmic background radiation in the 1960s, Hoyle's theory was discarded. The church father Basil the Great had some harsh words for those who think science is a juggernaut that inevitably crushes theology in its path: "The philosophers of Greece [i.e., the scientists of that age] have made much ado to explain nature, and not one of their systems has remained firm and unshaken, each being overturned by its successor. It is vain to refute them; they are sufficient in themselves to destroy one another."[5]

Yes, science and theology can conflict. But when they do, it's not clear which has to give way, science or theology. The problem with the conflict model is that it casts theology as the great obscurer and science as the great enlightener. This is, for instance, Richard Dawkins's line, as he declaims from his Oxford chair on science and culture. This was Andrew Dickson White's line a hundred years ago in his *History of the Warfare Between Science and Theology in Christendom*. It is a great theme and one endlessly played in the contemporary culture wars. Casting science as the great enlightener that has effectively refuted theology, however, hardly gets at the truth of the relation between the two.

Compartmentalization, complementarity and conflict all grasp some aspect of the relation between science and theology but then try to make that aspect the whole show. In place of these models I want to propose a fourth alternative, one that recognizes what is correct in these models, yet without being swayed to their extremes. I call this fourth option the *mutual support model*.[6] According to the mutual support model, theology and science overlap but are not coextensive. Where they overlap, one discipline can provide epistemic support for the other. Epistemic support is much more general than proof. Proof—as in decisive, once-and-for-all settlement of a question—if possible anywhere, is possible only in mathematics. The mutual support model has no stake in using theology to decisively prove or settle the claims of science, or vice versa.

Nonetheless, according to the mutual support model, theology can lend credence, increase the conditional probability of or render plausible certain scientific claims and not others. Likewise, science can do the same for theology. The Christian doctrine of creation supports a big-bang cosmology much better than it supports a steady-state cosmology. In the steady-state cosmology matter and space are infinite, and matter is constantly being created not by God but from a vacuum. Standard big-bang cosmology, on the other hand, implies a beginning that from a theological vantage is readily interpreted as a creation event.

The purpose of this chapter, then, is to argue for the mutual support model.[7] Within Christianity God has traditionally been revealed in two books—the book of Scripture, which is the Bible, and the book of nature, which is creation. Both books testify to the God who is their common author. Not only do these books agree, but each helps us make sense of the other. Much of the confusion in science and theology these days results from severing these books.

7.2 Epistemic Support

In his intellectual autobiography Rudolf Carnap observed, "If one is interested in the relations between fields which, according to customary academic divisions, belong to different departments, then one will not be welcomed as a builder of bridges, as one might have expected, but will rather be regarded by both sides as an outsider and troublesome intruder."[8] Carnap learned the hazards of interdisciplinary bridge-building from bitter experience. To this day philosophers recall how Carnap's efforts to relate philosophy and physics were obstructed during his stint at the University of Chicago's philosophy department in the 1940s and 1950s.

Since Carnap's day and in part because of Carnap's efforts, the bridges between philosophy and physics have become more firmly established, with philosophy of science and in particular philosophy of physics now accepted as legitimate subdisciplines of philosophy. Moreover certain philosophers of physics have through their work gained recognition in the physics community.[9]

Still it would be an overstatement to say that philosophers and physicists are engaged in active dialogue. Philosophy has traditionally been classified with the humanities, physics with the natural sciences. Much of what philosophers do and much of what physicists do simply don't intersect. A moral philosopher's meta-ethical ruminations on the nature of duty and a physicist's tinkering with test tubes in the laboratory do not seem to connect in any relevantly important ways. Moreover philosophers and physicists are likely to display the bias that comes from having invested one's life in a given endeavor, to wit, the view that one's own work has overriding significance and that other people's work, insofar as it is increasingly removed from one's own area of specialization, is also increasingly insignificant.

This excursion into the interdisciplinary dialogue between philosophy and physics and between the humanities and the natural sciences more generally spotlights the problem of interdisciplinary dialogue between theology and the natural sciences. Distinct disciplines have a hard time communicating, even those which on first impression we think would want to communicate (like philosophy and physics). How much more difficult is it then to get theology and science communicating when, especially over the last hundred years, they have been increasingly characterized in terms of conflict or compartmentalization (complementarity has been more an in-house position within the Christian community)?

Let us therefore suppose for the sake of argument that we are in a world not of ideal rational agents but of ideal amicable agents—amicable in the sense that the agents are willing to talk to, listen to and learn from each other. In such a world, would a dialogue between theology and science be fruitful? Would it further inquiry? Would it foster an increased understanding of the world? Would it yield a net gain of knowledge to both theologian and scientist? Or would only one side in the dialogue profit? Would such a dialogue constitute merely polite chitchat among members of different intellectual communities, who at the end of the day would conclude that nothing of any genuine consequence has been accomplished through such a dialogue?

Suppose that scientists and theologians are willing to communicate with and listen attentively to each other. Are there any good reasons to think that they will learn something from each other's discipline that will actually be valuable to their own? To be sure, both will learn new things from such a dialogue. The theologian may learn from the physicist that the universe began as an infinitely dense fireball known as the Big Bang, whereas the physicist may learn from the theologian that God created the world by means of a divine logos. So the theologian and the physicist each will have a new piece of information to add to her or his stock of knowledge. But how are these pieces of information to be integrated into the web of information that constitutes our knowledge of the world? And how might a theological piece of information affect a physicist's physical understanding of the world, and alternatively, how might a piece of information from physics affect a theologian's theological understanding of the world?

What underlies these questions is *epistemic support.* In the context of an interdisciplinary dialogue, epistemic support asks how acceptance of claims in one discipline justifies acceptance of claims in another. Now philosophers have written extensively about epistemic support, and their work here is directly relevant to the dialogue between theology and science. In developing the mutual support model for the relation between science and theology, I want to describe a conception of epistemic support that fosters a genuinely productive interdisciplinary dialogue between theology and science.

How then shall we characterize epistemic support between theology and science? What will it mean for a scientific (alternatively theological) claim A to support a theological (alternatively scientific) claim B? Does it mean that B follows as a logical deduction from A or that there is an airtight circumstantial case to be made for B given A or that it is irrational to reject B once A is taken for granted? Support in any of these senses is the very strong notion of *rational compulsion.* The notion of support argued for in this chapter will be considerably weaker and will be unpacked in terms of *explanatory power.*

Failure to distinguish between a strong and a weak form of epistemic support has led to confusions in the dialogue between science and theology. Consider, for instance, what Ernan McMullin means when he denies that the relation between the Big Bang and the creation of the universe by God can be characterized in terms of epistemic support:

> What one could say . . . is that if the universe began in time through the act of a Creator, from our vantage point it would look something like the Big Bang that cosmologists are talking about. What one cannot say is, first, that the Christian doctrine of Creation "supports" the Big Bang model, or, second, that the Big Bang model "supports" the Christian doctrine of Creation.[10]

Contra McMullin, I do want to *say* that the Big Bang supports the Christian doctrine of creation and vice versa.

The notion of support that I develop here will be sufficiently liberal to foster fruitful interdisciplinary dialogue, yet without requiring that scientific evidence compel religious beliefs or vice versa. Rational compulsion involves a far stronger notion of support than typically comes up within either science or theology, much less in the dialogue between the two. One feels rationally compelled to believe necessary truths like 2 + 2 = 4. One may even feel rationally compelled to believe in the existence of certain medium-sized objects like trees, cars and people.[11] Nevertheless a considerably weaker conception of epistemic support seems to prevail in science and theology and seems to be appropriate for characterizing any interdisciplinary connections between the two.

My primary task then is to delineate a conception of epistemic support whereby the interdisciplinary dialogue between science and theology does not reduce to idle chitchat but can instead engender deeper understanding and promote further inquiry. Such a conception of epistemic support is available and has been at the forefront of much recent work in the philosophy of science.[12] Nevertheless, before describing it, let us consider by way of negation the form epistemic support must not take if it is to foster genuinely productive interdisciplinary dialogue between theology and science.

7.3 Rational Compulsion

The bête noire that has at every turn obstructed meaningful dialogue between theology and science is the demand that epistemic support be conceived as some form of rational compulsion. "Rational compulsion" is my own term, but it seems to capture what has lain behind so many ill-starred attempts to bring science and theology into dialogue. It will therefore be helpful to consider this conception of epistemic support in some detail. First, let us be clear that rational compulsion constitutes a perfectly valid form of epistemic support. Indeed if A rationally compels B, then it is irrational to deny B if one affirms A. What's more, since no one wants to be charged with irrationality, anyone who affirms A and regards A as rationally compelling B will necessarily also affirm B and therefore regard A as epistemically supporting B.

In practice rational compulsion takes the form of an entailment relation, either strict or partial. For A to strictly entail B means that it is impossible for A to be true but B false (e.g., being six feet tall strictly entails being at least five feet tall). Strict entailment is typically what people mean when they refer to "deduction" or "demonstration" or "proof." On the other hand, for A to partially entail B means that the conditional probability of B given A is greater than the unconditional probability of B by itself (e.g., the probability of gaining tenure given that you've won a Nobel prize is greater than the probability of gaining tenure given no additional information). Partial entailment is sometimes called "probabilification." Partial entailment is a more general notion than strict entailment and properly subsumes it since A strictly entails B just in case the conditional probability of B given A is one (e.g., the probability of being unmarried given that you're a bachelor is one).[13]

Whether strict or partial, entailment is a logical relation, with the direction of the logic going from the thing doing the entailing to the thing entailed. In practice we know that A strictly entails B when we can find a logical argument that takes A as a premise and that by a series of logical manipulations (usually deductions according to certain inference rules) leads to B as a conclusion. On the other hand, we know that A partially entails B when we have reasonable ways of assigning probabilities to claims involving A and B and find that the conditional probability of B given A is greater than the unconditional probability of B by itself.

Both strict and partial entailment yield rational compulsion. This is immediately obvious for strict entailment. Indeed if it is impossible for B to be false if A is true, then if we affirm A, we had surely better affirm B also. Still we might wonder why partial entailment yields rational compulsion. Whereas strict entailment leaves no room for either (1) fallibility or (2) contingency or (3) degree or (4) doubt, partial entailment leaves room for all of these. If A strictly entails B, then (1) there is no possibility of being wrong about B if we are right about A; (2) B follows necessarily from A; (3) A epistemically supports B to the utmost and cannot be made to support B to a still higher degree; and (4) not only need we not but we also ought not doubt B if we trust A.

On the other hand, none of these properties holds in general for partial entailment. Consider the following two claims:

A: There will be a heavy snowfall tonight.
B: Schools will be closed tomorrow.

Suppose nine times out of ten when there is a heavy snow fall at night, schools are closed on the morrow. Then if we see heavy snow accumulating tonight, we have good reason to expect that school will be closed tomorrow. Nevertheless the four claims just made about strict entailment in the last paragraph fail to hold for partial entailment. Thus (1) even though A may hold, we may still be mistaken for holding B; (2) there is no necessary connection between A and B; (3) the relation of support between A and B admits of degrees (for instance, the relation would be still stronger if ninety-nine times out of a hundred school was closed following a heavy snow fall, weaker if only two times out of three); and (4) we are entitled to invest B with a measure of doubt even if we know A to be true.

Even so, partial entailment is rationally compulsive. To see this, consider the following thought experiment by C. S. Peirce:

> If a man had to choose between drawing a card from a pack containing twenty-five red cards and a black one, or from a pack containing twenty-five black cards and a red one, and if the drawing of a red card were destined to transport him to eternal felicity, and that of a black one to consign him to everlasting woe, it would be folly to deny that he ought to prefer the pack containing the larger portion of red cards, although, from the nature of the risk, it could not be repeated. . . . But suppose he should choose the red pack, and should draw the wrong card, what consolation would he have?[14]

Yes, you might end up with a black card if you choose from the deck consisting predominantly of red cards. But you will be much more likely to end up with a black card if you choose from the other deck. Hence if your aim is to avoid everlasting woe, you had better choose a card from the predominantly red deck. Now the injunction "you had better choose the red deck" is certainly a form of rational compulsion.

Thus rational compulsion arises even when we are dealing not with certainties but with probabilities. Suppose therefore that A and B are claims and that **P** is a probability that handles claims involving A and B. Then if $P(B\,|\,A)$ (the conditional probability of B given A) is greater than $P(B)$ (the unconditioned probability of B), we are rationally compelled or obligated to invest more credence in B on the assumption of A than in B taken by itself. Moreover since it is a basic property of probabilities that $P(B\,|\,A) = 1 - P(\sim B\,|\,A)$ ($\sim B$ is the negation of B), it follows that whenever $P(B\,|\,A)$ is greater than $1/2$, then $P(\sim B\,|\,A)$ is less than $1/2$. Thus if we know that A has happened and that $P(B\,|\,A)$ is greater than $1/2$, then if we must base a course of action on whether or not B occurs, we must suppose that B and not its negation will occur.[15] This shows that not only strict entailment but also partial entailment yields a form of rational compulsion.

The question remains, Why won't rational compulsion do as an account of epistemic support in the dialogue between science and theology? The problem with rational compulsion is twofold. For one, it is far too restrictive. The logic of rational compulsion is the logic of entailment, which is a very restricted type of logic. Indeed no field of inquiry short of mathematics could progress if it limited itself to the logic of strict or partial entailment. Rather most fields of inquiry require an alternate form of inference known variously as the "method of hypothesis," "abduction" or "inference to the best explanation." I'll consider this alternate form of inference in the next section. Suffice it to say, rational compulsion doesn't get you very far even when you're confined to a single discipline, much less when you have to span across disciplines.

The other problem with rational compulsion is that it is much better suited to defeating than fostering genuinely productive interdisciplinary dialogue. In the logic of entailment, which is the logic of rational compulsion, the direction of the logic as well as the direction of epistemic support move in the same direction. If A rationally compels B, then A strictly or partially entails B, *and* A epistemically supports B. The problem now is this. For a relation of epistemic support between A and B to serve any practical purpose, the thing that does the supporting, in this case A, must be taken for granted—A must be given. But once A is given, any consequences strictly or partially entailed by A, say B, must be accepted as well—after all, A rationally compels B.

This is by now old hat. But suppose next that A and B are claims from distinct disciplines. And suppose, as is sometimes though rarely the case, that A happens to strictly or partially entail B. Suppose further that two persons, Alice and Bob, are practitioners of the distinct disciplines represented respectively by A and B. Suppose finally that Alice is fully committed to A but that Bob finds B repugnant. For instance, in the debate between young-earth creationists and the scientific establishment, we might imagine Alice to be a member of the scientific establishment, Bob a young-earth creationist, A the claim that radiometric dating methods are sound and B the claim that the earth is several billion years old. In this case A does strictly entail B. But since Bob is committed to an earth that is only a few thousand years old, Bob finds B utterly unacceptable. What then does Bob do? The standard practice of young-earth creationists is to impugn A, that is, to reject the radiometric dating methods. As a result the interdisciplinary dialogue between young-earth creationists and the scientific establishment cannot even get off the ground. What is a fundamental assumption for Alice, namely A, becomes a point of contention for Bob.

Rational compulsion therefore serves the cause of interdisciplinary dialogue poorly since the most interesting possibility never occurs, to wit, Alice manages to convince Bob that B holds on the basis of A even though prior to the interdisciplinary encounter with Alice, Bob is firmly convinced that B does not hold. Rather than question established results of his own discipline, Bob will turn matters around and question the established results of the other side's discipline. The most interesting prospect for interdisciplinary dialogue therefore does not and cannot succeed.

Indeed, when limited to rational compulsion, interdisciplinary dialogue typically reduces to polite chitchat.[16] If nothing is riding on B, then Bob can graciously accept B if Alice is fully committed to A and A happens to entail B. Better yet, if Bob is already committed to B, then learning that Alice is committed to A and that A entails B amounts to a pat on the back for Bob, providing him with further support for B from Alice's discipline. In neither of these instances, however, is Bob learning anything genuinely new or significant about his discipline. In the one case, B is irrelevant to Bob's concerns; in the other, B simply receives further confirmation, something Bob neither needed nor sought.

The one case where rational compulsion can serve the cause of interdisciplinary dialogue is if Bob finds B important but is puzzled about B and has no way of determining the truth of B within his own discipline. Then if A rationally compels B and A is from another discipline, Bob will have learned something interesting about B from that other discipline. In practice, however, this possibility occurs infrequently. Moreover the reason this possibility occurs infrequently follows from the nature of the entailment relation that underlies rational compulsion: entailment is simply too strong for most interdisciplinary dialogues. Indeed there are not many interesting entailments that span across disciplines.

7.4 Explanatory Power

The dialogue between theology and science is singularly uninteresting if we have to limit our understanding of epistemic support to rational compulsion. Indeed an alternative understanding of epistemic support is needed if the interdisciplinary dialogue between science and theology is to be worth the bother. Fortunately such an alternative is available.[17] Although there are a number of ways to approach this alternative, I shall approach it through the concept of *explanatory power.*[18]

A little history will be useful to clarify the concept of explanatory power. During the nineteenth century C. S. Peirce devoted considerable energies to describing the modes of inference by which we derive conclusions from data. Because data are given and conclusions depend for their justification upon data, the relation of epistemic support is invariably directed from data to conclusion. Thus if A comprises the data and B the conclusion, we say A provides evidence for, confirms or epistemically supports B (where each of these expressions amounts to the same thing).

Now the thing Peirce observed is that the direction of the logic relating A and B need not go in the same direction as the relation of epistemic support between A and B. In the case of rational compulsion and entailment, as we saw in the last section, the directions are identical. Nevertheless it can happen that the relation of epistemic support goes in one direction, but the logic relating data and conclusion goes in the other. Peirce used the term *deduction* to characterize inference patterns whose logic and support relations were directed similarly, whereas he used the term *abduction* to characterize those where they were directed oppositely.[19]

The difference between these inference patterns becomes apparent from the argument schemas in figures 7.1 and 7.2.[20]

DATA: A is given and plainly true.
LOGIC: *But if A is true, then B is a matter of course.*
CONCLUSION: Hence, B must be true as well.

Figure 7.1. Deduction schema

DATA: The surprising fact A is observed.
LOGIC: *But if B were true, then A would be a matter of course.*
CONCLUSION: Hence, there is reason to suspect that B is true.

Figure 7.2. Abduction schema

Notice that the data and the conclusion of both schemas are identical, for in both instances we are given A and we conclude B. Yet the logic is entirely reversed. In the deduction schema the logic proceeds from A to B whereas in the abduction schema the logic proceeds from B to A.

The logic of the deduction schema is the *logic of entailment*. Once A is given, anything logically entailed by A must be accepted as well. The logic of the abduction schema, on the other hand, hinges on a quite different logic, one I call the *logic of explanation*. Once A is given, anything that neatly explains A becomes highly plausible. Within the abduction schema valid conclusions are therefore those that explain A.

The logic of explanation is incompatible with the logic of deduction. As far as the logic of deduction is concerned, the logic of explanation commits the fallacy of affirming the consequent. The fallacy of affirming the consequent is essentially a failure to acknowledge that antecedent conditions can be underdetermined, that is, a failure to recognize that the antecedent conditions for a given claim may be manifold and therefore not uniquely determined (= underdetermined).

For instance, suppose we know that Frank was promoted, and suppose we know that if Frank behaves obsequiously toward his boss, he will be sure to be promoted. It does not follow, therefore, as a logical deduction, that Frank did in fact behave obsequiously toward his boss. Frank may just be incredibly competent so that his boss decided to promote him despite his not being obsequious. Alternatively, Frank's mother may own the company, and so Frank's boss thought it wise to promote Frank even though Frank was at times downright rude. The point is that the explanation of Frank's promotion (whether it was on account of his obsequious behavior or whether it was on account of his mother being company owner or whatever) is not governed by the logic of deduction. Rational compulsion has no claim on the logic of explanation.

Peirce admitted as much when he wrote, "As a general rule [abduction] is a weak kind of argument. It often inclines our judgment so slightly toward its conclusion that we cannot say that we believe the latter to be true; we only surmise that it may be so."[21] Yet as a practical matter Peirce acknowledged that abduction often yields conclusions that are difficult to doubt even if they lack the compulsive force of the logic of deduction. For instance, Peirce argued that skepticism about the existence of Napoleon

Bonaparte was unjustified even though Napoleon's existence could only be known by abduction. As Peirce put it, "Numberless documents refer to a conqueror called Napoleon Bonaparte. Though we have not seen the man, yet we cannot explain what we have seen, namely, all these documents and monuments, without supposing that he really existed."[22] To this Peirce added, "There is no difference except one of degree between such an [historical] inference and that by which we are led to believe that we remember the occurrences of yesterday from our feelings as if we did so."[23]

To sum up, in the logic of deduction A epistemically supports B because A logically entails and therefore rationally compels B. On the other hand, in the logic of explanation, A epistemically supports B because B provides a good explanation of A. As Peirce showed, both logics constitute legitimate inference patterns and underwrite robust relations of epistemic support. Yet although these logics often work together, they are nevertheless distinct. Moreover the distinction must be maintained to avoid confusions.

What has happened to the logic of explanation and its conception of epistemic support since Peirce's day? The key development has been a generalization of Peircean abduction via the concept of explanatory power. Even though Peirce clearly distinguished deduction from abduction, there is a sense in which deduction still plays a central role within Peircean abduction. Recall the Peircean abduction schema in figure 7.2. Within the logic of this abduction schema, the prototypical example of B explaining A is the case where A follows as a logical deduction from B (i.e., B strictly entails or rationally compels A). Thus as an elementary example of abduction, Peirce considered the case where A = *every bean observed from the bag is white* and B = *all the beans in the bag are white*.[24] Here B not only explains A but actually entails A. (Indeed the logical deduction leading from B to A is immediate.)

It is in clarifying and generalizing the logic that connects data to conclusion that significant progress has been made in recent years. Explanatory power has become the guiding principle for characterizing this logic, with the question of what constitutes a best explanation occupying center stage. Thus philosophers of science have proposed three criteria that need to be satisfied for B to constitute the best explanation of A.

First, B must be *consonant* with A.[25] Thus instead of injecting discord or dissonance into our understanding of A, B must harmonize with A as well as the network of beliefs of which A is a part. In the network of beliefs that houses A, B too must find a ready home. Note that consonance is more than simply a coherentist requirement. Consonance involves both goodness of fit and aesthetic judgment. A and B must be not only at peace with one another but also adapted to each other. Like a hand in a glove, there has to be a fit.[26]

Second, B must *contribute* to A. Thus B must perform some useful work in helping to explain A. B must solve problems or answer questions pertinent to A which could not be handled without it. This second requirement is a corollary of Occam's razor, ensuring that adding B to our stock of beliefs won't be superfluous.

Third, as the best explanation, B must be the reigning *champion* among current competing explanations for A. B is therefore not the best explanation of A in any absolute sense. B must simply do a better job explaining A than any of its current competitors. Explanation is therefore viewed as inherently competitive, contrastive and fallible. Reigning champions stand ever in need of critical reexamination. Explanation invests its epistemic dollar with the current champion. This third requirement therefore ensures that explanation is simultaneously progressive and self-critical.[27]

How does epistemic support look when it is based on explanatory power rather than rational compulsion? The answer will by now be obvious. Instead of A epistemically supporting B because A rationally compels the acceptance of B, A now epistemically supports B because B is the best currently available explanation of A. Specifically this means that B is consonant with A, is a contributor to our understanding of A and is the current champion among competing explanations of A.

7.5 The Big Bang and Divine Creation

With explanatory power rather than rational compulsion characterizing epistemic support, the cosmological theory of the Big Bang and the Christian doctrine of divine creation can now be brought into a relation of mutual epistemic support. To show this in detail exceeds the scope of this chapter. Still a few brief observations will show what is at stake in relating the Big Bang and divine creation in terms of epistemic support (construed now within the logic of explanation).

Curiously, in the very passage where he denies that relations of epistemic support obtain between the big-bang model and the Christian doctrine of creation, Ernan McMullin actually opens the door to such relations. In a passage already quoted, McMullin remarks,

> What one could say . . . is that if the universe began in time through the act of a Creator, from our vantage point it would look something like the Big Bang that cosmologists are talking about. What one cannot say is, first, that the Christian doctrine of Creation "supports" the Big Bang model, or, second, that the Big Bang model "supports" the Christian doctrine of Creation.[28]

Yet if we take explanatory power as our basis for epistemic support, it seems that what McMullin denies in the second part of this quotation he actually affirms in the first part.

For consider what it means to say, "If the universe began in time through the act of a Creator, from our vantage point it would look something like the Big Bang that cosmologists are talking about." Doesn't this simply mean that if we assume the Christian doctrine of creation as a metaphysical hypothesis, then the Big Bang is the sort of cosmological theory we have reason to expect? And in terms of our criterion of consonance, doesn't this mean that the Christian doctrine of creation is consonant with the Big Bang? I submit that the answer to both questions is yes.

Suppose now we take the Big Bang as given (= data) and pose the question how we might best explain the Big Bang in metaphysical terms. The playing field is potentially quite large. Metaphysics offers a multitude of competing explanations on the nature and origin of the material universe, everything from solipsism to idealism to naturalism to theism. Nevertheless in practice we consider only the competing explanations advocated by parties in a dispute. Since McMullin's foil is the scientific naturalist, let us limit the competition to Christian theism and scientific naturalism.

If we limit our attention to these two choices, Christian theism and its doctrine of creation comes out the superior explanation of the Big Bang over any of the explanations offered to date by scientific naturalism. Consider the contortions that naturalistic scientists have inflicted on themselves, not in their metaphysical speculations but in their scientific theorizing, to avoid the Big Bang. For decades the scientific world resisted the Big Bang for no other reason than that it seems to require a beginning of time, which is not consonant with any credible form of naturalism. Einstein acknowledged this lack of consonance when he introduced his cosmological constant to maintain a static universe—a decision he came to regret, calling it the biggest blunder of his career.[29] Fred Hoyle acknowledged it as well when he put forward his steady-state theory to retain an eternal universe—despite its violation of the conservation of energy.[30]

The Christian doctrine of creation is consonant with the Big Bang and can justifiably be regarded a better explanation of the Big Bang than its naturalistic competitors. In the competition with naturalism, divine creation comes out the champion. Moreover, because the Big Bang is a putative scientific fact and because we are asking for a metaphysical account of that fact, it follows that the Christian doctrine of creation is not a superfluous addition to our understanding of the Big Bang. The Christian doctrine of creation contributes substantively to our metaphysical understanding of the Big Bang. Therefore, because the Christian doctrine of creation satisfies all three criteria characterizing best explanations, it may (in a competition with naturalism) plausibly be regarded as the best explanation of the Big Bang. Hence if we unpack epistemic support in terms of explanatory power rather than rational compulsion, we can conclude that *the Big Bang epistemically supports the Christian doctrine of creation.*

To be sure, this argument that the Big Bang epistemically supports the Christian doctrine of creation needs to be fleshed out. Still the general idea of how a fruitful interdisciplinary dialogue between theology and science should proceed will be clear. Note that in the example involving the Big Bang and the Christian doctrine of creation, I only examined the case of a scientific claim (i.e., the Big Bang) epistemically supporting a theological claim (the Christian doctrine of creation). We could of course turn this around. Thus we could fix the Christian doctrine of creation as data and ask which cosmological theory of the origin of the universe is best supported by the Christian doctrine of creation. The answer to this question is left as an exercise to the reader.[31]

7.6 Christ as the Completion of Science

The logic of explanation, especially with its emphasis on explanatory power and inference to the best explanation, makes possible a genuinely fruitful interdisciplinary dialogue between science and theology. Even so, to leave the discussion here would be unsatisfying. Theology has traditionally been called "the queen of the sciences." If humanity's chief truth consists in God's reconciling the world to himself through Christ, then theology should not be just one more discipline among others. To talk of theology in an interdisciplinary dialogue places theology on a par with other disciplines. To be sure, theology is a discipline and is in dialogue with other disciplines. But there is also a sense in which theology transcends, informs and unifies all disciplines. In closing this chapter I want therefore to consider what it means to assert the preeminence of Christian theology among the disciplines and particularly among the sciences. My thesis is that all disciplines find their completion in Christ and cannot be properly understood apart from Christ.

If we take seriously the word-flesh Christology of Chalcedon (i.e., the doctrine that Christ is fully human and fully divine)[32] and view Christ as the *telos* toward which God is drawing the whole of creation,[33] then any view of the sciences that leaves Christ out of the picture must be seen as fundamentally deficient. As Karl Barth consistently argued, Christology is not merely one of many Christian doctrines but the very lens through which alone it is possible to properly understand the panorama of human existence, and that includes all the special sciences as well as all other disciplines. Thus in writing his *Church Dogmatics*, Barth employed Christology as the lens through which to understand one major aspect of that panorama—no less the whole of Christian theology. I want to urge that we follow Barth's example and use Christology as the lens not just for understanding the whole of Christian theology, as Barth did in his *Church Dogmatics*, but even more ambitiously for understanding all the various disciplines.

This privileging of Christology as the lens through which to view the various disciplines won't violate the integrity of those disciplines. In cross-disciplinary studies, and especially when science and theology intersect, violence to the integrity of the respective disciplines is always a legitimate concern, for there is always the possibility that one will lose its integrity at the expense of the other.[34] The word-flesh Christology, however, safeguards against this violation of disciplinary integrity. The reason is straightforward. Because Christ is both fully divine and fully human, Christ can never be less than human. Thus whatever information the various disciplines offer needs to be taken seriously; indeed it will be taken seriously when construed through the christological lens, for these disciplines are human constructions, and Christ himself was human. Karl Marx's favorite maxim was *Nihil humani a me alienum puto* (nothing human is alien to me).[35] The Christian has more right than anyone to this maxim.

The christological lens is more than simply a principle for making sense of the various disciplines. Theologians recognize that theological inquiry always presupposes some consciousness of what hermeneutic principles are being employed, with the christological lens serving as a hermeneutic principle *par excellence*.[36] Hermeneutic principles, however, can be mere interpretive overlays, not entering substantively into the theories they are interpreting. But this is not the case with the christological lens. To be sure, Christ is the lens through which we as Christians view the panorama of existence. But Christ is also the incarnate Word who through the incarnation enters and transforms the whole of reality. We should therefore expect Christology to enter substantively into the various disciplines as well.

Typically when a lens is used to examine something, the lens is independent of the thing being examined. Thus when I look at a scene through binoculars, the scene itself need not contain any binoculars. But Christ is the new Adam who redefines creation by entering and transforming it. Thus when Christ is the lens through which we survey the world and the various disciplines that try to understand the world, we should expect the christological lens to focus on Christ as well. Indeed if the transformation Christ brings to the world is as radical as Scripture attests, as the christological lens surveys the world, we should expect Christ to be the principal object on which that lens gets focused.

But doesn't that entail conflating science and religion? If Christ enters substantively into our scientific theories, must not their scientific status be severely compromised? The answer is no. To see why the answer is indeed no and that there need never be any worry about smuggling Christ into our scientific theories and thereby undercutting them, we need to understand how Christ can enter substantively into a scientific theory without violating its integrity.

The point to understand here is that Christ is never an *addendum* to a scientific theory but always a *completion*. An addendum to a theory would look something like this: Erik Erikson proposed eight stages of psychosocial development: *trust versus mistrust, autonomy versus shame, initiative versus guilt, industry versus inferiority, identity versus role confusion, intimacy versus isolation, generativity versus stagnation, integrity versus despair.*[37] To treat Christ as an addendum to Erikson's theory might then take the form of adding a new theological stage of development to Erikson's scheme, say, the *Jesus versus Satan* stage. The absurdity of this move is evident, as is its violation of the integrity of Erikson's developmental scheme.

A completion, however, is entirely different from an addendum. To see how completions work, consider the following example from mathematics. In principle the applied mathematician can do everything he or she needs by working with rational numbers. (These are the numbers that can be represented by finite or repeating decimal expansions.) Rational numbers are the only numbers the applied mathematician ever encounters when working with a calculator or computer. In principle, therefore, the applied mathematician can make do entirely with rational numbers. Nevertheless it turns out that the mathematician's task becomes a lot easier when he or she embeds the rational numbers into the real numbers and uses the real numbers to derive formulas and equations. The real numbers are known as the completion of the rational numbers.[38]

The real numbers include both the rational numbers and the irrational numbers (these are numbers like π and the square root of 2, written $\sqrt{2}$, which require for their representation infinite and nonrepeating decimal expansions). Thus in going to the real numbers, the applied mathematician loses nothing that he or she had before in the rational numbers. Nevertheless the real numbers are not an artificial addendum to the rational numbers. The rational numbers, even though adequate for all the actual calculations that the applied mathematician ever makes, are *conceptually inadequate*.

A circle whose radius is given by a rational number q has circumference given by the irrational number $2\pi q$. A square whose side has length given by a rational number s has diagonal length given by the irrational number $\sqrt{2}s$.[39] The applied mathematician will in practice always end up approximating $2\pi q$ and $\sqrt{2}s$ with rational numbers. But the fact remains that in assigning rational approximations to the circumference of a circle and the diagonal of a square, the applied mathematician cannot escape that these inevitably are approximations whose validity as approximations depends on the real numbers that complete the rational numbers. In calculating the circumference of a circle and the diagonal length of a square, the applied mathematician is in the first place concerned with the actual circumference of that circle and the actual diagonal of that square, and not with their rational approximation. Rational approximations come afterward, being the best that applied mathematicians can do given their limitations as finite rational agents in a physical world.

The completion of the rational numbers by the real numbers illuminates Christology's role in the sciences. A scientist can investigate an aspect of the world without reference to Christ much as the applied mathematician can make his or her calculations without reference to the real numbers. But the validity of the scientist's insights can never be divorced from Christ, who through the incarnation enters, takes on and transforms the world and thus cannot help but pervade the scientist's domain of inquiry. So, too, the validity of the approximations that the applied mathematician makes can never be divorced from the real numbers that undergird and complete the rational numbers.

Even though the real numbers can be gotten from the rational numbers by adding the irrational numbers, the real numbers are not properly conceived as an addendum to the rational numbers. The real numbers do not merely include the rational numbers. Any real number that is not a rational number (i.e., every irrational number) is arbitrarily close to a rational number. One can think of it this way: If one takes a microscope, at any given finite level of magnification there is always a rational number that is indistinguishable from a given irrational number. Thus from a purely finite perspective it doesn't appear that there is anything else besides the rational numbers. Even so, without the real numbers undergirding the applied mathematician's calculations, the conceptual soundness of those calculations cannot be maintained, for circumferences of circles and diagonals of squares do not make sense in terms of rational numbers but only in terms of real numbers.

So, too, Christology tells us that the conceptual soundness of a scientific theory cannot be maintained apart from Christ. Christ is the light and life of the world. All things were created by him and for him. Christ defines humanity, the world and its destiny. It follows that a scientist, in trying to understand some aspect of the world, is in the first instance concerned with that aspect as it relates to Christ—and this is true regardless of whether the scientist acknowledges Christ. Only secondarily is the scientist concerned with obtaining a pragmatic understanding of that aspect of the world (e.g., the applied mathematician's calculations), a pragmatic understanding that will inevitably hinge on whatever theoretical constructs (e.g., the rational numbers) that the scientist has formulated.

Christ is indispensable to any scientific theory, even if its practitioners don't have a clue about him. The pragmatics of a scientific theory can, to be sure, be pursued without recourse to Christ. But the conceptual soundness of the theory can in the end only be located in Christ. Christ, as the completion of our scientific theories, maintains the conceptual soundness of those theories even as the real numbers maintain the conceptual soundness of the applied mathematician's calculations. Christ has assumed the fullness of our humanity and entered every aspect of our reality. He thereby renders all our studies the study of himself.

8

The Act of Creation

8.1 Creation as a Divine Gift

"Sing, O Goddess, the anger of Achilles son of Peleus, that brought countless ills upon the Achaeans."[1] In these opening lines of the *Iliad* Homer invokes the Muse. For Homer the act of creating poetry is a divine gift, one that derives from an otherworldly source and is not ultimately reducible to this world. This conception of human creativity as a divine gift pervaded the ancient world and was also evident among the Hebrews. In Exodus, for instance, we read that God filled the two artisans Bezaleel and Aholiab with wisdom so that they might complete the work of the tabernacle (Exodus 35:30-35).

The idea that creative activity is a divine gift has largely been lost these days. To ask a cognitive scientist, for instance, what made Mozart a creative genius is unlikely to prompt an appeal to God. A cognitive scientist who embraces neuropsychology may suggest that Mozart was blessed with a particularly fortunate collocation of neurons. One who prefers an information processing model of mentality may attribute Mozart's genius to some particularly effective computational modules. A cognitive psychologist taken with Skinner's behaviorism may attribute Mozart's genius to some particularly effective reinforcement schedules (perhaps imposed early in his life by his father, Leopold). And no doubt, in all of these explanations the cognitive scientist will invoke Mozart's natural genetic endowment. In place of a divine afflatus the modern cognitive scientist explains human creativity purely in terms of natural processes.

Who's right, the ancients or the moderns? My own view is that the ancients got it right. An act of creation is always a divine gift and cannot be reduced to purely naturalistic categories. To be sure, creative activity often involves the transformation of natural objects, like the transformation of a slab of marble into Michelangelo's David. But even when confined to natural objects, creative activity is never naturalistic without remainder. The divine is always present at some level and indispensable.

Invoking the divine to explain an act of creation is of course wholly unacceptable to the ruling intellectual elite. Naturalism, the view that nature is the ultimate reality, is the default position for all serious inquiry among our intellectual elite. From biblical studies to law to education to science to the arts, inquiry is allowed to proceed only under the supposition that nature is the ultimate reality. Naturalism denies any divine element to the creative act. By contrast, the Christian tradition plainly asserts that God is the ultimate reality and that nature itself is a divine creative act. Within Christian theism God is primary and fundamental, whereas nature is secondary and derivative. Naturalism, by contrast, asserts that nature is primary and fundamental.

Theism and naturalism provide radically different perspectives on the act of creation. Within theism any act of creation is also a divine act. Within naturalism any act of creation emerges from a purely natural substrate—the very minds that create are, within naturalism, the result of a long evolutionary process that itself was not created. The aim of this chapter then is to present a general account of creation that is faithful to the Christian tradition, that resolutely rejects naturalism and that engages contemporary developments in science and philosophy.

8.2 Naturalism's Challenge to Creation
Why should anyone want to understand the act of creation naturalistically? Naturalism, after all, offers fewer resources than theism. Naturalism simply gives you nature. Theism gives you not only nature but also God and anything outside of nature that God might have created. The

ontology of theism is far richer than that of naturalism. Why then settle for less?

Naturalists do not see themselves as settling for less. Instead they regard theism as saddled with a lot of extraneous entities that serve no useful function. The regulative principle of naturalism is Occam's razor. Occam's razor is a principle of parsimony that requires eliminating entities that perform no useful function. Using Occam's razor, naturalists attempt to slice away the superstitions of the past—and for naturalists the worst superstition of all is God. People used to invoke God to explain all sorts of things for which we now have perfectly good naturalistic explanations. Accordingly God is a superstition that needs to be excised from our understanding of the world. The naturalists' dream is to invent a theory of everything that entirely eliminates the need for God (Stephen Hawking is a case in point).[2]

Since naturalists are committed to eliminating God from every domain of inquiry, let us consider how successfully they have eliminated God from the act of creation. Even leaving aside the creation of the world and focusing solely on human acts of creation, do we find that naturalistic categories have fully explained human creativity? Occam's razor is all fine and well for removing stubble, but while we're at it let's make sure we don't lop off a nose or ear. With respect to human creativity, let's make sure that in eliminating God the naturalist isn't giving us a lobotomized account of human creativity. Einstein once remarked that everything should be made as simple as possible but not simpler. In eliminating God from the act of creation the naturalist needs to make sure that nothing of fundamental importance has been lost. Not only has the naturalist failed to provide this assurance, but there is good reason to think that any account of the creative act that omits God is necessarily incomplete and defective.[3]

What does naturalism have to say about human acts of creation? For the moment let's bracket the question of creativity and consider simply what it is for a human being to act. Humans are intelligent agents that act with intentions to accomplish certain ends. Although some acts by humans are creative, others are not. Georgia O'Keeffe's painting an iris is a creative act. Georgia O'Keeffe's flipping on a light switch is an act but not a creative act. For the moment, therefore, let us focus simply on human agency, leaving aside human creative agency.

How then does naturalism make sense of human agency? Although the naturalistic literature that attempts to account for human agency is vast, the naturalist's options are in fact quite limited. The naturalist's world is not a mind-first world. Intelligent agency is therefore in no sense prior to or independent of nature. Intelligent agency is neither sui generis nor basic. Intelligent agency is a derivative mode of causation that depends on underlying naturalistic—and therefore unintelligent—causes. Human agency in particular supervenes on underlying natural processes, which in turn are usually identified with brain function.[4]

It is important to distinguish the naturalist's understanding of causation from the theist's. Within theism God is the ultimate reality. Consequently whenever God acts, there can be nothing outside of God that compels God's action. God is not a billiard ball that must move when another billiard ball strikes it. God's actions are free, and though he responds to his creation, he does not do so out of necessity. Within theism, therefore, divine action is not reducible to some more basic mode of causation. Indeed within theism divine action is the most basic mode of causation since any other mode of causation involves creatures which themselves were created in a divine act.

Now consider naturalism. Within naturalism nature is the ultimate reality. Consequently whenever something happens in nature, there can be nothing outside of nature that shares responsibility for what happened. Thus when an event happens in nature, it is either because some other event in nature was responsible for it or because it simply happened, apart from any other determining event. Events therefore happen either because they were caused by other events or because they happened spontaneously. The first of these is usually called "necessity," the second "chance." For the naturalist, chance and necessity are the fundamental modes of causation. Together they constitute what are called "natural causes." Naturalism therefore seeks to account for intelligent agency in terms of natural causes.

How well have natural causes been able to account for intelligent agency? Cognitive scientists have achieved nothing like a full reduction. A full reduction of intelligent agency to natural causes would give a complete account of human behavior, intention and emotion in terms of neural processes. Nothing like this has been achieved. No doubt, neural processes are correlated with behavior, intention and emotion. Anger presumably is correlated with certain localized brain excitations. But localized brain excitations hardly explain anger any better than do overt behaviors associated with anger—like shouting obscenities.

Because cognitive scientists have yet to effect a full reduction of intelligent agency to natural causes, they speak of intelligent agency as *supervening* on natural causes. Supervenience is a hierarchical relationship between higher order processes (in this case intelligent agency) and lower order processes (in this case natural causes). What supervenience says is that the relationship between the higher and lower order processes is a one-way street, with the lower determining the higher. To say, for instance, that intelligent agency supervenes on neurophysiology is to say that once all the facts about neurophysiology are in place, all the facts about intelligent agency are determined as well. Supervenience makes no pretense at reductive analysis. It simply asserts that the lower level determines the higher level—how it does it, we don't know.[5]

Supervenience is therefore an insulating strategy, designed to protect a naturalistic account of intelligent agency until a full reductive explanation is found. Supervenience, though not providing a reduction, tells us that in principle a reduction exists. Given that nothing like a full reductive explanation of intelligent agency is at hand, why should we think that such a reduction is even possible? To be sure, if we knew that naturalism were correct, then supervenience would follow. But naturalism itself is at issue.

Neuroscience, for instance, is nowhere near achieving its ambitions, and that despite its strident rhetoric. Hardcore neuroscientists refer disparagingly to the ordinary psychology of beliefs, desires and emotions as "folk psychology." The implication is that just as "folk medicine" had to give way to "real medicine," so "folk psychology" will have to give way to a revamped psychology that is grounded in neuroscience. In place of talking cures that address our beliefs, desires and emotions, tomorrow's healers of the soul will manipulate brain states directly and ignore such outdated categories as beliefs, desires and emotions.[6]

At least so the story goes. Actual neuroscience research has yet to keep pace with its vaulting ambition. That should hardly surprise us. The neurophysiology of our brains is incredibly plastic and has proven notoriously difficult to correlate with intentional states. For instance, Louis Pasteur, despite suffering a cerebral accident, continued to enjoy a flourishing scientific career. When his brain was examined after he died, it was discovered that half the brain had completely atrophied.[7] How does one explain a flourishing intellectual life despite a severely damaged brain if mind and brain coincide?

Or consider a still more striking example. The December 12, 1980, issue of *Science* contained an article by Roger Lewin titled "Is Your Brain Really Necessary?" In the article Lewin reported a case study by John Lorber, a British neurologist and professor at Sheffield University:

> "There's a young student at this university," says Lorber, "who has an IQ of 126, has gained a first-class honors degree in mathematics, and is socially completely normal. And yet the boy has virtually no brain." The student's physician at the university noticed that the youth had a slightly larger than normal head, and so referred him to Lorber, simply out of interest. "When we did a brain scan on him," Lorber recalls, "we saw that instead of the normal 4.5-centimeter thickness of brain tissue between the ventricles and the cortical surface, there was just a thin layer of mantle measuring a millimeter or so. His cranium is filled mainly with cerebrospinal fluid."[8]

Against such anomalies, for cognitive neuroscientists to claim that brain determines mind hardly inspires confidence. Yet as Thomas Kuhn has taught us, a science that is progressing fast and furiously is not about to be derailed by a few anomalies.[9] Neuroscience is a case in point. For all the obstacles it faces in trying to reduce intelligent agency to natural causes, neuroscience persists in the Promethean determination to show that mind does ultimately reduce to neurophysiology. Absent a prior commitment to naturalism, this determination will seem misguided. On the other hand, given a prior commitment to naturalism, this determination is readily understandable.

8.3 Computational Reductionism

Understandable yes, obligatory no. Most cognitive scientists do not rest their hopes with neuroscience. Yes, if naturalism is correct, then a reduction of intelligent agency to neurophysiology is in principle possible. The sheer difficulty of even attempting this reduction, both experimental and theoretical, however, leaves many cognitive scientists looking for a more manageable field to invest their energies. As it turns out, the field of choice is computer science, especially its subdiscipline of artificial intelligence (abbreviated AI). Unlike brains, computers are neat and precise.

Also unlike brains, computers and their programs can be copied and mass-produced. Inasmuch as science thrives on replicability and control, computer science offers tremendous practical advantages over neurological research.

Whereas the goal of neuroscience is to reduce intelligent agency to neurophysiology, the goal of artificial intelligence is to reduce intelligent agency to computer algorithms. Since computers operate deterministically, reducing intelligent agency to computer algorithms would indeed constitute a naturalistic reduction of intelligent agency. Should artificial intelligence succeed in reducing intelligent agency to computation, cognitive scientists would still have the task of showing in what sense brain function is computational (alternatively, Marvin Minsky's dictum that the mind is a computer made of meat would still need to be verified). Even so, the reduction of intelligent agency to computation would go a long way toward establishing a purely naturalistic basis for human cognition.

An obvious question now arises: Can computation explain intelligent agency? First let's be clear that no actual computer system has come anywhere near to simulating the full range of capacities we associate with human intelligent agency. Yes, computers can do certain narrowly circumscribed tasks exceedingly well (like play chess). But require a computer to make a decision based on incomplete information and calling for common sense, and the computer will be lost. Perhaps the toughest problem facing artificial intelligence researchers is what's called the *frame problem*.[10] The frame problem is getting a computer to find the appropriate frame of reference for solving a problem.

Consider, for instance, the following story: A man enters a bar. The bartender asks, "What can I do for you?" The man responds, "I'd like a glass of water." The bartender pulls out a gun and shouts, "Get out of here!" The man says, "Thank you," and leaves. End of story. What is the appropriate frame of reference? No, this isn't a story by Franz Kafka. The key item of information needed to make sense of this story is this: The man has the hiccups. By going to the bar to get a drink of water, the man hoped to cure his hiccups. The bartender, however, decided on a more radical cure. By terrifying the man with a gun, the bartender cured the man's hiccups immediately. Cured of his hiccups, the man was grateful and left. Humans are able to understand the appropriate frame of reference for such stories immediately. Computers, on the other hand, haven't a clue.

Ah, but just wait. Give an army of clever programmers enough time, funding and computational power, and just see if they don't solve the frame problem. Naturalists are forever issuing such promissory notes, claiming that a conclusive confirmation of naturalism is right around the corner—just give our scientists a bit more time and money. This practice has appropriately been called "promissory materialism." Confronted with such promises, what's a theist to do? To refuse such promissory notes provokes the charge of obscurantism, but to accept them means suspending one's theism.

It is possible to reject promissory materialism without succumbing to obscurantism. The point to realize is that a promissory note need only be taken seriously if there is good reason to think that it can be paid. The artificial intelligence community has thus far offered no compelling reason for thinking that it will ever solve the frame problem. Indeed, computers that employ common sense to determine appropriate frames of reference continue utterly to elude computer scientists.[11]

Given the practical difficulties of producing a computer that faithfully models human cognition, the hardcore artificial intelligence advocate can change tactics and argue on theoretical grounds that humans are simply disguised computers. The argument runs something like this. Human beings are finite. Both the space of possible human behaviors and the space of possible sensory inputs are finite. For instance, there are only so many distinguishable word combinations that we can utter and only so many distinguishable sound combinations that can strike our eardrums. When represented mathematically, the total number of human lives that can be distinguished empirically is finite. Now it is an immediate consequence of recursion theory (the mathematical theory that undergirds computer science) that any operations and relations on finite sets are computable.[12] It follows that human beings can be represented computationally. Humans are therefore functionally equivalent to computers, Q.E.D.

This argument can be nuanced. For instance, we can introduce a randomizing element into our computations to represent quantum indeterminacy.[13] What's important here, however, is the gist of the argument. The argument asks us to grant that humans are essentially finite. Once that assumption is granted, recursion theory tells us that everything a finite being does is computable. We may never actually be able to build the machines that render us computable. But in principle we could, given enough memory and fast enough processors.

It's at this point that opponents of computational reductionism usually invoke Gödel's incompleteness theorem. Gödel's theorem is said to refute computational reductionism by showing that humans can do things that computers cannot—namely, produce a Gödel sentence. John Lucas made such an argument in the early 1960s, and his argument continues to be modified and revived.[14] Now it is perfectly true that humans can produce Gödel sentences for computational systems external to themselves. But computers can as well be programmed to compute Gödel sentences for computational systems external to themselves. This point is seldom appreciated but becomes evident from recursion-theoretic proofs of Gödel's theorem.[15]

The problem then is not to find Gödel sentences for computational systems external to oneself. The problem is for an agent to examine oneself as a computational system and therewith produce one's own Gödel sentence. If human beings are noncomputational, then there won't be any Gödel sentence to be found. If on the other hand, human beings are computational, then by Gödel's theorem, we won't be able to find our own Gödel sentences. And indeed we haven't. Our inability to translate neurophysiology into computation guarantees that we can't even begin computing our Gödel sentences if indeed we are computational systems. Yes, for a computational system laid out before us we can determine its Gödel sentence. Nevertheless we don't have sufficient access to ourselves to lay ourselves out before ourselves and thereby determine our Gödel sentences. It follows that neither Gödel's theorem nor our ability to prove Gödel's theorem shows that humans can do things that computers cannot.[16]

Accordingly Gödel's theorem fails to refute the argument for computational reductionism based on human finiteness. To recap that argument, humans are finite because the totality of their possible behavioral outputs and possible sensory inputs is finite. Moreover all operations and relations on finite sets are by recursion theory computable. Hence humans are computational systems. This is the argument. What are we to make of it? Despite the failure of Gödel's theorem to block its conclusion, is there a flaw in the argument?

8.4 Our Empirical Selves Versus Our Actual Selves

Yes, there is. The flaw consists in identifying human beings with their behavioral outputs and sensory inputs. Alternatively the flaw consists in reducing our humanity to what can be observed and measured. We are more than what can be observed and measured. Once, however, we limit ourselves to what can be observed and measured, we are necessarily in the realm of the finite and therefore computable. We can only make so many observations. We can only take so many measurements. Moreover our measurements never admit infinite gradations. (Indeed, there's always some magnitude below which quantities become empirically indistinguishable.) Our empirical selves are therefore essentially finite. It follows that unless our actual selves transcend our empirical selves, our actual selves will be finite as well—and therefore computational.

Roger Penrose understands this problem. In *The Emperor's New Mind* and in his more recent *Shadows of the Mind,* he invokes quantum theory to underwrite a noncomputational view of brain and mind.[17] Penrose's strategy is the same that we saw for Gödel's theorem: Find something humans can do that computers can't. There are plenty of mathematical functions that are noncomputable. Penrose therefore appeals to quantum processes in the brain whose mathematical characterization employs noncomputable functions.

Does quantum theory offer a way out of computational reductionism? I would say no. Noncomputable functions are an abstraction. To be noncomputable, functions have to operate on infinite sets. The problem, however, is that we have no observational experience of infinite sets or of the noncomputable functions defined on them. Yes, the mathematics of quantum theory employs noncomputable functions. But when we start plugging in concrete numbers and doing calculations, we are back to finite sets and computable functions.

Granted, we may find it convenient to employ noncomputable functions in characterizing some phenomenon. But when we need to say something definite about the phenomenon, we must supply concrete numbers, and suddenly we are back in the realm of the computable. Noncomputability exists solely as a mathematical abstraction—a useful abstraction, but an abstraction nonetheless. Precisely because our behavioral outputs and sensory inputs are finite, there is no way to test noncomputability against experience. All scientific data are finite, and any mathematical operations we perform on those data are computable. On strictly empirical grounds, noncomputable functions are therefore always dispensable, however elegant they may appear mathematically.

But there is a still deeper problem with Penrose's program to block computational reductionism. Suppose we could be convinced that there are processes in the brain that are noncomputational. For Penrose they are quantum processes, but whatever form they take, as long as they are natural processes, we are still dealing with a naturalistic reduction of mind. Computational reductionism is but one type of naturalistic reductionism—certainly the most extreme but by no means the only one. Penrose's program offers to replace computational processes with quantum processes. Quantum processes, however, are as fully naturalistic as computational processes. In offering to account for mind in terms of quantum theory, Penrose is therefore still wedded to a naturalistic reduction of mind and intelligent agency.

It's time to ask the obvious question: Why should anyone want to make this reduction? Certainly if we have a prior commitment to naturalism, we will want to make it. But apart from that commitment, why attempt it? As we've seen, neurophysiology hasn't a clue about how to reduce intelligent agency to natural causes (hence its continued retreat to concepts like supervenience, emergence and hierarchy—concepts which merely cloak ignorance).[18] We've also seen that no actual computational systems show any sign of reducing intelligent agency to computation. The argument that we are computational systems because the totality of our possible behavioral outputs and possible sensory inputs is finite holds only if we presuppose that we are nothing more than the sum of those behavioral outputs and sensory inputs. So, too, Penrose's argument that we are naturalistic systems because some well-established naturalistic theory (in this case quantum theory) characterizes our neurophysiology holds only if the theory does indeed accurately characterize our neurophysiology (itself a dubious claim given the frequency with which scientific theories are overturned) and so long as we presuppose that we are nothing more than a system characterized by some naturalistic theory.

Bottom line: The naturalistic reduction of intelligent agency is not the conclusion of an empirically based evidential argument but merely a straightforward consequence of presupposing naturalism in the first place. Indeed the empirical evidence for a naturalistic reduction of intelligent agency is wholly lacking. For instance, nowhere does Penrose write down the quantum mechanical Schrödinger equation for someone's brain and then show how actual brain states agree with brain states predicted by the Schrödinger equation. Physicists have a hard enough time writing down the Schrödinger equation for systems of a few interacting particles. Imagine the difficulty of writing down the Schrödinger equation for the multibillion neurons that constitute each of our brains. It won't happen. Indeed the only thing these naturalistic reductions of intelligent agency have until recently had in their favor is Occam's razor. And even this naturalistic mainstay is proving small comfort. Indeed recent developments in the theory of intelligent design are showing that intelligent agency cannot be reduced to natural causes. Let us now turn to these developments.

8.5 The Resurgence of Design

In arguing against computational reductionism both John Lucas and Roger Penrose attempted to find something humans can do that computers cannot. For Lucas it was to construct a Gödel sentence. For Penrose it was finding in neurophysiology a noncomputational quantum process. Neither of these refutations succeed against computational reductionism, much less against a general naturalistic reduction of intelligent agency. Nevertheless the strategy underlying these attempted refutations is sound, namely, to find something intelligent agents can do that natural causes cannot. We don't have to look far. All of us attribute things to intelligent agents that we wouldn't dream of attributing to natural causes. For instance, natural causes can throw Scrabble pieces on a board but cannot arrange the pieces into meaningful sentences. To obtain a meaningful arrangement requires an intelligent agent.

This intuition, that natural causes are too stupid to do the things that intelligent agents are capable of, has underlain the design arguments of past centuries. Throughout the centuries theologians have argued that nature exhibits features that nature itself cannot explain but that instead require an intelligence that transcends nature. As we saw in chapters four and five, design is witnessing a resurgence. Scientists are realizing that design can be rigorously formulated as a scientific theory. Indeed scientists now have a reliable criterion for identifying intelligently caused objects—the complexity-specification criterion. Specified complexity reliably signals design.

The implications of the complexity-specification criterion are significant not just for science but also for philosophy and theology. The power of this criterion resides in its generality. It would be one thing if the criterion only detected human agency. But as we've seen, it detects animal and extraterrestrial agency as well (see chapter five). Nor is it limited to intelligent agents that belong to the physical world. The fine-tuning of the universe is both complex and specified and readily yields design. So, too, Michael Behe's irreducibly complex biochemical systems readily yield design (see section 5.7). The complexity-specification criterion demonstrates that design pervades cosmology and biology.[19] Moreover it is a transcendent design, not reducible to the physical world. Indeed no intelligent agent who is strictly physical could have presided over the origin of the universe or the origin of life.

Unlike design arguments of the past, the claim that transcendent design pervades the universe is no longer a strictly philosophical or theological claim. It is also a fully scientific claim and follows directly from the complexity-specification criterion. In particular this is not an argument from ignorance. Just as physicists reject perpetual motion machines because of what they know about the inherent constraints on energy and matter, so too design theorists reject any naturalistic reduction of specified complexity because of what they know about the inherent constraints on natural causes. Natural causes are too stupid to keep pace with intelligent causes. We've suspected this all along. Intelligent design theory provides a rigorous scientific demonstration of this long-standing intuition. Let me stress, the complexity-specification criterion is not a principle that comes to us demanding our unexamined acceptance—it is not an article of faith. Rather it is the outcome of a careful and sustained argument about the precise interrelationships between necessity, chance and design.[20]

Demonstrating transcendent design in the universe is a scientific inference, not a philosophical pipedream (cf. appendix A.9). Once we understand the role of the complexity-specification criterion in warranting this inference, several things follow immediately: (1) Intelligent agency is logically prior to natural causation and cannot be reduced to it. (2) Intelligent agency is fully capable of making itself known against the backdrop of natural causes. (3) Any science that systematically ignores design is incomplete and defective. (4) Methodological naturalism, the view that science must confine itself solely to natural causes, far from assisting scientific inquiry, actually stifles it. (5) The scientific picture of the world championed since the Enlightenment is not just wrong but massively wrong. Indeed entire fields of inquiry, especially in the human sciences, will need to be rethought from the ground up in terms of intelligent design.[21]

8.6 The Creation of the World

I have devoted much of this chapter till now to contrasting intelligent agency with natural causes. In particular I have argued that empirical evidence fails to establish the reduction of intelligent agency to natural causes. I have also argued that no good philosophical arguments support that reduction. Indeed those arguments that do are circular, presupposing the very naturalism they are supposed to underwrite. My strongest argument against the sufficiency of natural causes to account for intelligent agency, however, comes from the complexity-specification criterion. This empirically based criterion reliably discriminates intelligent agency from natural causes. Moreover, when applied to cosmology and biology, it demonstrates not only the incompleteness of natural causes but also the presence of transcendent design.

Now within Christian theology there is one and only one way to make sense of transcendent design, and that is as a divine act of creation. I want therefore next to focus on divine creation, specifically on the creation of the world. My aim is to use divine creation as a lens for understanding intelligent agency generally. God's act of creating the world is the prototype for all intelligent agency (creative or not). Indeed all intelligent agency takes its cue from the creation of the world. How so? God's act of creating the world makes possible all of God's subsequent interactions with the world, as well as all subsequent actions by creatures within the world. God's act of creating the world is thus the prime instance of intelligent agency.

Let us therefore turn to the creation of the world as treated in Scripture. The first thing that strikes us is the mode of creation. God speaks and things happen. There is something singularly appropriate about this mode of creation. Any act of creation is the concretization of an intention by an intelligent agent. Now in our experience the concretization of an intention can occur in any number of ways. Sculptors concretize their intentions by chipping away at stone, musicians by writing notes on lined sheets of paper, engineers by drawing up blueprints. But in the final analysis all concretizations of intentions can be subsumed under language. For instance, a precise enough set of instructions in a natural language will tell the sculptor how to form the statue, the musician how to record the notes and the engineer how to draw up the blueprints. In this way language becomes the *universal medium* for concretizing intentions.

In treating language as the universal medium for concretizing intentions, we must be careful not to construe language in a narrowly linguistic sense (for example, as symbol strings manipulated by rules of grammar). The language that proceeds from God's mouth in the act of creation is not some linguistic convention. Rather as John's Gospel informs us, it is the divine *Logos*, the Word that in Christ was made flesh and through whom all things were created. This divine *Logos* subsists in himself and is under no compulsion to create. For the divine *Logos* to be active in creation, God must *speak* the divine *Logos*. This act of speaking always imposes a self-limitation on the divine *Logos*. There is a clear analogy here with human language. Just as every English utterance rules out those statements in the English language that were not uttered, so every divine spoken word rules out those possibilities in the divine *Logos* that were not spoken. Moreover, just as no human speaker of English ever exhausts the English language, so God in creating through the divine spoken word never exhausts the divine *Logos*.

Because the divine spoken word always imposes a self-limitation on the divine *Logos*, the two notions need to be distinguished. We therefore distinguish *Logos* with a capital L (that is, the divine Logos) from *logos* with a lowercase l (that is, the divine spoken word). Lacking a capitalization convention, the Greek New Testament employs *logos* in both senses. At the beginning of John's Gospel we read that "the *Logos* was made flesh, and dwelt among us" (John 1:14 KJV).[22] Here the reference is to the divine *Logos* who incarnated himself in Jesus of Nazareth. On the other hand, later in John's Gospel Jesus tells his disciples, "Now ye are clean through the *logos* which I have spoken unto you" (John 15:3 KJV).[23] Here the reference is to the divine spoken word by which people's hearts are purified.

Because God is the God of truth, the divine spoken word always reflects the divine *Logos*. At the same time, because the divine spoken word always constitutes a self-limitation, it can never comprehend the divine *Logos*. Furthermore because creation is a divine spoken word, it follows that creation can never comprehend the divine *Logos* either. This is why idolatry—worshiping the creation rather than the Creator—is so completely backwards, for it assigns ultimate value to something that is inherently incapable of achieving ultimate value. Creation, especially a fallen creation, can at best reflect God's glory. Idolatry, on the other hand, contends that creation fully comprehends God's glory. Idolatry turns the creation into the ultimate reality. We've seen this before. It is called naturalism. No doubt contemporary scientific naturalism is a lot more sophisticated than pagan fertility cults, but the difference is superficial. Naturalism is idolatry by another name.

We need at all costs to resist naturalistic construals of *logos* (whether *Logos* with a capital *L* or *logos* with a small *l*). Because naturalism has become so embedded in our thinking, we tend to think of words and language as purely contextual, local and historically contingent. On the assumption of naturalism, humans are the product of a blind evolutionary process that initially was devoid not only of humans but also of any living thing whatsoever. It follows that human language must derive from an evolutionary process that initially was devoid of language. Within naturalism, just as life emerges from nonlife, so language emerges from the absence of language.

Now it's certainly true that human languages are changing, living entities—one has only to compare the King James version of the Bible with more recent translations into English to see how much our language has changed in the last four hundred years. Words change their meanings over time. Grammar changes over time. Even logic and rhetoric change over time. What's more, human language is conventional. What a word means depends on convention and can be changed by convention. For instance, there is nothing intrinsic to the word *automobile* demanding that it denote a car. If we go with its etymology, we might just as well have applied *automobile* to human beings, who are after all "self-propelling." There is nothing sacred about the linguistic form that a word assumes. For instance, *gift* in English means a present, in German it means poison, and in French it means nothing at all. And of course, words only make sense within the context of broader units of discourse, like whole narratives.

For Christian theism, however, language is never purely conventional. To be sure, the assignment of meaning to a linguistic entity is conventional. Meaning itself, however, transcends convention. As soon as we stipulate our language conventions, words assume meanings and are no longer free to mean anything an interpreter chooses. The deconstructionist claim that "texts are indeterminable and inevitably yield multiple, irreducibly diverse interpretations" and that "there can be no criteria for preferring one reading to another" is therefore false.[24] This is not to preclude that texts can operate at multiple levels of meaning and interpretation. It is, however, to say that texts are anchored to their meaning and not free to float about indiscriminately.

Deconstruction's error traces directly to naturalism. Within naturalism there is no transcendent realm of meaning to which our linguistic entities are capable of attaching. As a result there is nothing to keep our linguistic usage in check save pragmatic considerations, which are always contextual, local and historically contingent. The watchword for pragmatism is expedience, not truth. Once expedience dictates meaning, linguistic entities are capable of meaning anything. Not all naturalists are happy with this conclusion. Philosophers like John Searle and D. M. Armstrong try simultaneously to maintain an objective realm of meaning and a commitment to naturalism.[25] They want desperately to find something more than pragmatic considerations to keep our linguistic usage in check. Insofar as they pull it off, however, they are tacitly appealing to a transcendent realm of meaning (cf. Armstrong's account of universals). As Alvin Plantinga has convincingly argued, objective truth and meaning have no legitimate place within a pure naturalism.[26] Deconstruction, for all its faults, has this in its favor: it is consistent in its application of naturalism to the study of language.

By contrast, *logos* resists all naturalistic reductions. This becomes evident as soon as we understand what *logos* meant to the ancient Greeks. For the Greeks *logos* was never simply a linguistic entity. Today when we think "word," we often think a string of symbols written on a sheet of paper. This is not what the Greeks meant by *logos*. *Logos* was a far richer concept for the Greeks. Consider the following meanings of *logos* from Liddell and Scott's *Greek-English Lexicon*:

☐ the word by which the inward thought is expressed (speech)
☐ the inward thought or reason itself (reason)

☐ reflection, deliberation (choice)
☐ calculation, reckoning (mathematics)
☐ account, consideration, regard (inquiry)
☐ relation, proportion, analogy (harmony, balance)
☐ a reasonable ground, a condition (evidence, truth)

Logos is therefore an exceedingly rich notion encompassing the entire life of the mind.

The etymology of *logos* is revealing. *Logos* derives from the Indo-European root *l-e-g*. This root appears in the Greek verb *lego*, which in the New Testament typically means "to speak." Yet the primitive meaning of *lego* is "to lay"; from there it came to mean "to pick up and gather"; then "to select and put together"; and hence "to select and put together words"; and therefore "to speak." As Marvin Vincent remarks in his New Testament word studies: "*logos* is a *collecting* or *collection* both of things in the mind, and of words by which they are expressed. It therefore signifies both the outward form by which the inward thought is expressed, and the inward thought itself, the Latin *oratio* and *ratio:* compare the Italian *ragionare*, 'to think' and 'to speak'."[27]

The root *l-e-g* has several variants. We've already seen it as *l-o-g* in *logos*. But it also occurs as *l-e-c* in *intellect* and *l-i-g* in *intelligent*. This should give one pause. The word *intelligent* actually comes from the Latin rather than from the Greek. It derives from two Latin words, the preposition *inter*, meaning "between," and the Latin (not Greek) verb *lego*, meaning "to choose or select." The Latin *lego* stayed closer to its Indo-European root meaning than its Greek cognate, which came to refer explicitly to speech. According to its etymology, intelligence therefore consists in *choosing between*.

We've seen this connection between intelligence and choice before, namely, in the complexity-specification criterion (see especially section 5.6). Specified complexity is precisely how we recognize that an intelligent agent has made a choice. It follows that the etymology of the word *intelligent* parallels the formal analysis of intelligent agency inherent in the complexity-specification criterion. The appropriateness of the phrase *intelligent design* now becomes apparent as well. Intelligent design is a scientific research program that seeks to understand intelligent agency by investigating specified complexity. But specified complexity is the characteristic trademark of choice. It follows that *intelligent design* is a thoroughly apt phrase, signifying that design is inferred precisely because an intelligent agent has done what only an intelligent agent can do, namely, make a choice.

If *intelligent design* is a thoroughly apt phrase, the same cannot be said for the phrase *natural selection*. The second word in this phrase, *selection*, is of course a synonym for *choice*. Indeed the *l-e-c* in *selection* is a variant of the *l-e-g* that in the Latin *lego* means "to choose or select," and that also appears as *l-i-g* in *intelligence*. Natural selection is therefore an oxymoron. It attributes the power to choose, which properly belongs only to intelligent agents, to natural causes, which inherently lack the power to choose. Richard Dawkins's concept of the blind watchmaker follows the same pattern, negating with *blind* what is affirmed in *watchmaker*. That's why Dawkins opens his book *The Blind Watchmaker* with the statement: "Biology is the study of complicated things that give the appearance of having been designed for a purpose."[28] Natural selection and blind watchmakers don't yield actual design but at best the appearance of design.

8.7 The Intelligibility of the World

Having considered the role of *logos* in creating the world, I want next to consider its role in rendering the world intelligible. To say that God through the divine *Logos* acts as an intelligent agent to create the world is only half the story. Yes, there is a deep and fundamental connection between God as divine *Logos* and God as intelligent agent—indeed the very words *logos* and *intelligence* derive from the same Indo-European root. The world, however, is more than simply the product of an intelligent agent. In addition, the world is intelligible.

We see this in the very first entity that God creates—light. With the creation of light, the world becomes a place that is conceptualizable and to which values can properly be assigned. To be sure, as God increasingly orders the world through the process of creation, the number of things that can be conceptualized increases, and the values assigned to things become refined. But even with light for now the only created entity, it is possible to conceptualize light, distinguish it from darkness and assign a positive value to light, calling it good. The world is thus not merely a place where God's intentions are fulfilled but also a place where God's intentions are intelligible. Moreover that intelligibility is as much moral and aesthetic as it is scientific.

God, in speaking the divine *Logos*, not only creates the world but also renders it intelligible. This view of creation has far-reaching consequences. For instance, the fact-value distinction dissolves opposite God's act of creation—indeed what is and what ought to be unite in God's original intention at creation. Consider, too, Einstein's celebrated dictum about the comprehensibility of the world. Einstein claimed: "The most incomprehensible thing about the world is that it is comprehensible." This statement, so widely regarded as a profound insight, is actually a sad commentary on naturalism. Within naturalism the intelligibility of the world must always remain a mystery. Within theism, on the other hand, anything other than an intelligible world would constitute a mystery.

God speaks the divine *Logos* to create the world and thereby renders the world intelligible. This fact is absolutely crucial to how we understand human language, and especially human language about God. Human language is a divine gift for helping us to understand the world and by understanding the world to understand God himself. This is not to say that we ever comprehend God as in achieving fixed, final and exhaustive knowledge of God. But human language does enable us to express accurate claims about God and the world. It is vitally important for the Christian to understand this point. Human language is not an evolutionary refinement of grunts and stammers formerly uttered by some putative apelike ancestors. We are creatures made in the divine image. Human language is therefore a divine gift that mirrors the divine *Logos*.

Consider what this conception of language does to the charge that biblical language about God is hopelessly anthropomorphic. We continue to have conferences in the United States with titles like "Reimagining God." The idea behind such conference titles is that all our references to God are human constructions and can be changed as human needs require new constructions. Certain feminist theologians, for instance, object to referring to God as father. God as father, we are told, is an outdated patriarchal way of depicting God that, given contemporary concerns, needs to be changed. "Father," we are told, is a metaphor co-opted from human experience and pressed into theological service. No, *No, NO!* This view of theological language is hopeless and destroys the Christian faith.

The concept father is not an anthropomorphism, nor is referring to God as father metaphorical. All instances of fatherhood reflect the fatherhood of God. It's not that we are taking human fatherhood and idealizing it into a divine father image à la Ludwig Feuerbach or Sigmund Freud. Father is not an anthropomorphism at all. It's not that we are committing an anthropomorphism by referring to God as father. Rather we are, as it were, committing a "theomorphism" by referring to human beings as fathers. We are never using the word *father* as accurately as when we attribute it to God. As soon as we apply *father* to human beings, our language becomes analogical and derivative.

We see this readily in Scripture. Jesus enjoins us to call no one father except God (Matthew 23:9). Certainly Jesus is not telling us never to refer to any human being as "father." All of us have human fathers, and they rightly receive that appellation. Indeed the fifth commandment tells us explicitly to honor our human fathers. But human fathers reflect a more profound reality, namely, the fatherhood of God.

Similarly consider how Jesus responds to a rich young ruler who addresses him as "good master." Jesus shoots back, "Why do you call me good? No one is good—except God alone" (Mark 10:18). Goodness properly applies to God. It's not an anthropomorphism to call God good. The goodness we attribute to God is not an idealized human goodness. God defines goodness. When we speak of human goodness, it is only as a reflection of the divine goodness.

This view, that human language is a divine gift for understanding the world and therewith God, is powerfully liberating. No longer do we live in a Platonic world of shadows from which we must escape if we are to perceive the divine light. No longer do we live in a Kantian world of phenomena that bars access to noumena. No longer do we live in a naturalistic world devoid of transcendence. Rather the world and everything in it becomes a sacrament, radiating God's glory. Moreover our language becomes capable of celebrating that glory by speaking truly about what God has wrought in creation.

The view that creation proceeds through a divine spoken word has profound implications not just for the study of human language but also for the study of human knowledge, or what philosophers call epistemology. For naturalism, epistemology's primary problem is unraveling Einstein's dictum: "The most incomprehensible thing about the world is that it is comprehensible." How is it that we can have any knowledge at all? Within naturalism there is no solution to this riddle.

Theism, on the other hand, faces an entirely different problem. For theism the problem is not how we can have knowledge but why our knowledge is so prone to error and distortion. The Judeo-Christian tradition attributes the problem of error to the Fall. At the heart of the Fall is alienation. Beings are no longer properly in communion with other beings. We lie to ourselves. We lie to others. And others lie to us. Appearance and reality are out of sync. The problem of epistemology within the Judeo-Christian tradition isn't to establish that we have knowledge but instead to root out the distortions that try to overthrow our knowledge.

On the view that creation proceeds through a divine spoken word, not only does naturalistic epistemology have to go by the board but so does naturalistic ontology. Ontology asks what are the fundamental constituents of reality. According to naturalism (and I'm thinking here specifically of the scientific naturalism that currently dominates Western thought), the world is fundamentally an interacting system of mindless entities (be they particles, strings, fields or whatever). Mind therefore becomes an emergent property of suitably arranged mindless entities. Naturalistic ontology is all backwards. If creation and everything in it proceeds through a divine spoken word, then the entities that are created don't suddenly fall silent at the moment of creation. Rather they continue to speak.

I look at a blade of grass and it speaks to me. In the light of the sun, it tells me that it is green. If I touch it, it tells me that it has a certain texture. It communicates something else to a chinch bug intent on devouring it. It communicates something else still to a particle physicist intent on reducing it to its particulate constituents. Which is not to say that the blade of grass does not communicate things about the particles that constitute it. But the blade of grass is more than any arrangement of particles and is capable of communicating more than is inherent in any such arrangement. Indeed its reality derives not from its particulate constituents but from its capacity to communicate with other entities in creation and ultimately with God himself.

The problem of being now receives a straightforward solution: To be is to be in communion, first with God and then with the rest of creation. It follows that the fundamental science, indeed the science that needs to ground all other sciences, is communication theory[29] and not, as is widely supposed, an atomistic, reductionist and mechanistic science of particles or other mindless entities, which then need to be built up to ever greater orders of complexity by equally mindless principles of association, known typically as natural laws. Communication theory's object of study is not particles but the information that passes between entities. Information in turn is just another name for *logos*. This is an information-rich universe. The problem with mechanistic science is that it has no resources for recognizing and understanding information. Communication theory is only now coming into its own. A crucial development along the way has been the complexity-specification criterion. Indeed specified complexity is precisely what's needed to recognize information.

Information—the information that God speaks to create the world, the information that continually proceeds from God in sustaining the world and acting in it and the information that passes between God's creatures—this is the bridge that connects transcendence and immanence. All of this information is mediated through the divine *Logos*, who is before all things and by whom all things consist (Colossians 1:17). The crucial breakthrough of the intelligent design movement has been to show that this great theological truth—that God acts in the world by dispersing information—also has scientific content. Information, whether divinely inputted or transmitted between creatures, is in principle capable of being detected via the complexity-specification criterion. Examples abound:

□ The fine-tuning of the universe and irreducibly complex biochemical systems are instances of specified complexity and signal information inputted into the universe by God at its creation.

□ Predictive prophecies in Scripture are instances of specified complexity and signal information inputted by God as part of his sovereign activity within creation.

□ Language communication between humans is an instance of specified complexity and signals information transmitted from one human to another.

The positivist science of the nineteenth and twentieth century was incapable of coming to terms with information. The science of the new millennium will not be able to avoid it. Indeed we already live in an information age.[30]

8.8 Creativity, Divine and Human

In closing this chapter I want to ask an obvious question: Why create? Why does God create? Why do we create? Although creation is always an intelligent act, it is much more than an intelligent act. The impulse behind creation is always to offer oneself as a gift. Creation is a gift. What's more, it is a gift of the most important thing we possess—ourselves. Indeed creation is the means by which a creator—divine, human or otherwise—gives oneself in self-revelation. Creation is not the neurotic, forced self-revelation offered on the psychoanalyst's couch. Nor is it the facile self-revelation of idle chatter. It is the self-revelation of labor and sacrifice. Creation always incurs a cost. Creation invests the creator's life in the thing created. When God creates humans, he breathes into them the breath of life—God's own life. At the end of the six days of creation God is tired—he has to rest. Creation is exhausting work. It is drawing oneself out of oneself and then imprinting oneself on the other.

Take the painter Vincent van Gogh, for instance. You can read all the biographies you want about him, but through it all van Gogh will still not have revealed himself to you. For van Gogh to reveal himself to you, you need to look at his paintings. As Christos Yannaras writes:

> We know the person of van Gogh, what is unique, distinct and unrepeatable in his existence, only when we see his paintings. There we meet a reason (*logos*) which is his only and we separate him from every other painter. When we have seen enough pictures by van Gogh and then encounter one more, then we say right away: This *is* van Gogh. We distinguish immediately the otherness of his personal reason, the uniqueness of his creative expression.[31]

The difference between the arts and the sciences now becomes clear. When I see a painting by van Gogh, I know immediately that it is his. But when I come across a mathematical theorem or scientific insight, I cannot decide who was responsible for it unless I am told. The world is God's creation, and scientists in understanding the world are simply retracing God's thoughts. Scientists are not creators but discoverers. True, they may formulate concepts that assist them in describing the world. But even such concepts do not bear the clear imprint of their formulators. Concepts like energy, inertia and entropy give no clue about who formulated them. Hermann Weyl and John von Neumann were both equally qualified to formulate quantum mechanics in terms of Hilbert spaces. That von Neumann, and not Weyl, made the formulation is now an accident of history. There's nothing in the formulation that explicitly identifies von Neumann. Contrast this with a painting by van Gogh. It cannot be confused with a Monet.

The impulse to create and thereby give oneself in self-revelation need not be grand but can be quite humble. A homemaker arranging a floral decoration engages in a creative act. The important thing about the act of creation is that it reveals the creator. The act of creation always bears the signature of the creator. It is a sad legacy of modern technology, and especially the production line, that most of the objects we buy no longer reveal their maker. Mass production is inimical to true creation. Yes, the objects we buy carry brand names, but in fact they are largely anonymous. We can tell very little about their maker. Compare this with God's creation of the world. Not one tree is identical with another. Not one face matches another. Indeed a single hair on your head is unique—there was never one exactly like it, nor will there ever be another to match it.

The creation of the world by God is the most magnificent of all acts of creation. It and humanity's redemption through Jesus Christ are the two key instances of God's self-revelation. The revelation of God in creation is typically called general revelation, whereas the revelation of God in redemption is typically called special revelation. Consequently theologians sometimes speak of two books, the book of nature, which is God's self-revelation in creation, and the book of Scripture, which is God's self-revelation in redemption. If you want to know who God is, you need to know God through both creation and redemption. According to Scripture, the angels praise God chiefly for two things: God's creation of the world and God's redemption of the world through Jesus Christ. Let us follow the angels' example.

> God moves in a mysterious way
> His wonders to perform;
> He plants His footsteps in the sea
> And rides upon the Storm.
>
> Deep in unfathomable mines
> Of never-failing skill,
> He treasures up His bright designs
> And works His sovereign will.

Ye fearful saints, fresh courage take;
The clouds ye so much dread
Are big with mercy and shall break
In blessings on your head.

His purposes will ripen fast,
Unfolding every hour;
The bud may have a bitter taste,
But sweet will be the flower.

Blind unbelief is sure to err
And scan His work in vain;
God is His own Interpreter
And He will make it plain.
(William Cowper, 1772)

Appendix
Objections to Design

Having outlined the positive case for design, I want in this appendix to address certain long-standing objections to design. The objections considered here cannot properly be called scientific objections. They do not, for instance, find fault with design by arguing that specified complexity (the criterion for detecting design) is imprecisely defined or cannot be empirically tested. Such scientific objections were addressed in the previous chapters. The objections considered here are better called "gatekeeper" objections. They find fault with design because of the threat that design is said to pose to science and not because the theoretical or empirical case for design is scientifically substandard. The impulse behind these objections is to keep the world safe for science and science safe from the world; the impulse is not to expand the boundaries of science and thereby enhance our knowledge of the world. This appendix therefore addresses nine principal objections for keeping design outside the pale of science:

1. Design substitutes extraordinary explanations where ordinary explanations will do and thereby commits a god-of-the-gaps fallacy.

2. There is nothing that cannot be explained by invoking design. Design explains everything and so explains nothing.

3. Design is nothing but scientific creationism cloaked in newer and more sophisticated terminology.

4. Design cannot properly be a part of science since scientific explanations are by definition naturalistic explanations whereas design is an irreducibly supernaturalistic explanation.

5. Design in biology is refuted by all the examples of suboptimal design. In particular, design cannot be reconciled with the problem of evil.

6. Design in nature is an anthropic coincidence or what's also called a selection effect. Yes, it's incredibly improbable that nature should be organized just the way it is; but if it weren't, we wouldn't be here to appreciate that fact.

7. Specified complexity is a purely mathematical construct and therefore irrelevant to biology. It cannot speak to biological concerns, only to mathematical concerns.

8. Design in biology is either an argument from analogy or an inductive generalization based on a sample of size zero. In neither case is design therefore a compelling argument.

9. There is a vast difference between mundane designers, like humans or extraterrestrials, and transcendent designers. We have no experience of transcendent designers and can make no scientific claims about them.

A.1 The God of the Gaps
Objection: Design substitutes extraordinary explanations where ordinary explanations will do and thereby commits a god-of-the-gaps fallacy.

I know no better place where the god-of-the-gaps fallacy is illustrated than in Daniel Defoe's classic tale *Robinson Crusoe*. Crusoe, a castaway on a deserted Caribbean island, describes what initially seemed like a miraculous intervention by God:

> I saw some few stalks of something green shooting out of the ground, which I fancied might be some plant I had not seen; but I was surprised and perfectly astonished, when after a little longer time I saw about ten or twelve ears come out, which were perfect green barley of the same kind as our European, nay, as our English barley.
>
> It is impossible to express the astonishment and confusion of my thoughts on this occasion; I had hitherto acted upon no religious foundation at all; indeed I had very few notions of religion in my head, nor had entertained any sense of anything that had befallen me, otherwise than as a

chance, or, as we lightly say, what pleases God; without so much as inquiring into the end of Providence in these things, or His order in governing events in the world. But after I saw barley grow there, in a climate which I know was not proper for corn, and especially that I knew not how it came there, it startled me strangely, and I began to suggest that God had miraculously caused this grain to grow without any help of seed sown, and that it was so directed purely for my sustenance on the wild miserable place.

This touched my heart a little and brought tears out of my eyes, and I began to bless myself, that such a prodigy of Nature should happen upon my account. . . . I not only thought these the pure productions of Providence for my support, but not doubting but that there was more in the place, I went all over the part of the island where I had been before, peering in every corner and under every rock, to see for more of it, but I could not find any.

At last it occurred to my thought that I had shook a bag of chickens' meat [i.e., grain or "corn"] out in that place, and then the wonder began to cease; and I must confess, my religious thankfulness to God's Providence began to abate too upon the discovering that all this was nothing but what was common; though I ought to have been as thankful for so strange and unforeseen Providence, as if it had been miraculous; for it was really the work of Providence as to me, that should order or appoint, that ten or twelve grains of corn should remain unspoiled (when the rats had destroyed all the rest), as if it had been dropped from Heaven; as also that I should throw it out in that particular place where, it being in the shade of a high rock, it sprang up immediately; whereas if I had thrown it anywhere else at that time, it had been burnt up and destroyed.[1]

Crusoe has committed a classic god-of-the-gaps fallacy. His mistake consists in employing an extraordinary explanation where an ordinary explanation will do, that is, in invoking God as the missing link in a causal chain where an ordinary natural cause will do. Consequently once Crusoe discovered the ordinary explanation of how English barley came to appear on his island (namely, that he by accident had dropped some barley seeds on the ground), Crusoe discarded the extraordinary explanation that a divine miracle had produced the barley.

Now the crucial question is whether employing design in science inevitably lands us in the same error, substituting an extraordinary explanation where an ordinary explanation will do. To see that design is capable of avoiding this error, it is necessary that we distinguish between two very different questions: (1) Did a designer act to bring about a given object or event? and if so (2) How did the designer act to bring about the given object or event? Let's call the first question the *detectability question* (i.e., Was it even a designer that brought about the given object or event?) and the second the *modality question* (i.e., By precisely what means was the object or event in question brought to pass?). The detectability question asks whether a designer acted at all and what warrant we have for thinking a designer acted. (This question was addressed in detail in chapter five.) The modality question, on the other hand, asks for a causal narrative describing precisely what happened in space and time to bring about the object or event under consideration.

Both these questions are implicit in the Crusoe example. According to Crusoe, a providential designer produced the English barley on his island. Having answered yes to the detectability question, Crusoe's first attempt at answering the modality question was to say that God produced the English barley by performing a miracle. Nevertheless even after it became clear to Crusoe that his answer to the modality question was incorrect and that an ordinary explanation would suffice, his answer to the detectability question remained unchanged. In Crusoe's mind God was still responsible for the barley growing on his island, only this time instead of specially creating an exact replica of English barley, God had arranged circumstances so that (1) some barley seeds were preserved from the rats on the ship, (2) the seeds made their way safely to shore and (3) they found fertile ground on the island. The end was the same, but the means differed. Thus instead of God acting outside ordinary natural processes, as Crusoe thought initially, God qua providence was working with, in and through nature to give Crusoe his English barley.

Of course, not just his answer to the modality question but also Crusoe's answer to the detectability question is open to dispute. For instance, once it's admitted that the barley came from the ship, the complexity-specification criterion of chapter five can no longer be satisfied. The point I want to stress, however, is that the detectability and modality questions are largely independent, with the correct answer or even lack of an answer to one question not necessarily affecting the correct answer to the other. For instance, given a Stradivarius violin, we are correct in answering the detectability question in the affirmative (i.e., the violin was indeed designed, and what's more, Stradivarius was the designer), even though we don't know how to answer the modality question—we don't know how Stradivarius made his violins. Lost arts are lost because we can no longer answer the modality question, not because our answer to the detectability question has changed. Answering yes to the detectability question is not to prejudge the modality question. Crusoe identified providence as responsible for the English barley he found growing on his island, but he initially understood providence as acting miraculously and then later as acting through perfectly ordinary natural causes.

But must the modality question always be answered without appealing to gaps in the chain of natural causes? Leaving room for such explanations is vital to scientific inquiry, for without the freedom to seriously entertain gaps in the causal nexus of nature, we place naturalism in a privileged position. There is no compelling reason why, in answering the modality question, we should in every instance be able, even in principle, to tell a gapless naturalistic narrative. Nor is it the case that the god-of-the-gaps always constitutes a fallacy. Indeed the fallacy arises only if an ordinary explanation suffices where an extraordinary explanation was previously invoked. But that ordinary explanations should *always* have this capacity cannot be justified. Whether an extraordinary explanation is appropriate depends on the event that needs to be explained and the circumstances surrounding the event.

With Crusoe's English barley an extraordinary explanation was inappropriate. Indeed, even if Crusoe were certain that he himself had not brought barley seeds to his island, appealing to a miracle would still have been dubious, for some Englishman might have been stranded on the same island before Crusoe and brought barley seeds with him. On the other hand, if Crusoe's foot had gotten crushed under a huge boulder so that Crusoe had to hack off part of his leg to get free and if subsequently he grew back a new foot, an extraordinary explanation would be required. Certainly Crusoe would be justified in saying that a miracle qua gap in the chain of natural causes had occurred, though whether he would be justified in attributing the miracle to the God of Christianity or some other religious faith is another matter.

I'm not arguing either for or against miracles here. My aim is simply to make sure that no answer to the modality question is ruled out of court on a priori grounds. Wittgenstein has remarked, "*Very* intelligent and well-educated people believe in the story of creation in the Bible, while others hold it as proven false, and the grounds of the latter are well known to the former."[2] British and American societies for psychical research have routinely had in their leadership Nobel laureates whose disciplines span the full range of the sciences.[3] Medical journals regularly report cases of spontaneous remissions for which no ordinary explanations are offered.[4] The physician and Nobel laureate Alexis Carrel claims himself to have witnessed miraculous cures which as far as he was concerned "are stubborn, irreducible facts, which must be taken into account."[5]

Of course there are plenty of intelligent people who hold the contrary view. David Hume's critique of miracles is well-known. Voltaire, though not an atheist, held that "to suppose that God will work miracles is to insult Him with impunity."[6] Spinoza had nothing but contempt for those "who will not cease from asking the causes of causes, until at last you fly to the will of God, the refuge for ignorance."[7] More recently we have seen the logical positivists insist that extraordinary explanations are pseudosolutions to pseudoproblems. And currently we have a scientific and philosophical elite at the *Skeptical Inquirer* who make it their business to debunk anything that smacks of the miraculous.[8]

How one answers the question of miracles is not the important thing here. The important thing is that extraordinary explanations not be prejudged and thereby ruled out of court by a prior commitment to naturalism, especially a naturalism purportedly underwritten by science. Suppose therefore we put naturalism aside. If we do, why should we think we've landed outside of science just because the modality question happens to receive an extraordinary explanation? Presumably, extraordinary explanations are extraordinary because they admit a gap in the chain of natural causes. Instead of having a chain of natural causes of the form

$$A \to B \to C \to D \to E \to F$$

(capital Roman letters here signify events, arrows signify natural causes), we thus have a chain in which one of the causal arrows is replaced by a gap, for instance,

$$A \rightarrow B \rightarrow C \quad \textit{gap} \quad D \rightarrow E \rightarrow F$$

Now what is it about the latter sequence of events, if anything, that places it beyond the pale of science? Certainly the individual events A through F are all open to scientific scrutiny. Moreover the arrows or causation connecting A to B and B to C as well as D to E and E to F are open to scientific scrutiny. Even the gap between C and D is open to scientific scrutiny in the sense that we can compare C with D and determine the nature of the discontinuity between C and D. What's more, D itself may clearly indicate marks of having been intelligently designed, issuing in a design inference that convincingly answers the detectability question even though the precise causal predecessors of D are unclear (cf. chapter five).

Indeed the only way the latter sequence of events can land us beyond the pale of science is if we add to it the claim that a supernatural agent manipulated C to produce D. In this case what pushes us beyond the pale of science is the inability of scientists as scientists to study the precise causal process that led from C to D (if indeed a supernatural agent employing supernatural means was responsible for bringing about D from C). But again it needs to be stressed that even if a supernatural agent was intervening in the causal nexus of nature, C and its causal precursors, D and its causal successors, the very gap between C and D and any marks upon D that reliably signal the activity of a designing intelligence are all open to scientific investigation. The old chestnut that miracles lie outside of science is true only in the very limited sense that the causal process that from antecedent circumstances led to the event designated a miracle lie beyond the scope of scientific investigation.

Nonetheless even the claim that an event was produced by processes beyond the scope of scientific investigation can itself be a scientific claim, or at least a metascientific claim that science ought to take seriously. Suppose some strange phenomenon M is observed ("M" for miracle). A search is conducted to discover a scientifically acceptable ordinary explanation for M. The search fails. Conclusion: no scientifically acceptable ordinary explanation exists. Is there a problem here? Physicist and philosopher of religion Ian Barbour thinks there is:

> We would submit that it is *scientifically stultifying* to say of any puzzling phenomenon that it is "incapable of scientific explanation," for such an attitude would undercut the motivation for inquiry. And such an approach is

also *theologically dubious,* for it leads to another form of the "God of the gaps," the *deus ex machina* introduced to cover ignorance of what may later be shown to have natural causes.[9]

To which C. A. Coulson adds, "When we come to the scientifically unknown, our correct policy is not to rejoice because we have found God; it is to become better scientists."[10]

No doubt there is something heroic in the sentiments expressed by Barbour and Coulson. Given a difficult problem, our proper attitude is not to capitulate and admit irremediable ignorance but rather to press on and struggle for a solution. If, however, no permissible solution to the problem exists (permissible in terms of the way the problem was formulated), are we to follow the example of Sisyphus, forever rolling the rock up the hill? When does determination become pigheadedness?

Barbour and Coulson are right to block lazy appeals to God within scientific explanation. But that is not the question here. The question is not whether God did it but whether science has the resources to provide an ordinary explanation for how M came about and whether science has the capacity to recognize when its resources are so limited. In *The Realm of the Nebulae* cosmologist Edwin Hubble claimed that "not until the empirical resources are exhausted, need we pass on to the dreamy realms of speculation."[11] When Hubble wrote this line in the 1930s, he clearly believed that the resources of science would never be exhausted and that our entrance into the dreamy realms of speculation could be postponed indefinitely. Nevertheless there is nothing to prevent empirical and theoretical resources from coming in limited supplies and getting exhausted, and in turn nothing to prevent scientists from recognizing when in fact these resources have been exhausted.

How long are we to continue a search before we have a right to give up the search and declare not only that continuing the search is vain but also that the very object of the search is nonexistent? There are times that searches must be continued against extreme odds. There are other times when searches are best given up. Despite Poseidon's wrath, Odysseus was right to continue seeking Ithaca. Sisyphus, on the other hand, should have given up rolling the rock up the hill long ago. We no longer look kindly on angle trisectors and circle squarers. We are amused by purported *perpetuum mobile* devices. Alchemists do not receive funding from the National Science Foundation. We deny the existence of unicorns, gnomes and fairy godmothers. In these cases we don't just say that the search for these objects is vain; we positively deny that the objects exist. Such denials, such claims that certain searches are vain, such admissions that certain modes of discourse cannot succeed in solving certain problems are widespread, both in and out of science. Stephen Meyer refers to them as "proscriptive generalizations."

There is no precise line of demarcation for deciding when a search is to be given up and when the object of a search is to be denied existence. Nevertheless I would offer a necessary condition. The failure in practice to discover a thing is good reason to doubt the thing's existence *only if* a diligent search for the thing has been performed. A full and efficient use of our empirical and theoretical resources for discovery should be made before we accept a proscriptive generalization. But once this has been done, to suppose that all the gaps in extraordinary explanations must be fillable by natural causes cannot be justified. Nor is it the case that one is necessarily blocking the path of inquiry by putting forward a proscriptive generalization which asserts that natural causes are incapable of filling a certain gap. Not all gaps are created equal. To assume that they are is to presuppose the very thing that is in question, namely, naturalism.

A.2 Intentionality Versus Design
Objection: There is nothing that cannot be explained by invoking design. Design explains everything and so explains nothing.

The problem with this objection is that it confuses design with intentionality.[12] Everything that's designed is, to be sure, intended. But not everything that's intended is designed. Suppose I place a mirror on top of my desk. The mirror's position is therefore intended. Nevertheless ordinary linguistic usage resists saying that the mirror's position is designed unless its position is also carefully calculated to accomplish some highly specific function. For instance, suppose someone I'm not too fond of is sitting at my desk and that I adjust the mirror so that it just manages to reflect the sun's rays into the person's eyes. In that case the mirror's position would not only be intended but also designed. If, on the other hand, I place the mirror on my desk simply to have a place for it and not to lose it, then its position would simply be intended without being designed.

What distinguishes design from intentionality is specified complexity (cf. chapter five). Things that are designed are both complex and specified.

Things that are intended without being designed lack one or both of these features. An illiterate person typing willy-nilly at a keyboard will produce a string of characters that is complex but not specified. A literate person typing the letters *t-h-e* produces a string of characters that is specified but not complex. A person (literate or illiterate) typing the letters *x-q-j* produces a string of characters that is neither complex nor specified. In each case these strings of characters are fully intended but not designed. Contrast this with Shakespeare writing one of his sonnets. Here the string of characters is both complex and specified. A Shakespearean sonnet is therefore not merely intended but also designed.

The objection that there is nothing that cannot be explained by invoking design is therefore mistaken. Whereas everything we observe might be intended, not everything we observe is designed. Design adds specified complexity to intentionality. Specified complexity reliably signals the presence of intentionality, or what in previous chapters we called "intelligent agency" or "intelligent causation." It follows that the first part of the objection we are considering becomes true if we replace *design* with the word *intention:* There is nothing that cannot be explained by invoking intention. Note, however, that replacing *design* with the word *intention* in the second part of this objection is false. To say that intention explains everything and therefore explains nothing is simply incorrect.

For instance, consider Frank, a disgruntled employee of a software development firm. Having received a pink slip, Frank decides to sabotage the software he's been working on. He knows the software is incredibly sensitive to copying errors, and one stray mark is liable to invalidate it. Frank therefore takes the source code and introduces a single letter change at some inconspicuous place in the program, say, by changing the conjunction *and* to *znd*. Without direct evidence of Frank's sabotage, this change would be attributed to a random copying error. Even so, it makes a big difference whether the change was due to a random copying error or a deliberate act of sabotage. Although everything might be intended, it is nonetheless informative to learn that something was intended rather than due to chance. The bottom line then is this: (1) not everything can be explained by invoking design; (2) everything can potentially be explained by invoking intentionality; and (3) intentionality can nonetheless serve as a nonvacuous explanation.

A.3 Scientific Creationism

Objection: Design is nothing but scientific creationism cloaked in newer and more sophisticated terminology.

Intelligent design needs to be distinguished from what is known as *creation science* or *scientific creationism.*[13] The most obvious difference between the two is that scientific creationism has prior religious commitments whereas intelligent design does not. Scientific creationism is committed to two religious presuppositions and interprets the data of science to fit those presuppositions. Intelligent design, on the other hand, has no prior religious commitments and interprets the data of science on generally accepted scientific principles. In particular, intelligent design does not depend on the biblical account of creation.

Scientific creationism holds to two presuppositions:

1. There exists a supernatural agent who creates and orders the world.

2. The biblical account of creation recorded in Genesis is scientifically accurate.

The supernatural agent presupposed by scientific creationism is usually understood as the transcendent personal God of the well-known monotheistic religions, specifically Christianity. This God is said to create the world out of nothing (i.e., without the use of pre-existing materials). Moreover the sequence of events by which this God creates is said to parallel the biblical record.

By contrast, intelligent design nowhere attempts to identify the intelligent cause responsible for the design in nature, nor does it prescribe in advance the sequence of events by which this intelligent cause had to act. Intelligent design holds to three tenets:

1. Specified complexity is well-defined and empirically detectable.

2. Undirected natural causes are incapable of explaining specified complexity.

3. Intelligent causation best explains specified complexity.

Design theorists hold these tenets not as religious presuppositions but as conclusions of sound scientific arguments (cf. chapter five).

Intelligent design is modest in what it attributes to the designing intelligence responsible for the specified complexity in nature. For instance, design theorists recognize that the nature, moral character and purposes of this intelligence lie beyond the remit of science. As Dean Kenyon and

Percival Davis remark in their text on intelligent design: "Science cannot answer this question; it must leave it to religion and philosophy."[14] Intelligent design as a scientific theory is distinct from a theological doctrine of creation. Creation presupposes a Creator who originates the world and all its materials. Intelligent design attempts only to explain the arrangement of materials within an already given world. Design theorists argue that certain arrangements of matter, especially in biological systems, clearly signal a designing intelligence.

Besides presupposing a supernatural agent, scientific creationism also presupposes the scientific accuracy of the biblical account of creation. Proponents of scientific creationism treat the opening chapters of Genesis as a scientific text and thus argue for a literal six-day creation, the existence of a historical Adam and Eve, a literal garden of Eden, a catastrophic worldwide flood, etc. Scientific creationism takes the biblical account of creation in Genesis as its starting point and then attempts to match the data of nature to the biblical account.

Intelligent design, by contrast, starts with the data of nature and from there argues to an intelligent cause responsible for the specified complexity in nature. Moreover in making such an argument, intelligent design relies not on narrowly held prior assumptions but on reliable methods developed within the scientific community for discriminating intelligently from naturally generated structures.[15] Scientific creationism's reliance on narrowly held prior assumptions undercuts its status as a scientific theory. Intelligent design's reliance on widely accepted scientific principles, on the other hand, ensures its legitimacy as a scientific theory.

These differences between intelligent design and scientific creationism have significant legal implications for the advancement of intelligent design in the public square. In formulating its position on scientific creationism in *Edwards v. Aguillard,* the Supreme Court cited the District Court in *McLean v. Arkansas Board of Education.* According to the court, scientific creationism is not just similar to the Genesis account of creation but is in fact identical to it and parallel to no other creation story.[16] Because scientific creationism corresponds point for point with the creation and flood narratives in Genesis, the Supreme Court found scientific creationism to be a religious doctrine and not a scientific theory.

The District Court in *McLean,* to which the Supreme Court appealed, listed six tenets as defining scientific creationism:[17]

1. There was a sudden creation of the universe, energy and life from nothing.

2. Mutations and natural selection are insufficient to bring about the development of all living kinds from a single organism.

3. Changes of the originally created kinds of plants and animals occur only within fixed limits.

4. There is a separate ancestry for humans and apes

5. The earth's geology can be explained via catastrophism, primarily by the occurrence of a worldwide flood.

6. The earth and living kinds had a relatively recent inception (on the order of ten thousand years).

These six tenets taken jointly define scientific creationism. The Supreme Court in *Edwards* ruled that taken jointly they may not be taught in public school science curricula. Nevertheless the court left the door open to some of these tenets taken individually.

Tenets 1, 5 and 6 are the most problematic for inclusion in public-school science curricula. Tenet 1 asserts the creation of the universe from nothing. Such an act of creation must by definition occur outside of space and time. More than rearranging a pre-existing universe, creation originates the universe itself. Consequently creation lies beyond the remit of science. Indeed creation is always a theological or philosophical doctrine.

Tenets 5 and 6, on the other hand, are subject to scientific investigation. Nevertheless the scientific warrant for tenets 5 and 6 must be sought outside intelligent design. Geology, for instance, can investigate the age of the earth and whether a worldwide flood killed all terrestrial life within the last several thousand years. But such investigations will proceed without considering specified complexity, that key trademark of intelligence.

Intelligent design has no stake in tenets 1, 5 and 6. Intelligent design requires an intelligent cause that is capable of arranging complex specified structures. That capacity to arrange matter, however, is exercised within space and time, and need not violate any laws of nature. Intelligent design does not require a creator that originates the space, time, matter and energy that together constitute the universe. Nor does intelligent design require any particular time-frame within which an intelligent cause must act. Nor for that matter does it require that any particular historical event must occur (like a worldwide flood 5,000 years ago). Intelligent design is compatible with a biophysical universe that developed over billions of years.

Tenets 3 and 4, by contrast, are legitimate subjects for consideration in public-school science curricula. These tenets, though largely rejected by the scientific community, are nonetheless debated within it. Moreover many active areas of research bear on tenets 3 and 4. Tenet 4 is really a special case of tenet 3. Whereas tenet 3 prescribes a limit to evolutionary change for organisms generally, tenet 4 prescribes such a limit specifically for primates.

It is a legitimate scientific question whether evolutionary processes have limits. According to the neo-Darwinian synthesis, there are no limits whatsoever: all organisms trace their ancestry back to an original single-celled organism (sometimes called the "protobiont"). This view is called "monophyly" or "common descent" and contrasts with "polyphyly," the view that some groups of organisms have separate ancestries.

Common descent, though widely held in the biological community, is nonetheless a legitimate subject for scientific debate. Actual scientific evidence, both experimental and paleontological, supports only limited variation within fixed boundaries, or what is called microevolution. Macroevolution—the unlimited capacity of organisms to transform beyond all boundaries—is an extrapolation from microevolution. As with all extrapolations it is legitimate to question whether this extrapolation is warranted. For instance, prominent naturalistic evolutionists like Stuart Kauffman, Rudolf Raff and George Miklos are actively investigating the warrant for this extrapolation.[18]

Intelligent design is compatible with both a single origin of life (i.e., common descent or monophyly) and multiple origins of life (i.e., polyphyly). Design theorists themselves are divided on this question. Dean Kenyon and Percival Davis, for instance, argue against common descent in *Of Pandas and People*.[19] On the other hand, in *Darwin's Black Box* Michael Behe provisionally accepts common descent.[20] Nonetheless design theorists agree that discussion of this question must not be shut down simply because a majority of biologists happen to embrace common descent. The limits of evolutionary change form a legitimate topic of scientific inquiry.[21] It is therefore illegitimate to exclude this topic from public-school science curricula.

Finally we come to tenet 2. This is the one tenet of scientific creationism that overlaps with intelligent design. It needs to be squarely addressed in public-school science curricula. Indeed any adequate treatment of biological evolution must consider the possibility that mutation and selection might be insufficient to explain the diversity of life. Only strict neo-Darwinists hold to the sufficiency of mutation and selection to produce the full diversity of living forms. All others regard the mutation-selection mechanism as to varying degrees incomplete. This includes not only scientific creationists and design theorists but also a significant number of theistic and naturalistic evolutionists. Well-known proponents of naturalistic evolution who argue against the sufficiency of the mutation-selection mechanism include Stephen Jay Gould, Stuart Kauffman, Ilya Prigogine, Manfred Eigen and Francis Crick.

Gould holds to a theory of "punctuated equilibria" in which organisms evolve in spurts, followed by long periods of stasis (i.e., lack of change).[22] Gould's theory offers no mechanism of organismal change, however. Kauffman and Prigogine look to the self-organizational properties of matter to supplement mutation and selection.[23] Manfred Eigen hopes to find the key to biological complexity in novel natural laws and algorithms.[24] Francis Crick thinks the problem of solving life's origin is so beyond the resources available on earth that life had to be seeded from outer space. (This is his theory of "directed panspermia.")[25]

Each of these scientists opposes the sufficiency of the mutation-selection mechanism on scientific grounds. For them the problem of biological complexity exceeds the capacity of mutation and selection. Design theorists agree. They too regard mutation and selection as insufficient to explain the origin and development of life. Likewise, their reasons for holding this view are strictly scientific. Design theorists argue that certain data of nature (e.g., Michael Behe's irreducibly complex biochemical systems) point decisively to the activity of a designing intelligence.

Skepticism and controversy about the sufficiency of mutation and natural selection is already part of mainstream science. To deny the controversy or to prevent its open discussion is dishonest and stifles scientific inquiry. The public square—and the public-school science curriculum in particular—needs to be careful about not suppressing dissent against a prevailing scientific view (in this case, neo-Darwinism with its mutation-selection mechanism) when that dissent is backed up with scientific evidence and argument. Intelligent design offers precisely such evidence and argument.

Intelligent design is not scientific creationism cloaked in newer and more sophisticated terminology. Intelligent design makes far fewer commitments than scientific creationism, carries far less baggage and consequently has far less chance of going wrong. Scientific creationism describes the origin of the universe, its duration, the mechanisms responsible for geological formations, the limits to evolutionary change and the beginnings of humanity, all the while conforming its account of creation to the first chapters of Genesis. In contrast, intelligent design makes no claims about the origin or duration of the universe, is not committed to flood geology, can accommodate any degree of evolutionary change, does not prejudge how human beings arose and does not specify in advance the mode by which a designing intelligence brought the first organisms into being.

Consequently it is mistaken and unfair to confuse intelligent design with scientific creationism. Intelligent design is a strictly scientific theory devoid of religious commitments. Whereas the Creator underlying scientific creationism conforms to a strict, literalist interpretation of the Bible, the designer underlying intelligent design is compatible with a much broader playing field. To be sure, the designer is compatible with the Creator-God of the world's major monotheistic religions like Judaism, Christianity and Islam. But the designer is also compatible with the watchmaker-God of the deists, the demiurge of Plato's *Timaeus* and the divine reason (i.e., *logos spermatikos*) of the ancient Stoics. One can even take an agnostic view about the designer, treating specified complexity as a brute unexplainable fact.[26] Unlike scientific creationism, intelligent design does not prejudge such questions as *Who is the designer?* or *How does the designer go about designing and building things?*

A.4 But Is It Science?

Objection: Design cannot properly be a part of science since scientific explanations are by definition naturalistic explanations whereas design is an irreducibly supernaturalistic explanation.

The charge is frequently made that design is not science. To make this charge stick, however, one needs to demonstrate that genuine science exhibits some feature that design lacks. Many such features have been proposed to date. Yet none has succeeded in showing that design stands outside science. Either the proposed feature is too lenient (thus including design after all) or too stringent (excluding not just design but other forms of inquiry that we do want to count as science), or it constitutes an arbitrary imposition on science, deliberately defining science so that it excludes design.

Consider, for instance, how the federal district court in *McLean v. Arkansas* (commonly known as the "Arkansas Creation Trial") defined science. That court listed five essential characteristics of science: guided by natural law, explanatory by natural law, testable against the empirical world, tentative and falsifiable.[27] Critics of design have since added to the list. What follows are the main objectives for keeping design out of science:

1. If it can't be measured or counted or photographed, then it can't be science—even if it's important.[28]

2. Intelligent design is necessarily unscientific because it (a) explains what is observable by what cannot be observed,[29] (b) is not falsifiable/verifiable,[30] (c) does not make predictions,[31] (d) provides no mechanisms,[32] (e) has no problem-solving capability[33] and (f) is not tentative.[34]

3. "[To explain via] a supernatural Designer is to explain precisely nothing, for it leaves unexplained the origin of the Designer. You have to say something like 'God was always there,' and if you allow yourself that kind of lazy way out, you might as well just say 'DNA was always there,' or 'Life was always there' and be done with it."[35]

4. "[Science understands] how things work [via] hierarchical reductionism. The hierarchical reductionist believes that carburettors [sic] are explained in terms of smaller units, which are explained in terms of [still] smaller units, which are ultimately explained in terms of the smallest of fundamental particles. Reductionism, in this sense, is just another name for an honest desire to understand how things work."[36]

5. "Even if [intelligent design] were totally successful in making its case as science, it would not yield a scientific explanation of origins. Rather, at most, it could prove that science shows that there can be no scientific explanation of origins. . . . Science by definition deals with the natural, the repeatable, that which is governed by law."[37]

6. "You can't (scientifically) study variables you can't test directly or indirectly. . . . As soon as [design theorists] invent a 'theo-meter,' maybe then we can test for [design]."[38]

Criticisms 1 and 2 derive from a variety of sources and are easily dispensed with. The claim that science is limited to what can be measured or counted or photographed and the claim that science is only in the business of explaining the observable by means of the observable do not stand up under scrutiny. Science posits a host of theoretical entities that no one has observed or in many instances has any hope of observing (e.g., quarks, superstrings and cold dark matter). Needless to say, such entities can't be photographed either. The notion that one gets science as soon as one puts numbers to things is also insupportable. For all its emphasis on numbers, biblical numerology is not science. On the other hand, despite its relative lack of mathematization, qualitative sciences like archaeology do belong to science.

Falsifiability has also proven problematic as a criterion for identifying science. According to this criterion, a theory is scientific if there are empirical grounds on which it can be falsified. Falsification, however, turns out to be difficult and in many cases impossible to achieve. As philosopher of science Elliott Sober has noted, a scientific theory invariably requires auxiliary assumptions to bring it in touch with observation.[39] This always leaves open the possibility that the auxiliary assumptions, and not the scientific theory itself, are responsible for a putative falsification. Similar observations hold for verifiability since auxiliary assumptions may shore up a theory that is in fact false.

Predictability is equally problematic. Many scientific theories attempt not so much to predict the future as to reconstruct the past (e.g., archaeology and anthropology). Theories about the evolution of life, for instance, are mainly concerned with reconstructing the past. They do, in a weak sense, predict what one should find in, say, the fossil record. But predictions of this sort are often impossible to confirm since, as evolutionary paleontologists are quick to note, "the absence of evidence is no evidence of absence."[40]

The requirement that a scientific theory must provide a causal mechanism is simply false. Newton's universal law of gravitation was no less a scientific theory because Newton failed—indeed refused—to postulate a mechanism for the regular pattern of attraction that his law described.[41] So too the claim that intelligent design has no problem-solving capability is false. Intelligent design solves many problems in biology (cf. chapters five and six). The question is not whether intelligent design has problem-solving capability but whether its solutions are valid. The validity of those solutions forms a legitimate subject for debate. But it is a scientific, not a religious, debate.

Finally, as for scientific theories being held tentatively, this simply isn't the way science works. No scientist with a career invested in a scientific theory is going to relinquish that theory easily. Biologist and philosopher Michael Ruse does not hold Darwinism tentatively when he proclaims: "Evolution is a fact, *fact, FACT!*"[42] Indeed Thomas Kuhn has argued that it takes a revolution to change scientific theories precisely because scientists do not hold them tentatively.[43]

Criticism 3 is by the zoologist Richard Dawkins. Dawkins criticizes design for committing an unacceptable regress in which the designer in turn needs to be explained. The problem with this criticism is that it can be applied whenever scientists introduce a novel theoretical entity. When Ludwig Boltzmann introduced his kinetic theory of heat back in the late 1800s and invoked the motion of unobservable particles (what we now call atoms and molecules) to explain heat, one might just as well have argued that such unobservable particles do not explain anything because they themselves need to be explained.[44]

It is always possible to ask for further explanation. Nevertheless at some point scientists stop and content themselves with the progress they have made. Boltzmann's kinetic theory explained things that the old phenomenological approaches to heat failed to explain—for instance, why shaking a container filled with a gas caused the temperature of the gas to increase. Whereas the old phenomenological approach provided no answer, Boltzmann's kinetic theory did: shaking the container caused the unobservable particles making up the gas to move more quickly and thus caused the temperature to rise.

So too with design, the question is not whether design theorists have resolved all lingering questions about the designing intelligence responsible for specified complexity in nature. Such questions will always remain. Rather the question is whether design does useful conceptual work, a question that Dawkins' criticism leaves unanswered. Design theorists argue that intelligent design is a fruitful scientific theory for understanding systems like Michael Behe's irreducibly complex biochemical machines. Their argument has to be taken on its own merits. It is a scientific argument.

Criticism 4 is also by Dawkins. Richard Dawkins, Daniel Dennett and many other scientists and philosophers are convinced that proper scientific explanations must be reductive, moving from the complex to the simple. Dawkins writes, "The one thing that makes evolution such a neat theory is that it explains how organized complexity can arise out of primeval simplicity."[45] Dennett views any scientific explanation that moves from simple to complex as "question-begging."[46] Dawkins explicitly equates proper scientific explanation with what he calls "hierarchical reductionism," according to which "a complex entity at any particular level in the hierarchy of organization" must properly be explained "in terms of entities only one level down the hierarchy."[47]

While no one will deny that reductive explanation is extremely effective within science, it is hardly the only type of explanation available to science. The divide-and-conquer mode of analysis behind reductive explanation has strictly limited applicability within science. Complex systems theory has long since rejected a reductive bottom-up approach to complex systems.[48] To properly understand a complex system requires a top-down approach that focuses on global relationships between parts as opposed to analysis into individual parts. The Santa Fe Institute, for instance, was founded to study systems of "simple interacting elements that [produce] through their aggregate behavior a global emergent order unpredictable simply through analysis of low-level interactions."[49] Likewise, a reductive mode of analysis is incapable of making headway with specified complexity (cf. CSI holism in section 6.5). Intelligent design is an integrative, top-down theory of complex structures. Integration is as much a part of science as reduction and analysis.

Criticisms 5 and 6 are respectively by Michael Ruse, a philosopher of biology, and Eugenie Scott, a physical anthropologist. Their criticisms can be taken as a piece and constitute what is typically regarded as the decisive objection against incorporating design into science. Ruse and Scott advocate a view that is with increasing frequency called *methodological naturalism*. According to this view, science must be confined exclusively to naturalistic explanations.[50]

Despite its apparent plausibility this criticism quickly breaks down once one attempts to define what it is for an explanation to be naturalistic. Presumably the established sciences, whose status as science is not controverted (unlike intelligent design), consist of naturalistic and only naturalistic explanations. In thereby relegating design to the realm of nonscience, Ruse and Scott imply that they possess reliable criteria for determining whether an explanation is naturalistic and therefore acceptable to science. Yet each of their criteria, insofar as it manages to exclude design from science, manages also to exclude things we definitely want to include within science.[51]

Must science deal exclusively with the repeatable? This clearly can't be the case. Big-bang cosmology is certainly part of science, but it bases its theorizing on a one-time event, namely, the Big Bang. Similarly in biology the origin of life, the origin of multicellular organisms, the origin of sexual reproduction and the origin of human beings are all unique events that are not in any clear sense repeatable. No scientist has come even close to repeating any of these events in the laboratory. Yet we certainly regard them as within the domain of science. Nor do we want to say that archaeologists, anthropologists and paleontologists are not doing science when they discover some unique artifact or feature of nature. The repeatability objection therefore fails.

Must science deal exclusively with what is governed by law? Although some philosophers and scientists hope that everything will one day be, at least in principle, explainable in terms of law, actual scientific practice assigns a rather limited place to law. Many special sciences, like archaeology and the search for extraterrestrial intelligence, study objects produced by intelligent agents and are thus not reducible to natural law.

But even such "hard sciences" as physics cannot be reduced to natural law. In the nineteenth century Ludwig Boltzmann explained heat in terms of the collision of what at the time were unobservable particles (what we now call atoms and molecules). Boltzmann demonstrated that his kinetic theory entailed the same ideal gas law that physicists already knew. Ernst Mach, Boltzmann's contemporary and nemesis, rejected the kinetic theory because it introduced unobservable entities and therefore did not confine itself to laws that could be empirically verified. The history of physics, however, has vindicated Boltzmann and indicted Mach. In specifying the microstructure of matter Boltzmann's kinetic theory yielded no new laws but did yield an abundance of theoretical insights for physics. (Indeed the entire field of statistical mechanics can be traced back to the kinetic theory.)[52]

The point is that science is not reducible to law, nor is it even desirable to try to reduce it to law. Science regularly introduces novel entities, metaphors and images.[53] Often these have no clear reference, cannot be measured and do not even make sense intuitively (e.g., the wave-particle duality of quantum physics). Despite all the idealizations about the scientific method and the proper content of science—idealizations that portray science as a logically tight and self-contained enterprise[54]—the actual practice of science follows no hard and fast rules. The Nobel laureate Percy Bridgman aptly described the scientific method as follows: "The scientific method, as far as it is a method, is nothing more than doing one's damnedest with one's mind, no holds barred."[55] The philosopher of science Paul Feyerabend, with the history of science to back him up, even went so far as to deny that there is a scientific method.[56]

What about testability? Must science deal exclusively with what is either directly or indirectly testable? Certainly it is a hallmark of science that any of its claims be open to criticism and subject to revision or refutation on the basis of new evidence or further theoretical insight. Science is therefore testable if by testable one means sensitive to new evidence and to further theoretical insight. Yet if this is what one means by testable, then design is certainly testable. Indeed it was in this sense that Darwin tested William Paley's account of design and found it wanting.[57] But testability is a double-edged sword. If it is possible for evidence to count against a claim, it must also be possible for evidence to confirm a claim. Testability is a symmetric notion. One cannot say, "Design isn't testable," and then turn around and say, "Darwin tested design and refuted it." Intelligent design is indeed testable, and it has been confirmed across a wide range of disciplines, spanning everything from natural history to molecular biology to information theory.

Finally, must science be confined exclusively to what is natural? Certainly science has nature as its proper object of study. Science seeks to study and explain the things that are happening in nature. But if studying nature is the sole criterion for determining whether an explanation is properly scientific, then design must constitute a part of science, for the specified complexity that intelligent design studies is identifiable throughout nature, notably in living things, and these form an integral part of nature. When design is faulted for not properly being a part of science, however, it is not for making living things an object of study. Rather it is for attributing living things to nonnaturalistic causes—to miracles and supernatural designers—and thereby making these non-naturalistic causes objects of study as well.

In answering this criticism let us first of all be clear that intelligent design does not require miracles. Just as humans do not perform miracles every time they act as intelligent agents, so there is no reason to assume that for a designer to act as an intelligent agent requires a violation of natural laws. There's an important contrast to keep in mind here. Science, according to Ruse and Scott, studies natural causes whereas to introduce design is to invoke supernatural causes. This is the wrong contrast. The proper contrast is between *undirected natural causes* on the one hand and *intelligent causes* on the other.

Intelligent causes can do things that undirected natural causes cannot. Undirected natural causes can explain how ink gets applied to paper to form a random inkblot but cannot explain an arrangement of ink on paper that spells out a meaningful message. To obtain such a meaningful arrangement requires an intelligent cause. Whether an intelligent cause is located within or outside nature (i.e., is respectively natural or supernatural) is a separate question from whether an intelligent cause has acted within nature. Design has no prior commitment to supernaturalism. Consequently science can offer no principled grounds for excluding design or relegating it to religion.

Given that design has no prior commitment to supernaturalism, what then is left of the criticism by Ruse and Scott against design? It seems that implicit in their requirement that scientific explanations be naturalistic is a theory of reference specifying what entities the terms in a scientific theory are permitted to refer to. In particular they seem to want to limit scientific terms to entities strictly locatable in space and time. According to such a theory of reference, the mere fact that a designer might not be locatable in space and time is enough to make explanations that invoke design nonnaturalistic and therefore nonscientific. Even those unobservable theoretical entities of physics like fields, potentials, quarks and strings are at least in principle locatable in space and time. But because a designer need not be, designers must be excluded from science.

I've just given what I take to be the most potent formulation of the criticism against design by Ruse and Scott. Yet even formulated this way, their criticism miscarries. For one thing, it presupposes a realist view of scientific explanation. If, for instance, one takes an antirealist view of scientific explanation, then the spatio-temporal location of the entities posited by a scientific theory becomes moot since space and time themselves become conceptual constructs. On an antirealist view, the important thing is not where those entities are located, since scientific theories describe not so much what is "out there" as they do our way of looking at the world. Thus the important thing in the antirealist view is whether the entities we posit are conceptually fruitful and empirically adequate and whether they offer superior explanatory power.[58]

If a theory of design in biology should prove successful, would it follow that the designer posited by this theory is real? Could an antirealist about science simply regard the designer as a regulative principle—a conceptually useful device for making sense out of certain facts of biology—without assigning the designer any weight in reality? Wittgenstein regarded the theories of Copernicus and Darwin not as true but as "fertile new points of view."[59] One's first interest as a scientist working on a theory of design is whether design provides powerful new insights and fruitful avenues of research. The metaphysics underlying such a theory, and in particular the ontological status of the designer, can then be taken up by philosophy and theology. Indeed one's metaphysics ought to be a matter of indifference to one's scientific theorizing about design. The fact that it is not for Ruse and Scott says more about their own biases than about the biases of design theorists, whose primary interest is to explore the fruitfulness of design for science.

The only reason for requiring science to rule out entities not locatable in space and time is that we know in advance that such entities do not exist, or if they do exist, that they can have no conceivable relevance to what happens in the world. Do such entities exist? Can they have empirical consequences? Are they relevant to what happens in the world? Such questions cannot be prejudged except on metaphysical grounds. To prejudge these questions the way Ruse and Scott do is therefore to make certain metaphysical commitments about what there is and what has the capacity to influence events in the world. Such commitments are utterly gratuitous to the practice of science.

A.5 Dysteleology

Objection: Design in biology is refuted by all the examples of suboptimal design. In particular, design cannot be reconciled with the problem of evil.

Intelligent design needs to be distinguished from *apparent design* on the one hand and *optimal design* on the other. Apparent design looks designed but really isn't. Optimal design is perfect design and hence cannot exist except in an idealized realm (sometimes called a "Platonic heaven"). Apparent and optimal design empty design of all practical significance.

A common strategy of opponents to design, like Stephen Jay Gould and Richard Dawkins, is to assimilate intelligent design to one of these categories—apparent or optimal design. The problem with this move is that it is an evasion. Indeed it utterly sidesteps the question of intelligent design. The automobiles that roll off the assembly plants in Detroit are intelligently designed in the sense that human intelligences are responsible for them. Nevertheless even if we think Detroit manufactures the best cars in the world, it would still be wrong to say they are optimally designed. Nor is it correct to say they are only apparently designed.

Within biology intelligent design holds that a designing intelligence is indispensable for explaining the specified complexity of living systems. Nevertheless, taken strictly as a scientific theory, intelligent design refuses to speculate about the nature of this designing intelligence. Whereas optimal design demands a perfectionistic designer who has to get everything just right, intelligent design fits our ordinary experience of design, which is always conditioned by the needs of a situation and therefore always falls short of some idealized global optimum.

No real designer attempts optimality in the sense of attaining perfect design. Indeed there is no such thing as perfect design. Real designers strive for *constrained optimization,* which is something completely different. As Henry Petroski aptly remarks in *Invention by Design,* "All design involves conflicting objectives and hence compromise, and the best designs will always be those that come up with the best compromise."[60] Constrained optimization is the art of compromise between conflicting objectives. This is what design is all about. To find fault with biological design because it misses an idealized optimum, as Stephen Jay Gould regularly does, is therefore gratuitous. Not knowing the objectives of the designer, Gould is in no position to say whether the designer has come up with a faulty compromise among those objectives.[61]

Nonetheless the claim that biological design is suboptimal has been tremendously successful at shutting down discussion about design. Interestingly, that success comes not from analyzing a given biological structure and showing how a constrained optimization for constructing that structure might have been improved. This would constitute a legitimate scientific inquiry so long as the proposed improvements can be concretely implemented and do not degenerate into wish fulfillment where one imagines some improvement but has no idea how it can be effected or whether it might lead to deficits elsewhere. Just because we can always imagine some improvement in design doesn't mean that the structure in question wasn't designed or that the improvement can be effected or that the improvement, even if it could be effected, would not entail deficits elsewhere.

The success of the suboptimality objection comes not from science at all but from shifting the terms of the discussion from science to theology.[62] In place of *How specifically can an existing structure be improved?* the question instead becomes *What sort of God would create a structure like that?* Darwin, for instance, thought there was just "too much misery in the world" to accept design: "I cannot persuade myself that a beneficent and omnipotent God would have designedly created the Ichneumonidae with the express intention of their feeding within the living bodies of Caterpillars, or that a cat should play with mice."[63] Other examples he pointed to included "ants making slaves" and "the young cuckoo ejecting its foster-brother."[64] The problem of suboptimal design is thus transformed into the problem of evil.

The problem of evil is to reconcile the following three propositions: (1) God is good. (2) God is all-powerful. (3) Evil exists. Since the existence of evil is taken for granted, the problem is to account for evil given that God is both good and all-powerful. If God is all-powerful but not good, there is no problem reconciling the existence of evil. (In that case God is free to be nasty.) Alternatively, if God is good but fails to be all-powerful, there is no problem reconciling the existence of evil. (In that case God means well but can't quite pull it off.)

Critics who invoke the problem of evil against design have left science behind and entered the waters of philosophy and theology. A torture chamber replete with implements of torture is designed, and the evil of its designer does nothing to undercut the torture chamber's design. The existence of design is distinct from the morality, aesthetics, goodness, optimality or perfection of design. Moreover specified complexity reliably signals design irrespective of whether design includes these additional features.

Some scientists, however, prefer to conflate science and theology. Consider the following criticism of design by Stephen Jay Gould:

> If God had designed a beautiful machine to reflect his wisdom and power, surely he would not have used a collection of parts generally fashioned for other purposes. . . . Odd arrangements and funny solutions are the proof of evolution—paths that a sensible God would never tread but that a natural process, constrained by history, follows perforce.[65]

Gould is here criticizing what he calls the "panda's thumb," a bony extrusion that helps the panda strip bamboo of its hard exterior and thus render the bamboo edible to the panda.

The first question that needs to be answered about the panda's thumb is whether it displays the clear marks of intelligence—namely, whether it is complex and specified. If so, then it is designed. If not, then it may be intended, but we cannot know for sure (see appendix A.2). The design theorist is not committed to every biological structure being designed. Mutation and selection do operate in natural history to adapt organisms to their environments. Perhaps the panda's thumb is such an adaptation. Nonetheless mutation and selection are incapable of generating specified complexity, and there are plenty of biological systems that exhibit specified complexity (see chapters five and six).

Once specified complexity has been established, it is a separate question whether a wise, powerful and beneficent God ought to have designed a complex specified structure one way or another. For the sake of argument, let's grant that certain designed structures are not just, as Gould puts it, "odd" or "funny," but even cruel. What of it? Philosophical theology has abundant resources for dealing with the problem of evil, maintaining a God who is both omnipotent and benevolent in the face of evil. The line I find most convincing is that evil always parasitizes good. Indeed all our words for evil presuppose a good that has been perverted. Impurity presupposes purity, unrighteousness presupposes righteousness, deviation presupposes a way (i.e., a *via*) from which we've departed, sin (the Greek *hamartia*) presupposes a target that was missed and so on.

Boethius put it this way in his *Consolation of Philosophy*: "If God exists whence evil; but whence good if God does not exist?"[66]

One looks at some biological structure and remarks, "Gee, that sure looks evil." Did it start out evil? Was that its function when a good and all-powerful God created it? Objects invented for good purposes are regularly co-opted and used for evil purposes. Drugs that were meant to alleviate pain become sources of addiction. Knives that were meant to cut bread become implements for killing people. Political powers that were meant to maintain law and order become the means for enslaving citizens.

This is a fallen world. The good that God initially intended is no longer fully in evidence. Much has been perverted. Dysteleology, the perversion of design in nature, is a reality. It is evident all around us. But how do we explain it? The scientific naturalist explains dysteleology by claiming that the design in nature is only apparent, that it arose through mutation and natural selection (or some other natural mechanism) and that imperfection, cruelty and waste are fully to be expected from such mechanisms. But such mechanisms cannot explain the specified complexity in nature. What's more, specified complexity signals actual design and not merely apparent design.

The design in nature is actual. More often than we would like, that design has gotten perverted. But the perversion of design—dysteleology—is not explained by denying design but by accepting it and meeting the problem of evil head on. The problem of evil is a theological problem. To force a resolution of the problem by reducing all design to apparent design is an evasion. It avoids both the scientific challenge posed by specified complexity, and it avoids the hard work of faith, whose job is to discern God's hand in creation despite the occlusions of evil.[67]

A.6 Just an Anthropic Coincidence

Objection: Design in nature is an anthropic coincidence or what's also called a selection effect. Yes, it's incredibly improbable that nature should be organized just the way it is; but if it weren't, we wouldn't be here to appreciate that fact.

There's a Gary Larson cartoon showing God, depicted as a white-haired old man in flowing robes, pulling a cake out of the oven. According to the caption, this is how God created the world. Although creating a cosmos and making a cake are hardly equivalent tasks, there is an important analogy between the two that is relevant to this objection. To design a world that supports human life requires that certain prior ingredients be in place. So, too, to make a cake that tastes good and is visually pleasing requires certain prior ingredients. What's more, not only do the ingredients have to be in place, but they have to be in the right proportion. Flour, water and yeast are fine, but if we have a ton of yeast for every microgram of flour and if all our water is frozen, our cake-making will never get started. So, too, if the proportions of carbon, hydrogen and oxygen in the universe diverge significantly from their present values, there wouldn't be any stars, much less habitable planets like ours that orbit stars.

Anthropic coincidences signify all the prior conditions that need to be precisely satisfied and correlated for human life to be possible. Often cosmologists refer to the totality of these coincidences as the "fine-tuning of the universe." For example, the fundamental forces of nature have to fall within very precise tolerances for the basic constituents of the universe to support life. If the strong nuclear force were slightly stronger, hardly any hydrogen would form because its nuclei would be unstable. If, on the other hand, it were slightly weaker, no elements other than hydrogen could form. Similarly if the force of gravity were slightly stronger, stars would burn out too rapidly to support life on surrounding planets. If, on the other hand, it were slightly weaker, there would not be enough heavy elements with which to build surrounding planets.[68]

Such anthropic coincidences abound. Hugh Ross collects them. In one of his more recent articles he lists over seventy from physics and cosmology.[69] Michael Denton, in his recent book *Nature's Destiny*, lists others from chemistry, geology and biology that are specifically required for human life.[70] With the emergence and development of the universe, we are in the position of a cook confronted with a cake requiring hundreds of ingredients, each given in just the right amounts and all amounts being precisely proportioned so that any divergence, whether in the amount of the ingredients or in their relative proportions, results in total failure of the cake.

Not surprisingly, scientists are asking themselves how all those "ingredients" needed to produce the universe came together in the first place. They offer two answers: chance and design. Of these, design has proven the only viable contender. For chance to be a viable contender, the probability of all the ingredients coming together to make life possible must not be too small. In fact it turns out to be virtually infinitesimal. As Roger Penrose remarks,

> How big was the original phase-space volume . . . that the Creator had to aim for in order to provide a universe compatible with the second law of thermodynamics and with what we now observe? . . . The Creator's aim must have been [precise] to an accuracy of one part in $10^{10^{123}}$. This is an extraordinary figure. One could not possibly even *write the number down* in full, in the ordinary denary notation: it would be "1" followed by 10^{123} successive "0"s! Even if we were to write a "0" on each separate proton and on each separate neutron in the entire universe—and we could throw in all the other particles as well for good measure—we should fall far short of writing down the figure needed. [Such is] the precision needed to set the universe on its course.[71]

To circumvent such vast improbabilities as one part in $10^{10^{123}}$, cosmologists like Alan Guth and Frank Tipler inflate the number of possible worlds where human beings might have arisen. Given an infinite number of possible worlds, any event that has positive probability, however small, is sure to happen in at least one of those possible worlds. So long as humanity has a positive probability of arising, it is therefore sure to arise in some possible world. And since only those worlds where humanity arises will have human beings that recognize their good fortune of being in a world that gave rise to them, chance becomes a perfectly acceptable way of accounting for humanity.

There is a catch, however: namely, the status of these possible worlds. Given infinitely many possible worlds, anything that's not logically impossible is sure to happen in at least one (and in fact infinitely many) of these possible worlds. The problem is that we have no evidence for any worlds other than our own. Moreover, since possible worlds are by definition causally inaccessible to our own actual world, there can be no evidence for their existence except that they render probable otherwise vastly improbable events. This move, to bolster an otherwise failing chance hypothesis by artificially inflating its probabilistic resources (i.e., the number of opportunities for the event) is statistically fallacious. I call it the *inflationary fallacy*.[72]

What then to do with these vast improbabilities? Many astronomers are opting for design. Even George Greenstein, who rejects design, muses, "As we survey all the evidence, the thought insistently arises that some super-natural agency . . . must be involved. Is it possible that suddenly, with-out intending to, we have stumbled upon scientific proof of the existence of a Supreme Being? Was it God who stepped in and so providentially crafted the cosmos for our benefit?"[73] In the same vein Fred Hoyle com-ments, "A commonsense interpretation of the facts suggests that a super intellect has monkeyed with physics, as well as chemistry and biology, and that there are no blind forces worth speaking about in nature."[74]

The universe just exactly suits us. Granted, it needs to suit us if we are going to be here at all. But that doesn't make the fine-tuning of the uni-verse any less amazing or chance any more plausible. We are not in the position of a lottery winner who knows there were many other lottery players competing with him or her. The lottery winner has positive evi-dence for other lottery players. Our universe is unique—we have no evi-dence for others like it. The fact that our universe happens to support life cannot therefore be explained by saying our universe was the lucky win-ner in a cosmic lottery in which most universes end up being lifeless. Our universe is fine-tuned, and chance is not a plausible explanation of its fine-tuning.

Biologists by and large agree. Most reject what could be called the "selection effect argument." According to this argument, just as the win-ner of a lottery is shocked at winning it, so we are shocked to have evolved. But the lottery was bound to have a winner, and so too some-thing was bound to have evolved. The appeal here is to a selection effect: Something vastly improbable was bound to happen, and so the fact that it happened to us (i.e., that we were selected—hence the name *selection effect*) does not preclude chance.[75] This argument is fallacious. It confuses a necessary condition (i.e., our being selected) with an explanation (i.e., why us).

The selection effect argument has been refuted by philosophers John Leslie, John Earman and Richard Swinburne.[76] It has also been refuted by biologists Francis Crick, Bernd-Olaf Küppers and Hubert Yockey.[77] Swin-burne's refutation is perhaps the most memorable:

> Suppose that a madman kidnaps a victim and shuts him in a room with a cardshuffling machine. The machine shuffles ten packs of cards simulta-neously and then draws a card from each pack and exhibits simultaneously

the ten cards. The kidnapper tells the victim that he will shortly set the machine to work and it will exhibit its first draw, but that unless the draw consists of an ace of hearts from each pack, the machine will simultaneously set off an explosion which will kill the victim, in consequence of which he will not see which cards the machine drew. The machine is then set to work, and to the amazement and relief of the victim the machine exhibits an ace of hearts drawn from each pack. The victim thinks that this extraordinary fact needs an explanation in terms of the machine having been rigged in some way. But the kidnapper, who now reappears, casts doubt on this suggestion. "It is hardly surprising," he says, "that the machine [drew] only aces of hearts. You could not possibly see anything else. For you would not be here to see anything at all, if any other cards had been drawn." But of course the victim is right and the kidnapper is wrong. There is indeed something extraordinary in need of explanation in ten aces of hearts being drawn. The fact that this peculiar order is a necessary condition of the draw being perceived at all makes what is perceived no less extraordinary and in need to explanation.[78]

In particular, selection effects do nothing to render chance an adequate explanation of specified complexity.[79]

A.7 Applying the Math to Biology
Objection: Specified complexity is a purely mathematical construct and therefore irrelevant to biology. It cannot speak to biological concerns, only to mathematical concerns.

This objection claims that mathematicians are muscling into the biologists' domain, trying to impose mathematical strictures that don't properly apply in biology. Biologists have been raising this objection at least since the 1966 Wistar Symposium when the mathematician Marcel Schützenberger challenged neo-Darwinism on complexity-theoretic grounds. At that symposium the biologists (notably C. H. Waddington and Ernst Mayr) simply dismissed Schützenberger's challenge. Instead of meeting his argument, they reasserted that here we are the result of evolution and hence something must be wrong with Schützenberger's analysis.[80]

Something is wrong indeed, but where does the fault lie? Is it that mathematicians have muscled into the biologists' domain or that biologists have discovered facts that are subject to mathematical analysis? Who gets to decide the relevance of mathematics to biology? Consider a postal worker who must deliver 101 letters to 100 mailboxes. There's a simple mathematical theorem known as the *pigeonhole principle,* which asserts that filling N slots with N+1 items entails that some slot will contain more than one item. Suppose now a mathematician tells the postal worker that one of those mailboxes will have to contain at least two letters. An irate postal worker may respond, "Who are you to tell me my business? What do you know about filling mailboxes with letters? Your pigeonhole principle is just a mathematical construct that is irrelevant to the actual stuffing of mailboxes with letters." Nonetheless, despite years of experience stuffing mailboxes, the postal worker is mistaken. The pigeonhole principle is all too relevant to the postal worker's task.

Specified complexity does indeed apply to biology. In fact it applies better to biology than it does to some of the toy examples considered in chapter five. This may seem counterintuitive since one's initial impulse is to think that specified complexity works just fine for toy examples, like writing letters on a page, but can't possibly work for biological reality, which is so much richer than these toy examples. At my public lectures on intelligent design, biologists often insist that one can't assign probabilities/complexities to biological systems with any degree of confidence (recall that the complexity in the complexity-specification criterion is actually a probability—something is complex to the degree that it is improbable; see section 5.3).

But in fact for many biological systems we can assign probabilities with more confidence than we can for toy examples. Take for instance the probability that by randomly throwing ink on a sheet of paper we should obtain the following phrase from *Hamlet:* METHINKS IT IS LIKE A WEASEL (see sections 5.3 and 6.5). What is the probability of getting this phrase by chance? A precise determination of probabilities is beyond our ability. Do we permit a host of typefaces, sizes, possible spatial positions and so on? Do we permit script or only Roman characters? Do we permit simple ciphers (e.g., a Caesar cipher that moves each letter a fixed number of letter spaces)? The possibilities are enormous and intractable.

That doesn't stop the probabilist, however. In practice a probabilist does not worry about all these possibilities but rather considers that this sequence of 28 letters and spaces is one in 27^{28} possible sequences of capital letters and spaces and then assigns this probability as an *upper bound* for the actual probability. The probabilist reasons as follows: "Even if you could by randomly spewing ink generate actual letters by chance (a generous concession at that), the probability of obtaining METHINKS IT IS

LIKE A WEASEL would still be no more than one in 27^{28}." Though not able to compute exact probabilities here, the probabilist is able reliably to assign upper bounds to these probabilities.

Now unlike the probabilist, who can do no better than compute upper bounds for the probabilities of letter sequences, the biologist is capable of computing probabilities for nucleotide and amino acid sequences exactly. Individual nucleotides and amino acids do not come in different sizes or fonts. They are not separated by different degrees of leading or kerning. The nucleotides in DNA can be stitched together in only one way, namely, along a sugar-phosphate backbone. So too the amino acids in a protein can be stitched together in only one way, namely, as peptide bonds. There are exactly four nucleotides that make up DNA and twenty amino acids that make up proteins. Nucleotides and amino acids are therefore alphabets whose sequencing does not allow the many degrees of freedom we encounter in ordinary writing.

Sequencing the letters from these alphabets is conceptually simpler than sequencing the letters from our everyday Roman alphabet. Because with our alphabet we have to worry about fonts, sizes, shading, leading, kerning and such, we have to idealize our probability calculations for letter sequences from the Roman alphabet. Thus we have to consciously ignore all the particularities of ink on paper and focus solely on the sequencing of Roman letters. As a result our probability calculations for Roman letter sequences are never exact but constitute an upper bound. On the other hand, the probability of getting a protein with 100 amino acids by chance is exactly one in 20^{100}. So, too, the probability of getting a particular DNA sequence of length 100 by chance is exactly one in 4^{100}.[81] Nucleotides and amino acids form alphabets. This is not a metaphor or analogy. It is literally true to say that DNA is a code and that the transcription-translation mechanism maps nucleotide sequences to amino acid sequences.[82]

This is not to say that all biological systems can be assigned exact probabilities. In the case of Michael Behe's irreducibly complex biochemical systems, we won't be able to calculate exact probabilities. Nonetheless we can calculate upper bounds for the probabilities of these systems. Behe's irreducibly complex biochemical systems are protein machines built from finitely many discrete proteins. Experimentally one can determine what are called *empirical probabilities* for the formation of functional proteins. To do this, one sequences amino acids in a test tube according to some stochastic process and then determines what proportion are functional. That experimentally determined proportion then determines what probabilists call an *empirical probability*. Similarly one can treat the individual proteins as givens and calculate the combinatorial possibilities of uniting the right proteins to form a given irreducibly complex biochemical machine. This combinatorial calculation then assigns an upper bound for the probability of such systems. None of this is far-fetched or bizarre. Indeed biologists are already doing such calculations.[83]

Mathematicians have not muscled into the biologists' domain. Rather biologists have uncovered certain facts to which mathematics applies. The application of mathematics to these facts has been unsettling for some biologists. Even so, the proper response of biologists is to meet this challenge of mathematics head on. The wrong response is to keep oneself uninformed about mathematics, assert that mathematics is largely irrelevant to the biological enterprise and continue business as usual. Disdain for mathematics does nothing to foster scientific inquiry. Mathematics does indeed elucidate biological complexity. It is ignorance or dogmatism to claim otherwise.

A.8 David Hume's Objections
Objection: Design in biology is either an argument from analogy or an inductive generalization based on a sample of size zero. In neither case is design therefore a compelling argument.

In his *Dialogues Concerning Natural Religion* David Hume raised two main criticisms against design. One criticism is that design at best constitutes a weak argument from analogy. The other criticism is that design fails as an inductive generalization since there is no prior sample on which to base it. Both Hume's criticisms miss the mark. Inferring design is neither an argument from analogy nor an inductive generalization but an inference to the best explanation. Inference to the best explanation, as we saw in chapter seven, remains a valid mode of scientific reasoning. Hume's refutation of design therefore attacks a straw man.

That design is merely an argument from analogy is perhaps the better known of Hume's criticisms. It is still the criticism that for many philosophers of religion remains decisive against design. Schematically an argument from analogy takes the following form: We are given two objects, U and V, which share certain properties, call them A, B, C and D. U and V are therefore similar with respect to A, B, C and D. Now suppose we know that U has some property Q, and suppose further that we want to determine whether V also has property Q. An argument from analogy then warrants that V has property Q because U and V share properties A, B, C and D, and U has property Q. In terms of premises and conclusion the argument from analogy therefore looks as in figure A.1.

In the case of Paley's watchmaker argument, U is a watch, V is an organism and the property Q is that something is intelligently designed. For the watch there is no question that it actually is intelligently designed. For the organism, on the other hand, this is not so clear. Yet because the watch and the organism share several features in common, call them A, B, C and D (functional interdependence of parts, self-propulsion, etc.), we are, according to the argument from analogy, warranted in concluding that organisms are also intelligently designed. In terms of premises and conclusion the argument looks as in figure A.2.

Although arguments from analogy can be intuitively appealing, they are not valid deductive arguments for which the truth of the premises guarantees the truth of the conclusion. Sometimes an argument from analogy leads us to the right conclusion as in figure A.3. But at other times it leads us astray, as in figure A.4.

> U has property Q.
> U and V share properties A, B, C and D.
> Therefore V also has property Q.

Figure A.1. An argument from analogy

> Watches are intelligently designed.
> Watches and organisms are similar.
> Therefore organisms are also intelligently designed.

Figure A.2. Paley's watchmaker argument à la Hume

The chief difficulty with arguments from analogy is that they are always also arguments from disanalogy. If U and V were identical, there would be no question about V having property Q if U has that property. The reason there is a question about V having property Q is because U and V are not identical. What this means schematically is that there are properties I, J, K and L that U possesses but which V does not possess. U has properties A, B, C and D, which V shares, but also properties I, J, K and L, which V does not share. Moreover U has property Q. The big question, therefore, is whether Q is a property like A, B, C and D, which V shares with U, or whether Q is a property like I, J, K and L, which V does not share with U. Without additional information the argument from analogy has no way of deciding this question.

By itself, therefore, the argument from analogy provides no compelling support for its conclusion. The property that stands in question, here Q, might just as well be part of the disanalogy as part of the analogy. At best, therefore, the argument from analogy gives us reason to suspect that two objects that share similarities might share still an additional similarity. Analogies may thus point us to further analogies. Yet without additional information we can draw no definite conclusion.[84]

> In human beings, the blood circulates.
> Human beings and dogs are similar.
> Therefore in dogs, the blood circulates.

Figure A.3. A correct conclusion from analogy

> In human beings, the blood circulates.
> Human beings and plants are similar.
> Therefore in plants, the blood circulates.

Figure A.4. An incorrect conclusion from analogy

If the design argument is nothing but an argument from analogy, then it is a very weak argument indeed. Fortunately there is much more to the design argument than an analogy. Elliott Sober, for instance, in his text on the philosophy of biology cashes out the design argument not as an argument from analogy nor even as an inductive argument but as an inference to the best explanation. As he puts it,

> Hume did not think of the design argument [as an inference to the best explanation]. For him . . . it [was] an argument from analogy, or an induc-

tive argument. This alternate conception of the argument makes a great deal of difference. Hume's criticisms are quite powerful if the argument has the character he attributes to it. But if the argument is, as I maintain, an inference to the best explanation, Hume's criticisms entirely lose their bite.[85]

Thus instead of construing Paley's argument as an argument from analogy, Sober develops it as an inference to the best explanation:

[Paley's] argument involves comparing two different arguments—the first about a watch, the second about living things. We can represent the statements involved in the watch argument as follows:

A: The watch is intricate and well suited to the task of timekeeping.

W_1: The watch is the product of intelligent design.

W_2: The watch is the product of random physical processes.

Paley claims that $P(A \mid W_1) \gg P(A \mid W_2)$ [i.e., the probability of A given that W_1 is the case is *much bigger* than the probability of A given that W_2 is the case]. He then says that the same pattern of analysis applies to the following triplet of statements:

B: Living things are intricate and well-suited to the task of surviving and reproducing.

L_1: Living things are the product of intelligent design.

L_2: Living things are the product of random physical processes.

Paley argues that if you agree with him about the watch, you also should agree that $P(B \mid L_1) \gg P(B \mid L_2)$. Although the subject matters of the two arguments are different, their logic is the same. Both are inferences to the best explanation in which the Likelihood Principle [a statistical principle which says that for a set of competing hypotheses, the hypothesis that confers maximum probability on the data is the best explanation] is used to determine which hypothesis is better supported by the observations.[86]

Sober therefore views the design argument as a perfectly reasonable argument. Yet if the design argument is such a great argument, why doesn't Sober subscribe to it? Enter Charles Darwin. Darwin threw a new hypothesis into the mix. In Paley's day there were only two competing hypotheses to explain the data B (= *Living things are intricate and well-suited to the task of surviving and reproducing*). These hypotheses were L_1 (= *Living things are the product of intelligent design*) and L_2 (= *Living things are the product of random physical processes*). Given only L_1 and L_2, L_1 is the clear winner. But with the Darwinian revolution, Sober now has a third hypothesis, L_3: *Living things are the product of variation and selection*. According to Sober, once the playing field is increased to include the Darwinian hypothesis L_3, L_1 no longer fares very well. To be sure, L_1 still explains the data B quite nicely. But it fails, according to Sober, to account for additional data like the fossil record, suboptimality of design and vestigial organs. Prior to Darwin, Paley had offered what was the best explanation of life. With Darwin the best explanation shifted.

Inference to the best explanation is inherently competitive (cf. section 7.4). Best explanations are not best across all times and circumstances. Rather they are best relative to the hypotheses currently available and the background information we have to evaluate those hypotheses. Sober therefore has to leave the door open to design even though he doesn't think it very likely that design will ever pose a serious threat to Darwinism. He concedes, "Perhaps one day, [design] will be formulated in such a way that the auxiliary assumptions it adopts are independently supported. My claim is that no [design theorist] has succeeded in doing this yet."[87] The burden of this book has been to show that design remains a live issue and can once again be formulated as the best explanation for the origin and development of life.

Hume's other criticism of the design argument was that it constitutes a failed inductive generalization. Since, as we've just seen, the design argument is an inference to the best explanation, and since an inference to the best explanation need not be an inductive generalization, Hume's second criticism of the design argument fails as well. Sober elaborates:

> [Hume] contends that if we are to have good reason to think that the organisms in *our* world are the product of intelligent design, then we must have looked at lots of *other* worlds and observed intelligent designers producing organisms there. But how many such worlds have we observed? The answer is, *not even one*. So the inductive argument is as weak as it possibly could be; its sample size is zero.
>
> Once again, it is important to see that an inference to the best explanation need not obey the rules that Hume stipulates. For example, consider the suggestion by Alvarez *et al*. [1980] that the mass extinction that occurred at the end of the Cretaceous period was caused by a large meteorite crashing to earth and sending up a giant dust cloud. Although there is plenty of room to disagree about whether this is plausible, . . . it is quite irrelevant that we have never witnessed meteorite strikes producing mass extinctions "in other

worlds." Inference to the best explanation is different from an inductive sampling argument.[88]

Although Sober is right to identify the design argument as an inference to the best explanation, to leave the matter here does not go far enough. Design is not merely an argument but also a scientific theory. Specified complexity in particular provides an information-theoretic apparatus for understanding the designed features of the physical world. Whereas the work of a design argument is done as soon as one uncovers a designing intelligence, this is only the start for a theory of intelligent design. To analyze the information in a designed structure, to trace its causal history, to determine its function and to ascertain how it could have been constructed are just a few of the questions that a theory of intelligent design addresses. Intelligent design far exceeds the design arguments of the past.

A.9 Mundane Versus Transcendent Designers
Objection: There is a vast difference between mundane designers, like humans or extraterrestrials, and transcendent designers. We have no experience of transcendent designers and can make no scientific claims about them.

According to this objection, we know what it is for a mundane designer to act as an intelligent cause, but when it comes to a transcendent designer, we haven't a clue. But how do we know that a mundane designer has acted as an intelligent cause? We *never* have direct contact with a designer's internal psychological states—and this is true for both mundane and transcendent designers. We know we are dealing with an intelligent cause only through the effects that such causes leave behind. Intelligence is *always* inferred. Knowledge of intelligence is never a direct intuition.

Indeed the whole point of Michael Behe's irreducible complexity and my own specified complexity is that these are empirical features of *mundane objects* that reliably signal intelligent causation. Whether these mundane objects trace their causal histories through mundane or transcendent designers is irrelevant. When we see irreducible complexity or specified complexity, we know that an intelligent cause has been present and acted—even if we know nothing else. This is not an argument from ignorance. Behe and I offer in-principle arguments for why undirected natural causes (i.e., chance, necessity or some combination of the two) cannot produce irreducible and specified complexity. Moreover we offer sound arguments for why intelligent causation best explains irreducible and specified complexity. The ontological status of that intelligent cause simply does not arise in the analysis. Consequently there is no principled way to make the analytic cut between mundane and transcendent designers. The only way to make this cut is by presupposing naturalism, which is precisely the point at issue.

Thomas Reid understood this point clearly. He understood that the capacity of humans to infer intelligence from events and circumstances in the physical world is an indispensable component of human rationality, a point that the rationalist and empiricist critiques of design never adequately grasped. To refute these critiques Reid gave an account of how we infer intelligent agency that remains valid to this day. To be sure, Reid did not develop a full-fledged criterion of design (like irreducible or specified complexity). Nevertheless his intuitions were so good and his response to David Hume so perceptive that it is fitting to conclude this appendix with a sample of Reid's thoughts on design.

The following passage is taken from Reid's lectures on natural theology. He delivered these lectures at the University of Glasgow during February and March of 1780. (Hume's *Dialogues Concerning Natural Religion* appeared in 1779.) What follows is an abridged version of the seventh of these lectures. I've modernized punctuation and spelling. Here is the text:

> A man's wisdom can be known only by its effects, by the signs of it in his conduct—his eloquence by the signs of it in his discourse. In this same manner we judge of his courage, and strength of mind, and of all his other virtues. It is only by their effects that we can discern these qualities of his mind.
>
> Yet it may be observed that we judge of these *talents* with as little hesitation as if they were objects of our senses. One we pronounce to be a perfect idiot incapable of doing any thing that will be valid in law; another to have understanding and to be accountable for his actions. One we pronounce to be open, another cunning. One ignorant, another knowing. Every man of common understanding forms such judgments of those he converses with. He can no more avoid it than he can [avoid] seeing objects that are placed before his eyes.
>
> Yet in all these the talent is not immediately perceived; [rather] it is discerned only by the effects it produces. From this it is evident that it is no less

a part of the human constitution to judge of powers by their effects than of corporeal objects by the senses. We see that such judgments are common to all men and absolutely necessary in the affairs of life. Now every judgment of this kind is only an application of that general rule, that from marks of intelligence and wisdom in effects a wise and intelligent cause may be inferred. . . .

Cicero in his tract *De Natura Deorum* speaks thus: Can anything done by chance have all the marks of design? If a man throws dies and both turn up aces, if he should throw 400 times, would chance throw up 400 aces? Colors thrown carelessly upon a canvas may come up to appear as a human face, but would they form a picture beautiful as the pagan Venus? A hog grubbing in the earth with his snout may turn up something like the letter A, but would he turn up the words of a complete sentence?

Thus, in order to show the absurdity of supposing what has the marks of design could arise from chance, [Cicero] gives a variety of examples where the absurdity is palpable. . . . And we find other authors arguing in the same way. The ingenious Mr. Hutchinson . . . has drawn arguments from chances to show that a regular arrangement of parts must proceed from designs—that they could not proceed from chances. It may be remarked that this doctrine of chances as a branch of mathematics is not yet a hundred years old, but the truth of this principle [that design may be inferred from the marks of design] has gained the assent of all since the beginning of the world. . . .

The most direct attack against this principle has been made by Mr. Hume, who puts an argument against it in the mouth of an Epicurean [cf. Hume's *Dialogues Concerning Natural Religion*], on which he seems to lay great stress. It is this, that the production of the universe is a singular effect, to which there is no similar instance. Therefore, we can draw no conclusion from it, whether it is made by wisdom and intelligence or without. I shall consider a little the form of this objection.

The amount of it is this, that if we were accustomed to see worlds produced, some by wisdom and others without it, and saw always such worlds as ours produced by a wise cause, the conclusion would then be [that] this world of ours was made by wise contrivance. But as we have no experience of this kind, therefore we can conclude nothing about the matter. This conclusion of his is built on the supposition of past experience finding two things constantly united. But this I showed to be a mistake. [Earlier in the lecture Reid argued, "Experience may show us a constant conjunction between two things in those cases where both are perceived. But if one only is perceived, experience never can show it constantly conjoined with the other." And since intelligence never is directly perceived but only inferred, Hume's claim that the design argument constitutes a species of induction cannot be right.]

No man ever saw wisdom, and if he does not [infer wisdom] from the marks of it, he can form no conclusions respecting anything of his fellow creatures. How should I know that any of this audience have understanding? It is only by the effects of it on their conduct and behavior, and this leads me to suppose that such behavior proceeds only from understanding.

But says Hume, unless you know it by experience, you know nothing of it. If this is the case, I never could know it at all. Hence it appears that whoever maintains that there is no force in the [general rule that from marks of intelligence and wisdom in effects a wise and intelligent cause may be inferred], denies the existence of any intelligent being but himself. He has the same evidence for wisdom and intelligence in God as in a father or brother or friend. He infers it in both from its effects, and these effects he discovers in the one as well as the other.[89]

Notes

Chapter 1: Recognizing the Divine Finger

[1]Episode 2F10, "And Maggie Makes Three," original airdate January 22, 1995.

[2]*If A, then B* is logically equivalent to *If not B, then not A.*

[3]From Hanson's well-known essay titled "What I Do Not Believe," quoted in Bruce Gordon, "Living Reasons: Blaise Pascal and the Rationality of Religious Belief," *Foundations* 5, no. 1 (1997): 6. Hanson's challenge parallels Cleanthes' remark in David Hume's *Dialogues Concerning Natural Religion* (1779; reprint, Buffalo, N.Y.: Prometheus, 1989), p. 37:

> Suppose, therefore, that an articulate voice were heard in the clouds, much louder and more melodious than any which human art could ever reach: Suppose, that this voice were extended in the same instant over all nations, and spoke to each nation in its own language and dialect: Suppose, that the words delivered not only contain a just sense and meaning, but convey some instruction altogether worthy of a benevolent Being, superior to mankind: Could you possibly hesitate a moment concerning the cause of this voice? and must you not instantly ascribe it to some design or purpose?

[4]The relevant rule of logic is called *modus ponens:* Given the conditional *If A, then B* and the statement *A*, the statement *B* follows immediately.

[5]According to 1 John 4:12, no human being has ever seen God.

[6]Although the following sections focus on examples from Scripture, we need hardly confine our attention here. The ancients throughout the Mediterranean world understood this general scheme for validating decisions through signs. See, for instance, Deborah Bennett, *Randomness* (Cambridge, Mass.: Harvard University Press, 1998), pp. 74-75.

Nor do we need to confine our attention to antiquity. The Jewish rabbis also understood the general scheme for validating decisions through signs. Thus Rabbi Isaac ben Mosheh Aramah, writing in the fifteenth century, described the use of lots by which Jonah was found guilty of bringing disaster to his fellow seafarers: "For it is impossible for it to be otherwise than that the lot should fall on one of them whether he be innocent or guilty. . . . However, the meaning of their statement 'let us cast lots' is to cast lots *many times.* Therefore the plural—*goralot*—is used rather than [the singular]. . . . They did so and *cast lots many times* and every time the lot fell on Jonah and consequently the matter was verified for them. It follows then that the casting of *a* lot indicates primarily a reference to chance" (quoted in Bennett, *Randomness*, p. 75).

Bennett comments (*Randomness*, pp. 75-76):

> The cast of a single lot is considered to be chance, whereas a cast many times repeated is considered to be a sign of God and therefore not chance. In a similar fashion, the Rabbi remarks on the role of chance in the selection of lots for the scapegoat, again emphasizing that the achievement of the good omen of the lot "for the Lord" in the right hand ought only to be considered a [sign] if it happens many times.

For a lot to land repeatedly in the same way would be extraordinary (in modern terms, highly improbable) and thus, according to Rabbi ben Mosheh Aramah, clearly signified the divine will.

[7]I am indebted to Jack Collins for drawing my attention to this example.

[8]Origen, *Origen Against Celsus*, The Ante-Nicene Fathers 4, ed. A. Roberts and J. Donaldson (Grand Rapids, Mich.: Eerdmans, 1989), pp. 395-669.

[9]Miguel de Unamuno, *The Tragic Sense of Life* (1913; reprint, New York: Dover, 1990), chap. 8.

[10]Skeptics are fond of pointing to the neo-Pythagorean philosopher Apollonius of Tyana as a messiah figure who supposedly demonstrated many of the same signs as Jesus, including a

miraculous birth. But in the case of Apollonius it's clear that the parallels with Jesus were concocted by anti-Christian writers to "disparage the uniqueness of the Christian Gospel" (see F. L. Cross, ed., *The Oxford Dictionary of the Christian Church*, 2nd ed., s.v. "Apollonius of Tyana"). For a more extensive account of Apollonius, see Everett Ferguson, *Backgrounds of Early Christianity*, 2nd ed. (Grand Rapids, Mich.: Eerdmans, 1993), pp. 361-63. One contemporary skeptic who in his public lectures gets anti-Christian mileage out of Apollonius is Michael Shermer. Cf. his *Why People Believe Weird Things: Pseudoscience, Superstition and Other Confusions of Our Time* (New York: W. H. Freeman, 1998). The only well-substantiated accounts of a virgin birth and a bodily resurrection are those of Jesus.

[11]Cf. 2 Peter 1:20-21 (KJV): "No prophecy of the scripture is of any private interpretation. For the prophecy came not in old time by the will of man: but holy men of God spake as they were moved by the Holy Ghost."

[12]Friedrich Schleiermacher, the father of liberal theology, championed this view, and it is still with us (see chapter two).

[13]See William Dembski, *The Design Inference* (Cambridge: Cambridge University Press, 1998), chap. 2.

[14]Ibid., chap. 1.

Chapter 2: The Critique of Miracles

[1]Friedrich Schleiermacher, *The Christian Faith*, ed. H. R. Mackintosh and J. S. Stewart (1830; reprint, Edinburgh: T & T Clark, 1989), p. 60.

[2]Spinoza's treatment of miracles in his *Tractatus Theologico-Politicus* set the tone for the Enlightenment. See Baruch Spinoza, *Tractatus Theologico-Politicus*, trans. S. Shirley, intro. B. S. Gregory (1670; reprint, Leiden: Brill, 1989), chap. 6.

[3]See Norman L. Torrey, *Voltaire and the English Deists* (New Haven, Conn.: Yale University Press, 1930).

[4]Lessing's classic statement of this thesis is "Accidental truths of history can never become the proof of necessary truths of reason." See Gotthold Ephraim Lessing, *On the Proof of the Spirit and Power*, in *Lessing's Theological Writings*, ed. and trans. H. Chadwick (1777; reprint, Stanford, Calif.: Stanford University Press, 1967), p. 53.

[5]David Hume, *Dialogues Concerning Natural Religion* (1779; reprint, Buffalo, N.Y.: Prometheus, 1989).

[6]For Kant's rejection of the proofs for God's existence, see Immanuel Kant, *Critique of Pure Reason*, trans. N. K. Smith (1787; reprint, New York: St. Martin's, 1929), pp. 495-524. For his treatment of God as a regulative ideal, see Immanuel Kant, *Critique of Practical Reason* (1788; reprint, New York: Liberal Arts Press, 1956), pp. 128-36.

[7]Schleiermacher, *Christian Faith*, p. 60.

[8]At the very opening of the *Summa Theolgiae* Thomas Aquinas shows how distinct sciences can come to identical conclusions (e.g., astronomy and physics both coming to the conclusion that the earth is round). Aquinas's view is that theology and philosophy overlap substantially, and where they overlap they agree. Since what is known philosophically is for Aquinas known apodeictically, philosophical knowledge, which by its very nature comprises truths of reason, can for Aquinas establish truths of the Christian faith. See Thomas Aquinas, *God and the Order of Creation: Summa Theologiae*, vol. 1 in *The Basic Writings of Saint Thomas Aquinas*, ed. A. C. Pegis (1270; reprint, New York: Random House, 1945), p. 6.

[9]In his *Institutes* Calvin writes, "Most people believe that there is a God, and they consider that the gospel history and the remaining parts of the Scripture are true. Such a judgment is on a par with the judgments we ordinarily make concerning those things which are either narrated as having once taken place, or which we have seen as eyewitnesses." See John Calvin, *Institutes of the Christian Religion*, The Library of Christian Classics 20, ed. J. T. McNeill, trans. F. L. Battles (1559; reprint, Philadelphia: Westminster Press, 1960), 3.2.9. Calvin regards such a faith, however, as totally inadequate: "Most

people, when they hear [the term *faith*] understand nothing deeper than a common assent to the gospel history. In fact, when faith is discussed in the schools, they call God simply the object of faith, and by fleeting speculations, as we have elsewhere stated, lead miserable souls astray rather than direct them to a definite goal." See Calvin, *Institutes*, 3.2.1. Calvin denies that mere assent to the gospel history is adequate for eliciting faith. The point to recognize, however, is that Calvin does not dispute that assent to the "gospel history" is fully rational and well-supported.

[10]Quoted from Gregory's introduction to Spinoza's *Tractatus Theologico-Politicus*, p. 27.

[11]Ibid.

[12]Ibid.

[13]Ibid., p. 30.

[14]Spinoza was a thoroughgoing elitist. He sharply distinguished the masses of common people from the enlightened philosophers like himself. Contrast this with Christ who appealed to the masses and rejected the intellectuals of his day, to wit, the Pharisees.

[15]H. van der Loos, *The Miracles of Jesus* (Leiden: Brill, 1965), pp. 6-7.

[16]Spinoza, *Tractatus Theologico-Politicus*, p. 126.

[17]David Hume, *An Enquiry Concerning Human Understanding* (1748; reprint, LaSalle, Ill.: Open Court, 1958), chap. 10.

[18]Spinoza, *Tractatus Theologico-Politicus*, p. 124.

[19]Against Spinoza's epistemological critique, one can argue that knowledge of a universal negation does not demand an explicit identification and rejection of each thing being quantified over. Yes, for an event E to be a miracle, it must be the case that for all natural laws L, L does not explain E. It does not follow, however, that for a subject S to know that E is a miracle, S has to explicitly identify each possible natural law L and then verify that L does not explain E. Scientists claim to know plenty of universal negations without ever having explicitly identified and rejected everything to which those negations might apply.

For example, physicists are convinced there are no perpetual motion machines. They maintain this conviction without examining all the mechanical devices in the universe, much less determining for each of these devices whether its motion eventually halts. Physicists have theoretical reasons for rejecting perpetual motion machines, most notably the second law of thermodynamics. So too there can be theoretical reasons for thinking that natural laws are incapable of explaining an event—and thus for designating an event a miracle—apart from a complete and explicit examination of every single natural law which might explain that event. See for instance my article "On the Very Possibility of Intelligent Design" in J. P. Moreland, ed., *The Creation Hypothesis* (Downers Grove, Ill.: InterVarsity Press, 1994), pp. 113-38.

[20]Quoted in Richard Brandt, *The Philosophy of Schleiermacher: The Development of His Theory of Scientific and Religious Knowledge* (New York: Harper, 1941), p. 36.

[21]Friedrich Schleiermacher, *On Religion: Speeches to Its Cultured Despisers*, trans. J. Oman (1799; reprint, Louisville, Ky.: Westminster John Knox, 1994), p. 40.

[22]Brandt, *Philosophy of Schleiermacher*, p. 146.

[23]Compare bk. 1, def. 7 in Spinoza's *Ethics* with Schleiermacher, *Christian Faith*, §81.2, p. 334.

[24]For a helpful historical discussion of the traditional understanding of miracles, see Loos, *Miracles of Jesus*, pp. 37-42.

[25]Schleiermacher, *Christian Faith*, §47, p. 180.

[26]Ibid., §14.3, p. 71.

[27]Ibid., §47, pp. 181-82. Actually Schleiermacher introduces an unnecessary subtlety at this point in the argument, distinguishing miracles in which something that was supposed to happen fails to happen (negative miracles) from miracles in which something that was not supposed to happen does happen (positive miracles). The logic is the same for both cases, however, since in either case something still happens. (Even the failure of some event happening constitutes an event.)

[28]A condition *If A, then B* is said to constitute an entailment relation between A and B provided that it is impossible for B to be false if A is true. The conditional *If the president likes me, I'll be promoted* may be true but does not constitute an entailment relation since there may be circumstances outside the president's control that prevent me from being promoted even if the president likes me, i.e., it is possible for me to miss being promoted even if the president likes me. On the other hand, the conditional *If the president fires me, I shall not be promoted* is necessarily true and constitutes an entailment relation since there is no possibility of me being promoted once I have been fired.

[29]Quoted in Brandt, *The Philosophy of Schleiermacher*, p. 214.

[30]Isaac Newton, *Isaac Newton's Papers and Letters on Natural Philosophy*, ed. I. B. Cohen (Cambridge, Mass.: Harvard University Press, 1958), p. 302.

[31]Nancy R. Pearcey and Charles B. Thaxton, *The Soul of Science* (Wheaton, Ill.: Crossway, 1994), p. 90.

[32]More than half of Newton's writings were concerned solely with religion and alchemy (see Gregory's introduction to Spinoza, *Tractatus Theologico-Politicus*, p. 9).

[33]John Locke, *An Essay Concerning Human Understanding*, ed. A. C. Fraser (1690; reprint, Oxford: Clarendon Press, 1894), p. 382. See also the paragraphs on miracles in John Locke, *The Reasonableness of Christianity* (1695; reprint, Washington, D.C.: Regnery Gateway, 1989).

[34]Hume, *An Enquiry Concerning Human Understanding*, chap. 10.

[35]Peter Lipton's model of Inference to the Best Explanation (IBE) has no way of precluding "divine intervention" as the best explanation for a given phenomenon (Lipton, *Inference to the Best Explanation* [London: Routledge, 1991]).

[36]G. K. Chesterton, *The Quotable Chesterton*, ed. G. J. Marlin, R. P. Rabatin and J. L. Swan (Garden City, N.Y.: Image, 1987), p. 336.

[37]Raymond Bradley and Norman Swartz, *Possible Worlds: An Introduction to Logic and Its Philosophy* (Indianapolis: Hackett, 1979), pp. 147-49.

[38]Alan Richardson (*The Miracle-Stories of the Gospels* [United States: Harper & Brothers, 1942], p. 127) takes this position in discussing Jesus' miracles: "Only those who came in faith understood the meaning of the acts of power. That is why any discussion of the Gospel miracles must begin, as we began, with a consideration of the biblical theology, with the faith which illuminates their character and purpose."

[39]See Loos, *Miracles of Jesus*, p. 43.

[40]F. R. Tennant, *Miracle and Its Philosophical Presuppositions* (Cambridge: Cambridge University Press, 1925), p. 10.

[41]Process theologians, for instance, do this all the time. See Anna Case-Winters, *God's Power: Traditional Understandings and Contemporary Challenges* (Louisville, Ky.: Westminster John Knox, 1990), pt. 3.

[42]Schleiermacher and Spinoza employ the language of "ordination," "will" and "decrees" throughout their work and use these terms synonymously. When applied to God this language signifies the necessity of what is determined coming to pass. See Schleiermacher, *Christian Faith*, §54, p. 211ff., as well as Spinoza, *Tractatus Theologico-Politicus*, chap. 6, for examples of how they use these terms.

[43]Schleiermacher, *Christian Faith*, §47, p. 180.

[44]Ibid.

[45]In my subsequent discussion of efficacious prayer I have found Nancey Murphy's article "Does Prayer Make a Difference?" particularly helpful. This article appears in Ted Peters, ed., *Cosmos as Creation* (Nashville: Abingdon, 1989), pp. 235-45.

[46]Cf. Schleiermacher's discussion of human responsibility for sin in Schleiermacher, *Christian Faith*, §81.2, p. 334.

[47]Roy Weatherford, *The Implications of Determinism* (London: Routledge, 1991), p. 28.

[48]For a detailed treatment of methodological naturalism, see J. P. Moreland's article "Theistic Science and Methodological Naturalism" in Moreland, *Creation Hypothesis*, pp. 41-66.

[49]See Loos, *Miracles of Jesus*, pp. 6-8.

[50]John D. Barrow, *Theories of Everything: The Quest for Ultimate Explanation* (New York: Fawcett Columbine, 1991).

[51]Dudley Shapere, *Reason and the Search for Knowledge: Investigations in the Philosophy of Science* (Dordrecht: Reidel, 1984), pp. xix-xx.

Chapter 3: The Demise of British Natural Theology

[1]Strictly speaking, there has been not just one design argument but rather a whole family of design arguments. Nevertheless the common feature of these arguments is to look to some aspect of nature exhibiting the "marks of intelligence" (a phrase commonly employed by Thomas Reid), and from thence infer that a designer is responsible for those marks of intelligence. Cf. William Dembski, "The Design Argument," in *The History of Science and Religion in the Western Tradition: An Encyclopedia*, ed. G. B. Ferngren (New York: Garland, forthcoming).

[2]David Hull, *Darwin and His Critics: The Reception of Darwin's Theory of Evolution by the Scientific Community* (Cambridge, Mass.: Harvard University Press, 1973), p. 26.

[3]Typical in this regard are Adrian Desmond and James Moore, *Darwin* (New York: Warner, 1991); Michael Ruse, *Darwinism Defended* (Reading, Mass.: Addison-Wesley, 1982); Richard Dawkins, *The Blind Watchmaker* (New York: Norton, 1987); along with Hull, *Darwin and His Critics*. Even Peter Bowler and Neil Gillespie, who try to put as good a face on British natural theology as they can, reach the same conclusion; see Peter Bowler, *Evolution: The History of an Idea*, rev. ed. (Berkeley: University of California Press, 1989), and Neal Gillespie, *Charles Darwin and the Problem of Creation* (Chicago: University of Chicago Press, 1977).

In *The Strategy of Life: Teleology and Mechanics in Nineteenth Century German Biology* (Dordrecht: Reidel, 1982), Timothy Lenoir, who critiques Darwinism from the perspective of the nineteenth-century German teleomechanists (e.g., von Baer), nevertheless consistently distances the German teleomechanists from the British natural theologians. Thus in his discussion of von Baer and the German tradition in biology, Lenoir writes, "von Baer's position had nothing whatever to do with the suspension of natural laws through the intervention of a creator. . . . The origins of life are not to be dissociated from the organization of matter obeying physico-chemical laws" (p. 263).

As we shall see in the course of this chapter, miraculous interventions by a Creator were not necessary to the British natural theologians' conception of teleology, though in practice many of the British natural theologians did see teleology as mediated through divine miracles (cf. Buckland's "creative interference" later in this chapter). On the other hand, that there was an intelligent agent who by foresight and deliberate action—whether in violation or in harmony with natural laws—produced the cosmos, was an essential component of British natural theology. This latter notion was also rejected by the German teleo-mechanists. As Lenoir notes, "The German tradition . . . never made use of the design argument or the notion of a purposeful divine architect. This position was expunged by Kant as having no place in natural science" (p. 4).

[4]Elliott Sober, *Philosophy of Biology* (Boulder, Colo.: Westview, 1993), p. 29.

[5]Ibid., p. 52.

[6]The increasing tendency, however, was for God to act in concert with natural laws rather than by overriding them. This point will become clearer as we proceed.

[7]See, for instance, David Livingstone's account of Asa Gray in *Darwin's Forgotten Defenders: The Encounter Between Evangelical Theology and Evolutionary Thought* (Grand Rapids, Mich.: Eerdmans, 1987), pp. 60-64.

[8]The term *empirical content* will come up a number of times in this chapter, so it will help to have a definition. A proposition has empirical content if it rules out certain possible observations. As Robert Stalnaker puts it, "Content requires contingency. To learn something, to acquire information, is to rule out possibilities. To understand the information conveyed in a communication is to know what possibilities would be excluded by its truth" (Stalnaker,

Inquiry [Cambridge, Mass.: MIT Press, 1984], p. 85). By extension we then define a scientific theory as having empirical content if it entails or renders probable a proposition that has empirical content.

Now the crucial claim of natural theologians like Paley and Reid was that natural theology, and in particular design, had empirical content. Whether they were right is of course another matter, but what is clear is that since Darwin, design has largely been stripped of its empirical content. Thus it is possible for the contemporary philosopher of religion Richard Swinburne to advocate design and yet assert, "Complex animals and plants can be produced through generation by less complex animals and plants . . . and simple animals and plants can be produced by natural processes from inorganic matter" (Swinburne, *The Existence of God* [Oxford: Oxford University Press, 1979], p. 135). Another example of design without empirical content is Howard Van Till's notion of "creaturely capacities"—capacities implanted by God in nature to achieve the divine purposes yet with no possibility of being tested empirically (Howard Van Till, "Is Special Creationism a Heresy?" *Christian Scholar's Review* 22, no. 4 [1993]: 380-95).

⁹Sober, for instance, finds deficient Hume's arguments against design in the *Dialogues Concerning Natural Religion*. According to Hume the design argument is either an argument from analogy or an inductive generalization based on a sample of size zero so that in neither case can design constitute a compelling argument. But according to Sober, not only can the design argument be cashed out as an inference to the best explanation (a form of inference whose logic is distinct from arguments by analogy and inductive arguments and which thereby avoids Hume's objections entirely—see Peter Lipton, *Inference to the Best Explanation* [London: Routledge, 1991]), but the British natural theologians, notably Paley, did in fact cash it out this way (in particular, Paley's design argument does not stand or fall with his watchmaker analogy). According to Sober, Hume was therefore barking up the wrong tree (*Philosophy of Biology*, p. 33ff.). See also appendix A.8.

¹⁰Colin Brown, *Miracles and the Critical Mind* (Grand Rapids, Mich.: Eerdmans, 1984), p. 29.

¹¹Desmond and Moore, *Darwin*, p. 213.

¹²Ibid., p. 219.

¹³Others who have held that chair include Isaac Newton, Paul Dirac and Stephen Hawking.

¹⁴Buckland's Bridgewater treatise was on geology and mineralogy. See William Buckland, *Geology and Mineralogy Considered in Reference to Natural Theology* (London: Pickering, 1836).

¹⁵Desmond and Moore, *Darwin*, p. 213. Cf. Charles Babbage, *The Ninth Bridgewater Treatise* (London: Murray, 1836).

¹⁶This holds even if we allow for a probabilistic component in the laws.

¹⁷Thomas Reid, *Lectures on Natural Theology*, ed. E. Duncan and W. R. Eakin (1780; reprint, Washington, D.C.: University Press of America, 1981), p. 59.

¹⁸Gillespie, *Charles Darwin*, p. 146.

¹⁹Ibid.

²⁰Quoted from Desmond and Moore, *Darwin*, p. 603. Darwin made these remarks in 1873.

²¹Quoted from the second edition of the *OED*, s.v. "agnostic" and "agnosticism."

²²Desmond and Moore, *Darwin*, p. 568.

²³John Warwick Montgomery, "Is Man His Own God," in *Christianity for the Tough Minded: Essays in Support of an Intellectually Defensible Religious Commitment*, ed. J. W. Montgomery (Minneapolis: Bethany House, 1973), pp. 24-25.

²⁴See Gillespie, *Charles Darwin*, pp. 149-51.

²⁵See Reid, *Lectures on Natural Theology*, and William Paley, *Natural Theology: Or Evidences of the Existence and Attributes of the Deity Collected from the Appearances of Nature* (1802; reprint, Boston: Gould & Lincoln, 1852).

²⁶See Babbage's *Ninth Bridgewater Treatise;* and Charles Lyell, *Sir Charles Lyell's Scientific Journals on the Species Question*, ed. L. G. Wilson (New Haven, Conn.: Yale University Press, 1970), pp. 328, 408, 415, 426.

[27]Dawkins, *Blind Watchmaker*, p. 6.

[28]Cf. Desmond and Moore, "Never an Atheist," chap. 41 in *Darwin*.

[29]Hume, for instance, considers the following Epicurean move:

> A finite number of particles is only susceptible of finite transpositions: and it must happen, in an eternal duration, that every possible order or position must be tried an infinite number of times. This world, therefore, with all its events, even the most minute, has before been produced and destroyed, and will again be produced and destroyed, without any bounds and limitations. No one, who has a conception of the power of infinite, in comparison of finite, will ever scruple this determination.

David Hume, *Dialogues Concerning Natural Religion* (1779; reprint, Buffalo, N.Y.: Prometheus, 1989), p. 67.

[30]Dawkins, *Blind Watchmaker*, p. 6.

[31]It's not until the 1930s, with the work of the statistician Ronald Fisher and the geneticist J. B. S. Haldane, that the Darwinian mechanism came into its own in the neo-Darwinian synthesis.

[32]Gillespie, *Charles Darwin*, p. 147. The quote from Wright can be found in Hull, *Darwin and His Critics*, p. 386. For critical reviews of Darwin's work by Darwin's contemporaries see the latter source. Desmond and Moore, *Darwin*, chap. 38 presents a nice synopsis of the nineteenth-century criticisms against Darwin's selectionist mechanism.

[33]Cf. Robert Chambers, *Vestiges of the Natural History of Creation* (London: Churchill, 1844), which, though the most widely regarded of the British evolutionary writings prior to Darwin's *Origin of Species*, could not properly be regarded as a rigorous scientific text.

[34]Lenoir, *Strategy of Life*, p. 248.

[35]Hull, *Darwin and His Critics*, pp. 268-69.

[36]To this day a suitably updated version of Darwinism, known as the neo-Darwinian synthesis, remains the best naturalistic account available to explain life.

[37]Phillip Johnson, *Darwin On Trial* (Downers Grove, Ill.: InterVarsity Press, 1991).

[38]Preeminent among the faults of British natural theology was its identification of the designer of nature with a pre-packaged conception of the Christian God. Christian dogma spelled out a designer/deity satisfying a list of perfections which seemed irreconcilable with the imperfections scientists, and especially biologists, were discovering in nature. British natural theology, with its emphasis on the benevolence of the designer/deity, failed properly to appreciate the brutality and suffering found in nature (cf. Paley, *Natural Theology*, chap. 26). Darwin exploited this weakness: "I cannot persuade myself that a beneficent and omnipotent God would have designedly created the Ichneumonidae [parasitic wasps] with the express intention of their feeding within the living bodies of Caterpillars" (Francis Darwin, ed., *The Life and Letters of Charles Darwin* [London: Murray, 1887], 2:303-12, and also Gillespie, *Charles Darwin*, chap. 5-6). The fact is, however, that design does not entail optimal design, perfection or lack of suffering. Stripped of a priori theological presuppositions, the core idea of British natural theology, i.e., design, is much more difficult to refute.

[39]Francis Darwin, *Life and Letters*, 2:7.

[40]The logic here is itself suspect. For instance, physicists routinely explain events in terms of entities that not only have not been observed but may not even in principle be observable, e.g., the dark matter that is supposed to account for galaxies not flying apart (see Malcolm Longair, "The New Astrophysics," in *The New Physics*, ed. Paul Davies [Cambridge: Cambridge University Press, 1989], pp. 163-64). The point is that there are no hard and fast rules for what entities and causal processes a scientist can employ to explain an event and still remain a scientist.

[41]Dawkins makes the same point (*Blind Watchmaker*, pp. 7-8):

I feel more in common with the Reverend William Paley than I do with the distinguished modern philosopher, a well-known atheist, with whom I once discussed [the complexity of living things]. I said that I could not imagine being an atheist at any time before 1859, when Darwin's *Origin of Species* was published. "What about Hume?", replied the philosopher. "How did Hume explain the organized complexity of the living world?", I asked. "He didn't", said the philosopher, [to which he added,] "Why does it need any special explanation?" Paley knew that it needed a special explanation; Darwin knew it, and I suspect that in his heart of hearts my philosopher companion knew it too.

[42]For ease of exposition I shall in the sequel use the word *contrivance* to signify both the intentional products of an intelligent agent (i.e., actual contrivances) as well as things that only look as though they were produced by an intelligent agent (i.e., apparent contrivances). Human artifacts are actually contrived. On the other hand, if Darwin is right, living systems are only apparently contrived. The point to realize, however, is that even apparent contrivance requires an explanation, for there are a lot of things in the world that are not even apparently contrived—like the rocks strewn about by an avalanche.

[43]Charles Hodge, *What Is Darwinism? and Other Writings on Science & Religion*, ed. M. A. Noll and D. N. Livingstone (1874; reprint, Grand Rapids, Mich.: Baker, 1994), pp. 86-89.

[44]Though Paley defended miracles as part of his general defense of the veracity of Christianity (cf. William Paley, *A View of the Evidences of Christianity*, annotations by R. Whately [1794; reprint, Murfreesboro, Tenn.: Dehoff, 1952]), a defense of miracles is notably absent from his text on natural theology (cf. Paley, *Natural Theology*).

[45]This is clear from the first two chapters of Paley's *Natural Theology*. For instance, in discussing his watchmaker example Paley writes: "Arrangement, disposition of parts, subserviency of means to an end, relation of instruments to a use, imply the presence of intelligence and a mind." Whether these are sufficient criteria wherewith accurately to identify intelligent agency is of course open to dispute. Paley's use of these criteria, however, is clear enough: he treats them as sufficient to signal "the presence of intelligence." In particular he does not need these criteria mediated by miracles. Reid (*Lectures on Natural Theology*, pp. 51-59) makes the same point, and in my view even more clearly than Paley. See appendix A.9.

[46]See L. P. Gerson, *God and Greek Philosophy: Studies in the Early History of Natural Theology* (London: Routledge, 1990).

[47]Reid, *Lectures on Natural Theology*, pp. 51-59.

[48]See Gerson, *God and Greek Philosophy*, as well as Roy Weatherford, *The Implications of Determinism* (London: Routledge, 1991).

[49]John Tyndall, *Fragments of Science* (New York: Appleton, 1897), 2:136-37.

[50]*Phaedo* 98, in Plato, *The Collected Dialogues of Plato, Including the Letters*, ed. E. Hamilton and H. Cairns (Princeton, N.J.: Princeton University Press, 1961), p. 80.

[51]Jacques Monod, *Chance and Necessity* (New York: Vintage, 1972), p. 21.

[52]Mark Noll and David Livingstone, "Charles Hodge and the Definition of Darwinism" in Hodge, *What is Darwinism?* p. 42.

[53]See Brown, *Miracles and the Critical Mind*, p. 9; and *The Trinity* 3.9.16, in Augustine, *The Trinity*, The Fathers of the Church 55, trans. S. McKenna (Washington, D.C.: The Catholic University of America Press, 1963), p. 112.

[54]See Van Till, "Is Special Creationism a Heresy?"

Chapter 4: Naturalism & Its Cure

[1]Cf. 1 Corinthians 2:14, especially in the original Greek. The contrast is between *pneumatikos* (spiritual) and *psychikos* (soulish or natural).

[2]Alexander Schmemann, *For the Life of the World* (Crestwood, N.Y.: St. Vladimir's Press, 1988), p. 100.

[3]Ainslie T. Embree, ed., *The Hindu Tradition: Readings in Oriental Thought* (New York: Vintage, 1966), p. 9.

[4]Ibid.

[5]Maximus the Confessor writes in *The Four Hundred Chapters on Love* (in *Maximus Confessor: Selected Writings*, The Classics of Western Spirituality [New York: Paulist Press, 1985], I:5; I:7):

> If all things have been made by God and for his sake, then God is better than what has been made by him. The one who forsakes the better and is engrossed in inferior things shows that he prefers the things made by God to God himself. . . .
>
> If the soul is better than the body and God incomparably better than the world which he created, the one who prefers the body to the soul and the world to the God who created it is no different from idolaters.

[6]See William Dembski, "The Design Argument," in *The History of Science and Religion in the Western Tradition: An Encyclopedia*, ed. G. B. Ferngren (New York: Garland, forthcoming).

[7]William Paley, *Natural Theology: Or Evidences of the Existence and Attributes of the Deity Collected from the Appearances of Nature* (1802; reprint, Boston: Gould & Lincoln, 1852).

[8]See Michael Behe, *Darwin's Black Box* (New York: Free Press, 1996); Dean Overman, *A Case Against Accident and Self-Organization* (Lanham, Md.: Rowman & Littlefield, 1997); William Dembski, ed., *Mere Creation* (Downers Grove, Ill.: InterVarsity Press, 1998); and William Dembski, *The Design Inference* (Cambridge: Cambridge University Press, 1998).

[9]See Dembski, *Design Inference*, chap. 1.

[10]For more on the connection between design and information see chapter six. See also Werner Gitt, *In the Beginning Was Information*, trans. J. Kies (Bielefeld, Germany: Christliche Literatur-Verbreitung, 1997).

[11]See respectively Behe, *Darwin's Black Box*, pp. 39-45; Marcel-Paul Schützenberger, "The Miracles of Darwinism," *Origins & Design* 17, no. 2 (1996): 10-15; and William Dembski, "Intelligent Design as a Theory of Information," *Perspectives on Science and Christian Faith* 49, no. 3 (1997): 180-90.

[12]Paley, "The Goodness of the Deity," chap. 26 in *Natural Theology*.

[13]See Dembski, *Design Inference*.

[14]Del Ratzsch, "Design, Chance and Theistic Evolution," in Dembski, *Mere Creation*, p. 294.

[15]See Charles Thaxton, Walter Bradley and Roger Olsen, *The Mystery of Life's Origin* (New York: Philosophical Library, 1984), pp. 22-24.

[16]Private communication.

[17]See Howard Van Till, "The Fully Gifted Creation," in *Three Views on Creation and Evolution*, eds. J. P. Moreland and John Mark Reynolds (Grand Rapids, Mich.: Zondervan, 1999), pp. 161-218. Van Till and others resist the designation "theistic evolution" because it emphasizes the evolutionary process at the expense of the Creator who is responsible for the process. Nonetheless "theistic evolution" is the term that's more widely known, and my characterization of it fits those who, like Van Till, accept that the biological community has essentially gotten the scientific theory of evolution correct and who, also like Van Till, empty creation of empirical content. Theistic evolutionists, evolutionary creationists and proponents of a fully gifted creation never specify what difference their theism makes for their science. Only if their theism makes a concrete, empirical difference for their science could they be regarded as design theorists.

[18]The theistic evolutionist would deny that these natural processes are in fact undirected. But to claim that they are directed is not an empirical statement for the theistic evolutionist, but a statement of faith. A tornado and its path of destruction may be subsumed under divine providence but only as a faith commitment. Science as such would be unable to

detect any directedness in the tornado. The point of intelligent design is that there are events in the world which science as such can reliably attribute to intelligence. For theistic evolutionists everything is designed, but nothing can be scientifically known to be designed.

[19]See Thomas Aquinas's *Summa Contra Gentiles*, in *Introduction to St. Thomas Aquinas*, ed. A. C. Pegis (New York: Modern Library, 1948), III.38.

[20]Cf. the theology of Karl Barth. Barth wrote: "There simply cannot be any scientific questions, objections, or even aids from natural science in respect of what holy scripture and the Christian church understand by God's work of creation," quoted in Eberhard Busch, *Karl Barth: His Life from Letters and Autobiographical Texts* (Grand Rapids, Mich.: Eerdmans, 1994), p. 316.

[21]Cf. Arthur Peacocke, *Theology for a Scientific Age* (Oxford: Basil Blackwell, 1990), pp. 182-83.

[22]See Behe, *Darwin's Black Box.*

[23]See Thaxton et al., *The Mystery of Life's Origin*; Percival Davis and Dean Kenyon, *Of Pandas and People*, 2nd ed. (Dallas: Haughton, 1993); Behe, *Darwin's Black Box*; and Stephen Meyer, "The Origin of Life and the Death of Materialism," *The Intercollegiate Review* 31, no. 2 (1996): 24-43.

[24]Daniel Dennett even suggests "quarantining" those who teach their children that evolution by natural selection is false (*Darwin's Dangerous Idea* [New York: Simon & Schuster, 1995], p. 519).

[25]Cf. Phillip E. Johnson, *Reason in the Balance: The Case Against Naturalism in Science, Law and Education* (Downers Grove, Ill.: InterVarsity, 1995).

[26]Michael Ruse, *Darwinism Defended* (Reading, Mass.: Addison-Wesley, 1982), p. 58.

[27]George Gaylord Simpson, *The Meaning of Evolution*, rev. ed. (New Haven, Conn.: Yale University Press, 1967), p. 345.

[28]See Ronald Numbers, *Darwinism Comes to America* (Cambridge, Mass.: Harvard University Press, 1998), pp. 9, 11.

[29]The exact quote from Dawkins is as follows: "It is absolutely safe to say that if you meet somebody who claims not to believe in evolution, that person is ignorant, stupid, or insane (or wicked, but I'd rather not consider that)" (Richard Dawkins, review of *Blueprints* by Donald Johanson and Maitland Edey, *New York Times*, April 9, 1989, sec. 7, p. 34).

[30]See Johnson, *Reason in the Balance*; Alvin Plantinga, "Methodological Naturalism," pts. 1 and 2, *Origins & Design* 18, no. 1 (1997): 18-27, and 18, no. 2 (1997): 22-34.

[31]Michael Denton, *Evolution: A Theory in Crisis* (Bethesda, Md.: Adler & Adler, 1986).

[32]Thomas Kuhn, *The Structure of Scientific Revolutions*, 2nd ed. (Chicago: University of Chicago Press, 1970); Larry Laudan, *Progress and Its Problems: Towards a Theory of Scientific Growth* (Berkeley: University of California Press, 1977).

[33]Dennett, *Darwin's Dangerous Idea*, p. 63.

[34]Malcolm Muggeridge, *The End of Christendom* (Grand Rapids, Mich.: Eerdmans, 1980), p. 59.

Chapter 5: Reinstating Design Within Science

[1]See Aristotle *Metaphysics* 5.2, in *The Basic Works of Aristotle*, ed. R. McKeon (New York: Random House, 1941), p. 752.

[2]Francis Bacon, *The Advancement of Learning*, Great Books of the Western World 30, ed. R. M. Hutchins (1605; reprint, Chicago: Encyclopedia Britannica, 1952).

[3]Monod writes, "The cornerstone of the scientific method is the postulate that nature is objective. In other words, the *systematic* denial that 'true' knowledge can be got at by interpreting phenomena in terms of final causes—that is to say, of 'purpose' " (Jacques Monod, *Chance and Necessity* [New York: Vintage, 1972], p. 21).

[4]Jaki writes: "I want no part whatever with the position . . . in which science is surreptitiously taken for a means of elucidating the utterly metaphysical question of purpose"

(Stanley Jaki, *Chesterton, a Seer of Science* [Urbana: University of Illinois Press, 1986], pp. 139-40 n. 2).

[5]Richard Dawkins, *The Blind Watchmaker* (New York: Norton, 1986), p. 1.

[6]Francis Crick, *What Mad Pursuit* (New York: Basic Books, 1988), p. 138.

[7]Eliot Marshall, "Medline Searches Turn Up Cases of Suspected Plagiarism," *Science* 279 (January 1998): 473-74.

[8]Charles Darwin, *On the Origin of Species* (1859; reprint, Cambridge, Mass.: Harvard University Press, 1964), p. 482.

[9]Michael Behe, *Darwin's Black Box* (New York: Free Press, 1996).

[10]See St. Bonaventure, *The Soul's Journey into God*, in *Bonaventure*, ed. E. Cousins, Classics of Western Spirituality (ca. 1260; reprint, New York: Paulist Press, 1978), chap. 1.

[11]Hugh Ross, *The Fingerprint of God*, 2nd ed. (Orange, Calif.: Promise, 1991).

[12]For a full account see my book *The Design Inference* (Cambridge: Cambridge University Press, 1998). There I refer to an sp/SP criterion (specification/small probability criterion). This criterion is equivalent to the complexity-specification criterion developed here.

[13]Michael Polanyi, "Life Transcending Physics and Chemistry," *Chemical and Engineering News*, August 21, 1967, pp. 54-66; Michael Polanyi, "Life's Irreducible Structure," *Science* 113 (1968): 1308-12; Timothy Lenoir, *The Strategy of Life: Teleology and Mechanics in Nineteenth Century German Biology* (Dordrecht: Reidel, 1982), pp. 7-8. See also Hubert Yockey, *Information Theory and Molecular Biology* (Cambridge: Cambridge University Press, 1992), p. 335.

[14]Dembski, *Design Inference*, chap. 5.

[15]Unfortunately the scientific community uses not the true explanatory filter but the following naturalized version of it:

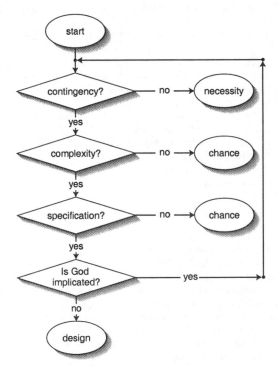

The naturalized explanatory filter

To see that this is in fact how the scientific community sanitizes design, consider the following admonition by Julian Huxley: "In any case, if we repudiate creationism, divine or vitalistic guidance, and the extremer forms of orthogenesis, as originators of adaptation, we must (unless we confess total ignorance and abandon for the time any attempts at explanation) invoke natural selection" (*Evolution: The Modern Synthesis* [London: George Allen & Unwin, 1945], p. 473). Huxley guarantees that design will be ruled out a priori and that explanations of biological complexity cycle endlessly between chance and necessity.

[16]This section summarizes chapter five of Dembski, *Design Inference*.

[17]For an exact treatment of complexity theory see Dembski, *Design Inference*, chap. 4.

[18]Ibid., chap. 5.

[19]Martin Gardner, "Arthur Koestler: Neoplatonism Rides Again," *World*, August 1, 1972, pp. 87-89.

[20]Walter Martin, *The Kingdom of the Cults*, rev. ed. (Minneapolis: Bethany House, 1985), pp. 127-30.

[21]Dembski, *Design Inference*, sec. 6.5.

[22]Bruce Alberts, "The Cell as a Collection of Protein Machines: Preparing the Next Generation of Molecular Biologists," *Cell*, February 8, 1998, p. 291.

[23]Behe, *Darwin's Black Box*, pp. 39-45.

[24]Ibid., p. 39.

[25]Ibid., pp. 69-72.

[26]See, for example, Nicholas Gaiano, Adam Amsterdam, Koichi Kawakami, Migeul Allende, Thomas Becker and Nancy Hopkins, "Insertional Mutagenesis and Rapid Cloning of Essential Genes in Zebrafish," *Nature* 383 (1996): 829-32; Carolyn K. Suzuki, Kitaru Suda, Nan Wang and Gottfried Schatz, "Requirement for the Yeast Gene *LON* in Intramitochondrial Proteolysis and Maintenance of Respiration," *Science* 264 (1994): 273-76; Qun-Yong Zhou, Carol J. Qualfe and Richard D. Palmiter, "Targeted Disruption of the Tyrosine Hydroxylase Gene Reveals that Catecholamines are Required for Mouse Fetal Development," *Nature* 374 (1995): 640-43.

[27]Arno Wouters, "Viability Explanation," *Biology and Philosophy* 10 (1995): 435-57.

[28]Behe, *Darwin's Black Box*.

[29]Dawkins, *Blind Watchmaker*, p. 9.

[30]John W. Bodnar, Jeffrey Killian, Michael Nagle and Suneil Ramchandani, "Deciphering the Language of the Genome," *Journal of Theoretical Biology* 189 (1997): 183.

[31]See Percival Davis and Dean Kenyon, *Of Pandas and People*, 2nd ed. (Dallas: Haughton, 1993), p. 128.

[32]See Del Ratzsch, "Design, Chance & Theistic Evolution," in *Mere Creation*, ed. W. A. Dembski (Downers Grove, Ill.: InterVarsity Press, 1998), p. 294.

[33]See J. Budziszewski, *Written on the Heart: The Case for Natural Law* (Downers Grove, Ill.: InterVarsity Press, 1997).

[34]For a powerful critique of evolutionary psychology see Jeffrey Schloss, "Evolutionary Accounts of Altruism & the Problem of Goodness by Design," in Dembski, *Mere Creation*, pp. 236-61.

[35]Martin Heidegger, *Being and Time*, in *Basic Writings*, ed. D. F. Krell (New York: Harper & Row, 1977), p. 51.

Chapter 6: Intelligent Design as a Theory of Information

[1]Manfred Eigen, *Steps Towards Life: A Perspective on Evolution*, trans. P. Woolley (Oxford: Oxford University Press, 1992), p. 12.

[2]Keith Devlin, *Logic and Information* (New York: Cambridge University Press, 1991), p. 1.

[3]Robert Stalnaker, *Inquiry* (Cambridge, Mass.: MIT Press, 1984), p. 85.

[4]Fred Dretske, *Knowledge and the Flow of Information* (Cambridge, Mass.: MIT Press, 1981), p. 4.

[5]ASCII = American Standard Code for Information Interchange.

[6]Claude Shannon and Warren Weaver, *The Mathematical Theory of Communication* (Urbana: University of Illinois Press, 1949), p. 32.

[7]Peter Medawar, *The Limits of Science* (New York: Harper & Row, 1984), pp. 78-82.

[8]See William Dembski, *The Design Inference* (Cambridge: Cambridge University Press, 1998), chap. 4.

[9]Eigen, *Steps Towards Life*, p. 12.

[10]Michael Behe, *Darwin's Black Box* (New York: Free Press, 1996). See also section 5.7 of this book.

[11]John Barrow and Frank Tipler, *The Anthropic Cosmological Principle* (Oxford: Oxford University Press, 1986).

[12]David Bohm, *The Undivided Universe: An Ontological Interpretation of Quantum Theory* (London: Routledge, 1993), pp. 35-38.

[13]Rolf Landauer, "Information Is Physical," *Physics Today*, May 1991, p. 26.

[14]Roy Frieden, *Physics from Fisher Information: A Unification* (Cambridge: Cambridge University Press, 1998).

[15]David J. Chalmers, *The Conscious Mind: In Search of a Fundamental Theory* (New York: Oxford University Press, 1996), chap. 8.

[16]The nonrandom strings form a very small (i.e., highly improbable and therefore highly complex) set within the space of all possible strings, most of which are random in the sense of being noncompressible. The nonrandom strings are also specified (compressibility provides the specification). See Andrei N. Kolmogorov, "Three Approaches to the Quantitative Definition of Information," *Problemy Peredachi Informatsii* (in translation) 1, no. 1 (1965): 3-11; Gregory J. Chaitin, "On the Length of Programs for Computing Finite Binary Sequences," *Journal of the Association for Computing Machinery* 13 (1966): 547-69.

[17]What I'm calling "law" throughout the remainder of this chapter is a special case of what in chapter five I called "necessity." Except for logical necessity the two notions are largely interchangeable, though scientists tend to prefer "law," whereas philosophers are equally content with "law" or "necessity."

[18]Eigen, *Steps Towards Life*, p. 12.

[19]Cf. Dretske, *Knowledge and the Flow of Information*, and Susantha Goonatilake, *The Evolution of Information: Lineages in Gene, Culture and Artefact* (London: Pinter, 1991). Both of these books are typical of naturalistic accounts of information—they focus exclusively on the flow of information but ignore the origin of information. Naturalistic accounts of the flow of information are all fine and well but do nothing to account for the origin of information.

[20]Klaus Weihrauch, *Computability* (Berlin: Springer-Verlag, 1987), p. 107. A universal Turing machine is an algorithm capable of running all other algorithms.

[21]For popular accounts of this enterprise, see Steven Levy, *Artificial Life: The Quest for a New Creation* (New York: Pantheon, 1992); and Mitchell Waldrop, *Complexity: The Emerging Science at the Edge of Order and Chaos* (New York: Simon & Schuster, 1992).

[22]See Heinz-Otto Peitgen, Harmut Jürgens and Dietmar Saupe, *Chaos and Fractals: New Frontiers of Science* (New York: Springer-Verlag, 1992), chap. 14.

[23]See Leon Brillouin, *Science and Information Theory*, 2nd ed. (New York: Academic Press, 1962), pp. 267-69, where he makes this point beautifully. Brillouin quotes a delightful passage from Edgar Allen Poe, who, commenting as far back as 1836 on Babbage's inference engine, understood clearly that deterministic systems are incapable of attaining to "the intellect of man." Brillouin concludes thus: "[A] machine does not create any new information, but it performs a very valuable transformation of known information. It would be very interesting to find some measure of this transformation and to compute its value, but up to now no method has been discovered to evaluate this work." Brillouin wrote this back in the 1950s. Since then such measures for the transformation of information have been developed. They are called *complexity measures*. Indeed an entire new discipline has developed since Brillouin's prescient observation, to wit, *complexity theory*. For an introduction to complexity theory, see Dembski, *Design Inference*, chap. 4.

[24]Emile Borel, *Probabilities and Life*, trans. M. Baudin (New York: Dover, 1962), p. 28.

[25]See Dembski, *Design Inference*, sec. 6.5.

[26]Bernd-Olaf Küppers, *Information and the Origin of Life* (Cambridge, Mass.: MIT Press, 1990), p. 59.

[27]Richard Dawkins, *The Blind Watchmaker* (New York: Norton, 1987), pp. 139, 145-46.

[28]See Stewart Ethier and Thomas Kurtz, *Markov Processes: Characterization and Convergence* (New York: John Wiley, 1986), pp. 49-50.

[29]Ibid., p. 50.

[30]For a sampling of the types of problems genetic algorithms are capable of solving, see Melanie Mitchell, *An Introduction to Genetic Algorithms* (Cambridge, Mass.: MIT Press, 1996).

[31]See David Wolpert and William Macready, "No Free Lunch Theorems for Optimization," *IEEE Transactions on Evolutionary Computation* 1, no. 1 (1997): 67-82; and Joseph Culberson, "On the Futility of Blind Search: An Algorithmic View of 'No Free Lunch,' " *Evolutionary Computation* 6, no. 2 (1998): 109-27.

[32]See Samuel Karlin and Howard Taylor, *A First Course in Stochastic Processes*, 2nd ed. (New York: Academic Press, 1975); and by the same authors, *A Second Course in Stochastic Processes* (New York: Academic Press, 1981).

[33]Medawar, *Limits of Science*, pp. 78-82.

[34]See Michael Denton, *Nature's Destiny* (New York: Free Press, 1998), pp. 269-73; and Behe, *Darwin's Black Box*, p. 5.

[35]Cf. Paul Nelson, *Common Descent, Generative Entrenchment and the Epistemology of Evolutionary Inference*, in *Evolutionary Monographs*, ed. L. Van Valen (Chicago: University of Chicago Press, forthcoming).

[36]See Timothy Lenoir, *The Strategy of Life: Teleology and Mechanics in Nineteenth Century German Biology* (Dordrecht: Reidel, 1982).

[37]Dawkins, *Blind Watchmaker*, pp. 13, 316; Daniel Dennett, *Darwin's Dangerous Idea* (New York: Simon & Schuster, 1995), p. 153.

[38]The textual transmission of the New Testament is a wonderful place to begin for understanding the problems facing textual critics. See Bruce Metzger, *The Text of the New Testament: Its Transmission, Corruption and Restoration* (Oxford: Oxford University Press, 1992).

[39]Hubert Yockey, *Information Theory and Molecular Biology* (Cambridge: Cambridge University Press, 1992), p. 335.

[40]Carlos F. Amábile-Cuevas, Maura Cárdenas-García and Mauricio Ludgar, "Antibiotic Resistance," *American Scientist* 83 (1995): 324.

[41]Lynn Margulis, *Symbiosis in Cell Evolution: Microbial Communities in the Archean and Proterozoic Eons*, 2nd ed. (New York: Freeman, 1993).

[42]Franklin Harold, "From Morphogenes to Morphogenesis," *Microbiology* 141 (1995): 2765.

[43]Scott Gilbert, *Developmental Biology*, 3rd ed. (Sunderland, Mass.: Sinauer, 1991), pt. I.

[44]Cf. Jacques Monod, *Chance and Necessity* (New York: Vintage, 1972), p. 12.

[45]For a more thorough account of what I'm calling "modification," see John A. Endler and Tracy McLellan, "The Processes of Evolution: Toward a Newer Synthesis," *Annual Review of Ecology and Systematics* 19 (1988): 396, table 1; and James D. Watson, et al., *Molecular Biology of the Gene*, 4th ed. (Menlo Park, Calif.: Benjamin/Cummings, 1987), chaps. 10-12.

[46]Amábile-Cuevas et al., "Antibiotic Resistance," p. 324.

[47]See Behe, *Darwin's Black Box*; and Siegfried Scherer, "Basic Functional States in the Evolution of Light-Driven Cyclic Electron Transport," *Journal of Theoretical Biology* 104 (1983): 289-99.

[48]Dawkins's recent metaphor of climbing a mountain is therefore utterly inappropriate. Dawkins's Mount Improbable cannot be climbed. Its face is sheer, and the Darwinian mechanism is incapable of scaling it. Cf. Richard Dawkins, *Climbing Mount Improbable* (New York: Norton, 1996).

[49]This is by far the most common case in biology (see Behe, *Darwin's Black Box,* chap. 8).

[50]See Alexander G. Cairns-Smith, *Seven Clues to the Origin of Life* (Cambridge: Cambridge University Press, 1985); and Alexander G. Cairns-Smith and H. Hartman, eds., *Clay Minerals and the Origin of Life* (Cambridge: Cambridge University Press, 1986).

[51]This is Michael Corey's preferred option (Corey, *Back to Darwin: The Scientific Case for Deistic Evolution* [Lanham, Md.: University Press of America, 1994]).

[52]See Ronald Numbers, *The Creationists: The Evolution of Scientific Creationism* (New York: Alfred A. Knopf, 1992), p. 245.

[53]Cf. Stuart Kauffman, *The Origins of Order: Self-Organization and Selection in Evolution* (Oxford: Oxford University Press, 1993); Stuart Kauffman, *At Home in the Universe* (Oxford: Oxford University Press, 1995); and Christopher Langton, ed., *Artificial Life III: Proceedings of the Workshop on Artificial Life Held June 1992 in Santa Fe, New Mexico,* Santa Fe Institute Studies in the Sciences of Complexity 17 (Redwood City, Calif.: Addison-Wesley, 1994).

[54]See Nelson, *Common Descent.*

Chapter 7: Science & Theology in Mutual Support

[1]Jean Pond refers to this model also as an *independence model.* This alternate usage is entirely appropriate. See Richard Carlson, ed., *Science & Christianity: Four Views* (Downers Grove, Ill.: InterVarsity Press, forthcoming).

[2]The late Donald MacKay was a leading light in the American Scientific Affiliation and a key proponent of complementarity. See his *Human Science and Human Dignity* (Downers Grove, Ill.: InterVarsity Press, 1979), p. 30. In Carlson's *Science & Christianity,* Howard Van Till refers to a *partnership model.* Although he resists the term "complementarity," Van Till's partnership model exhibits the same conceptual independence between science and theology inherent in the complementarity model.

[3]Richard Dawkins supports a particularly virulent form of the conflict model: "I think a case can be made that faith is one of the world's great evils, comparable to the smallpox virus but harder to eradicate" ("Is Science a Religion?" *The Humanist* 57 [January/February 1997]: 26). Adolf Hitler apparently thought that the same case could be made: "The reason why the ancient world was so pure, light, and serene was that it knew nothing of the two great scourges: the pox and Christianity," quoted from *Hitler's Table Talk* (1941-1943), in Alan Bullock's *Hitler: A Study in Tyranny,* rev. ed. (New York: Harper & Row, 1964), p. 672.

[4]Charles Hodge, *Systematic Theology,* 3 vols. (1873; reprint, Grand Rapids, Mich.: Eerdmans, 1981), 1:59.

[5]Basil, *Hexaemeron,* The Nicene and Post-Nicene Fathers of the Christian Church 8, 2nd series, ed. P. Schaff and H. Wace (Grand Rapids, Mich.: Eerdmans, 1989), p. 53.

[6]Stephen Meyer refers to this model alternatively as a "qualified agreement model" or an "epistemic support model." See Carlson, *Science & Christianity.*

[7]Section 7.2 closely follow my article with Stephen Meyer titled "Fruitful Interchange or Polite Chitchat? The Dialogue Between Theology and Science," *Zygon* 33, no. 3 (1998): 415-30.

[8]Rudolf Carnap, "Carnap's Intellectual Autobiography," in *The Philosophy of Rudolf Carnap,* ed. P. A. Schilpp (LaSalle, Ill.: Open Court, 1963), p. 11.

[9]Names that come to mind here include Abner Shimony, who holds doctorates in both physics and philosophy; David Malament, who has proven technical mathematical results in general relativity; and Arthur Fine, who has done original work on the foundations of quantum mechanics.

[10]Ernan McMullin, "How Should Cosmology Relate to Theology?" in *The Sciences and Theology in the Twentieth Century,* ed. A. R. Peacocke (Notre Dame, Ind.: University of Notre Dame Press, 1981) p. 39.

[11]Cf. Wittgenstein's remark: "I am sitting with a philosopher in the garden; he says again and again, 'I know that that's a tree,' pointing to a tree that is near us. Someone else arrives and hears this, and I tell him: 'This fellow isn't insane. We are only doing philosophy.' "

From Ludwig Wittgenstein, *On Certainty* (New York: Harper & Row, 1969), p. 61e, no. 467.

[12]Here I am thinking especially of the work of Imre Lakatos, "Falsification and the Methodology of Scientific Research Programmes," in *Criticism and the Growth of Knowledge,* ed. I. Lakatos and A. Musgrave (Cambridge: Cambridge University Press, 1970), pp. 91-196; Larry Laudan, *Progress and Its Problems: Toward a Theory of Scientific Growth* (Berkeley: University of California Press, 1977); Nancey Murphy, *Theology in the Age of Scientific Reasoning* (Ithaca, N.Y.: Cornell University Press, 1990); and Peter Lipton, *Inference to the Best Explanation* (London: Routledge, 1991).

[13]A detailed treatment of partial entailment may be found in Ernest Adams, *The Logic of Conditionals* (Dordrecht: Reidel, 1975).

[14]Charles S. Peirce, "The Red and the Black," in *The World of Mathematics,* 4 vols., ed. J. R. Newman (1878; reprint, Redmond, Wash.: Tempus, 1988), pp. 1313-14.

[15]Things become more complicated if beside probabilities we introduce utilities and thus have to balance the utility associated with a consequence against its probability. (See Richard Jeffrey, *The Logic of Decision,* 2nd ed. [Chicago: University of Chicago Press, 1983], chap. 1.) Nevertheless, for simply apportioning our beliefs to the likelihood of events, probabilities are all we need.

[16]Clearly there are exceptions. The conflict between the scientific establishment and young-earth creationists is a case in point.

[17]This section summarizes Stephen Meyer's treatment of explanation in "Of Clues and Causes: A Methodological Interpretation of Origin of Life Studies" (Ph.D. diss., University of Cambridge, 1990).

[18]Imre Lakatos, for instance, uses the phrase "heuristic power," whereas Larry Laudan speaks of "problem solving ability." See Lakatos, "Falsification and the Methodology of Scientific Research Programmes"; and Laudan, *Progress and Its Problems.*

[19]Charles S. Peirce, *Collected Papers,* ed. C. Hartshorne and P. Weiss (Cambridge, Mass.: Harvard University Press, 1931), 2:372-88.

[20]Meyer, "Clues and Causes," p. 25.

[21]Peirce, *Collected Papers,* 2:375.

[22]Ibid:

[23]Ibid.

[24]Ibid., 2:374.

[25]Synonyms and close relatives of *consonance* abound in the philosophical literature. These include *coherence, consistency* and *consilience* (to name just a few that begin with the letter *c*). I prefer *consonance* in part because it evokes the psychological notion of "cognitive dissonance." Among theologians concerned with theology-science interconnections, *consonance* seems to be gaining ground in recent days. Cf. Ted Peters, *Cosmos as Creation: Theology and Science in Consonance* (Nashville: Abingdon, 1989).

[26]Cf. Lipton, *Inference to the Best Explanation,* pp. 114-22, as well as John Leslie's notion of a "neat explanation" in *Universes* (London, Routledge, 1989).

[27]Cf. Lipton, *Inference to the Best Explanation.*

[28]McMullin, "How Should Cosmology Relate to Theology?" p. 39.

[29]So Einstein told George Gamow in a conversation around 1947 (George Gamow, *My World Line* [New York: Viking, 1970], p. 44.).

[30]See Stanley Jaki, *God and the Cosmologists* (Washington, D.C.: Regnery Gateway, 1989), pp. 64-70.

[31]As for the logic of explanation connecting intelligent design and the Christian doctrine of creation, I offer that as a doctoral dissertation topic.

[32]Cf. James Loder and W. Jim Neidhardt, *The Knight's Move: The Relational Logic of the Spirit in Theology and Science* (Colorado Springs: Helmers & Howard, 1992), chap. 5. The definition of Chalcedon starts, "Following the Holy Fathers, we all with one accord teach men to acknowledge one and the same Son, our Lord Jesus Christ, at once complete in Godhead and complete in manhood, truly God and truly man," quoted from Loder and Neidhardt,

Knight's Move, p. 81.

[33]"In him all things in heaven and on earth were created, things visible and invisible. . . . All things have been created through him and for him. He himself is before all things, and in him all things hold together. . . . In him all the fullness of God was pleased to dwell, and through him God was pleased to reconcile to himself all things, whether on earth or in heaven, by making peace through the blood of his cross" (Colossians 1:16-20 NRSV).

[34]Cf. Kuyper's doctrine of the various spheres and departments of life in Abraham Kuyper, *Lectures on Calvinism* (Grand Rapids, Mich.: Eerdmans, 1994).

[35]Eugene Kamenka, ed., *The Portable Karl Marx* (New York: Viking Penguin, 1983), p. 53.

[36]See Anthony Thiselton, *New Horizons in Hermeneutics* (Grand Rapids, Mich.: Zondervan, 1992).

[37]Erik Erikson, *Childhood and Society*, 2nd ed. (New York: Norton, 1963), chap. 7.

[38]See Walter Rudin, *Principles of Mathematical Analysis*, 3rd ed. (New York: McGraw-Hill, 1976), pp. 8-11.

[39]According to Morris Kline, "The discovery of incommensurable ratios [i.e., irrational numbers] is attributed to Hippasus of Metapontum (5th cent. B.C.). The Pythagoreans were supposed to have been at sea at the time and to have thrown Hippasus overboard for having produced an element in the universe which denied the Pythagorean doctrine that all phenomena in the universe can be reduced to whole numbers or their ratios." This desire for neat, self-contained explanations did not stay confined to the Pythagoreans but in our day remains typical of Enlightenment rationalism and scientific naturalism. Christ always destroys our neat categories. For the quote from Morris Kline, see his *Mathematical Thought from Ancient to Modern Times* (New York: Oxford University Press, 1972), 1:32.

Chapter 8: The Act of Creation

[1]Homer, *The Iliad*, trans. S. Butler, Great Books of the Western World 4, ed. R. M. Hutchins (Chicago: Encyclopaedia Britannica, 1952), 1.1, p. 3.

[2]Cf. Stephen Hawking, *A Brief History of Time: From the Big Bang to Black Holes* (New York: Bantam, 1988); and John Barrow, *Theories of Everything: The Quest for Ultimate Explanation* (New York: Fawcett, 1991).

[3]Cf. William Dembski, "The Incompleteness of Scientific Naturalism," in *Darwinism: Science or Philosophy?* ed. J. Buell and V. Hearn (Dallas: Foundation for Thought and Ethics, 1994).

[4]Consider the following statement by Michael Gazzaniga (Gazzaniga, ed., *The Cognitive Neurosciences* [Cambridge, Mass.: MIT Press, 1995], p. xiii):

> At some point in the future, cognitive neuroscience will be able to describe *the algorithms* that drive structural neural elements into the physiological activity that results in perception, cognition, and perhaps even consciousness. To reach this goal, the field has departed from the more limited aims of neuropsychology and basic neuroscience. Simple descriptions of clinical disorders are a beginning, as is understanding basic mechanisms of neural action. The future of the field, however, is in working toward a science that truly relates brain and cognition *in a mechanistic way*. That task is not easy, and many areas of research in the mind sciences are not ready for that kind of analysis. Yet that is the objective. (Emphasis added).

[5]See Paul Teller, "A Poor Man's Guide to Supervenience and Determination," *Southern Journal of Philosophy* 22, supplement (1984): 137-62. According to Stephen Schiffer,

> "Supervenience" is a primitive metaphysical relation between properties that is distinct from causation and more like some primitive form of entailment. . . . I therefore find it more than a little ironic, and puzzling, that supervenience is nowadays being heralded as a way of making non-pleonastic, irreducibly non-natural mental properties cohere with an acceptably naturalistic solution to the mind-body problem. . . .

The appeal to a special primitive relation of "supervenience" . . . is obscurantist. Supervenience is just epiphenomenalism without causation.

From *The Remnants of Meaning* (Cambridge, Mass.: MIT Press, 1987), pp. 153-54.
[6]See Stephen Stich, *From Folk Psychology to Cognitive Science: The Case Against Belief* (Cambridge, Mass.: MIT Press, 1983).
[7]As Stanley Jaki observes in *Brain, Mind and Computers* (South Bend, Ind.: Gateway Editions, 1969), pp. 115-16,

A brain may largely be deteriorated and still function in an outstanding way. . . . A famous case is that of Pasteur, who at the height of his career suffered a cerebral accident, and yet for many years afterwards did research requiring a high level of abstraction and remained in full possession of everything he learned during his first forty some years. Only the autopsy following his death revealed that he had lived and worked for years with literally one half of his brain, the other half being completely atrophied.

[8]Roger Lewin, "Is Your Brain Really Necessary?" *Science* 210 (1980): 1232.
[9]See Thomas Kuhn, *The Structure of Scientific Revolutions*, 2nd ed. (Chicago: University of Chicago Press, 1970).
[10]John Haugeland, *Artificial Intelligence: The Very Idea* (Cambridge, Mass.: MIT Press, 1985), pp. 203-11.
[11]This is not to say there has been no research on the frame problem. Roger Schank's research on scripts was some of the early work in this area. Nonetheless the range of applicability of this work tends to be highly constricted and fails to capture the flexibility and adaptability of humans in deploying common sense. Cf. Robert Schank, *The Cognitive Computer: On Language, Learning and Artificial Intelligence* (Reading, Mass.: Addison-Wesley, 1984).
[12]Hartley Rogers Jr., *Theory of Recursive Functions and Effective Computability* (Cambridge, Mass.: MIT Press, 1987), chap. 5.
[13]See José Balcázar, Josep Díaz and Joaquim Gabarró, *Structural Complexity I* (Berlin: Springer-Verlag, 1988), chap. 6.
[14]John Lucas, "Minds, Machines and Gödel," *Philosophy* 36 (1961): 120-24.
[15]See, for example, Klaus Weihrauch, *Computability* (Berlin: Springer-Verlag, 1987), pp. 260-64.
[16]This was the upshot of John McCarthy's book review of *Emperor's New Mind* by Roger Penrose, *Bulletin of the American Mathematical Society* 23, no. 2 (1990): 606-16.
[17]Roger Penrose, *The Emperor's New Mind* (Oxford: Oxford University Press, 1989); Roger Penrose, *Shadows of the Mind* (Oxford: Oxford University Press, 1994).
[18]Cf. Stephen Schiffer, *Remnants of Meaning*, pp. 153-54.
[19]See, for instance, Michael Denton, *Nature's Destiny: How the Laws of Biology Reveal Purpose in the Universe* (New York: Free Press, 1998).
[20]For the details, refer to William Dembski, *The Design Inference* (Cambridge: Cambridge University Press, 1998).
[21]See William Dembski, ed., *Mere Creation: Science, Faith & Intelligent Design* (Downers Grove, Ill.: InterVarsity Press, 1998).
[22]*Logos* substituted for *word*.
[23]*logos* substituted for *word*.
[24]Quotes taken from Ronald Thiemann, *Constructing a Public Theology* (Louisville, Ky.: Westminster John Knox, 1991), pp. 45-46. Thiemann himself was not here endorsing these positions.
[25]See John Searle, *The Construction of Social Reality* (New York: Free Press, 1995), chaps. 7-9; and D. M. Armstrong, *Universals: An Opinionated Introduction* (Boulder, Colo.: Westview, 1989).
[26]Alvin Plantinga, "Is Naturalism Irrational?" chap. 12 in *Warrant and Proper Function*

(Oxford: Oxford University Press, 1993).

[27]Marvin Vincent, "John 1:1-5," in *Vincent's Word Studies in the New Testament* (Peabody, Mass.: Hendrickson, 1984).

[28]Richard Dawkins, *The Blind Watchmaker* (New York: Norton, 1986), p. 1.

[29]See Roy Frieden's ground-breaking book *Physics from Fisher Information: A Unification* (Cambridge: Cambridge University Press, 1998). Frieden reconceptualizes the whole of physics in terms of information and thus in terms of communication theory.

[30]Paul Davies writes,

> Anyone who invested in information technology stocks will have seen their shares rocket recently. After years of hype, the information revolution is finally here. As the futurist George Gilder points out, telecommunications networks carry more valuable goods than all the world's supertankers. . . . If information is indeed poised to replace matter as the primary 'stuff' of the world, then an even bigger prize may lie in store. One of the oldest problems of existence is the duality between mind and matter. In modern parlance, brains (matter) create thoughts (mental information). Nobody knows how. But if matter turns out to be a form of organised information, then consciousness may not be so mysterious after all.

From "Bit Before It?" *New Scientist,* January 30, 1999, p. 3.

[31]Christos Yanaras, *Elements of Faith: An Introduction to Orthodox Theology* (Edinburgh: T & T Clark, 1991), pp. 44-45.

Appendix: Objections to Design

[1]Daniel Defoe, *Robinson Crusoe* (1719; reprint, New York: Signet Classic, 1980), pp. 81-82.

[2]Ludwig Wittgenstein, *On Certainty* (New York: Harper & Row, 1969), p. 43e, no. 336. The emphasis is Wittgenstein's.

[3]Arthur Koestler, *The Roots of Coincidence* (New York: Random House, 1972); and Dean Radin, *The Conscious Universe* (San Francisco: Harper, 1997).

[4]Even the archskeptic and debunker James Randi admits as much when he cites *Acta Orthopaedica Scandinavica:* "A histologically confirmed malignant, primary bone tumour in the [left] pelvis, presumably an osteosarcoma, underwent spontaneous regression. The large tumour was inoperable and gave rise to severe pain as well as difficulty in walking. After 2 years of progression, with increasing destruction of the pelvic bones, the clinical and radiological condition improved spontaneously, and at present the patient is alive, almost symptom-free, after 6 years follow-up." Quoted in James Randi, *The Faith Healers* (Buffalo, N.Y.: Prometheus, 1987), pp. 28-29.

[5]Alexis Carrel, *Man the Unknown* (New York: Harper & Brothers, 1936), p. 148.

[6]Stanley Jaki, *Miracles and Physics* (Front Royal, Va.: Christendom Press, 1989), p. 39 n. 36.

[7]Baruch de Spinoza, *Ethics,* trans. W. H. White, revised by A. H. Stirling, Great Books of the Western World 31, ed. R. M. Hutchins (1675; reprint, Chicago: Encyclopedia Britannica, 1952), p. 371.

[8]The *Skeptical Inquirer* is published by the Committee for the Scientific Investigation of Claims of the Paranormal, P. O. Box 703, Amherst, NY, 14226, www.csicop.org. Cf. also Michael Shermer, *Why People Believe Weird Things: Pseudoscience, Superstition and Other Confusions of Our Time* (New York: Freeman, 1997).

[9]Ian Barbour, *Issues in Science and Religion* (London: SCM Press, 1966), p. 390.

[10]C. A. Coulson, *Science and Religion: A Changing Relationship* (Cambridge: Cambridge University Press, 1955), p. 2.

[11]Edwin Hubble, *The Realm of the Nebulae* (New Haven, Conn.: Yale University Press, 1936), p. 202.

[12]I am indebted to Diogenes Allen for pointing out to me the distinction between intentionality and design. The distinction came up in a discussion of Austin Farrer's understanding

of divine action.

[13]For this portion of the appendix, I'm indebted to Mark DeForrest for sharing with me an unpublished manuscript on the difference between intelligent design and scientific creationism.

[14]Percival Davis and Dean Kenyon, *Of Pandas and People,* 2nd ed. (Dallas: Haughton, 1993), p. 7.

[15]William Dembski, *The Design Inference* (Cambridge: Cambridge University Press, 1998), chaps. 2 and 7.

[16]*Edwards v. Aguillard,* 482 U.S. 578 (1987).

[17]Ronald Numbers, *The Creationists* (New York: Knopf, 1992), p. x.

[18]See Stuart Kauffman, *The Origins of Order: Self-Organization and Selection in Evolution* (New York: Oxford University Press, 1993); Rudolf Raff, *The Shape of Life: Genes, Development and the Evolution of Animal Form* (Chicago: University of Chicago Press, 1996); Bernard John and George L. G. Miklos, *The Eukaryote Genome in Development and Evolution* (London: Allen & Unwin, 1988); G. L. G. Miklos and K. S. W. Campbell, "From Protein Domains to Extinct Phyla: Reverse Engineering Approaches to the Evolution of Biological Complexities," in *Early Life on Earth, Nobel Symposium No. 84,* ed. S. Bengtson (New York: Columbia University Press, 1993).

[19]Davis and Kenyon, *Pandas and People,* pp. 98-113.

[20]Behe writes: "I find the idea of common descent (that all organisms share a common ancestor) fairly convincing, and have no particular reason to doubt it." Michael Behe, *Darwin's Black Box* (New York: Free Press, 1996), p. 5.

[21]See Lane Lester and Raymond Bohlin, *The Natural Limits to Biological Change,* 2nd ed. (Dallas: Probe Books, 1989).

[22]Niles Eldredge and Stephen Jay Gould, "Punctuated Equilibria: An Alternative to Phyletic Gradualism," in *Models in Paleobiology,* ed. T. J. M. Schopf (San Francisco: Freeman, Cooper, 1973), pp. 82-115.

[23]Kauffman, *Origins of Order;* Ilya Prigogine and Isabelle Stengers, *Order Out of Chaos* (New York: Bantam, 1984).

[24]Manfred Eigen, *Steps Towards Life: A Perspective on Evolution,* trans. P. Woolley (Oxford: Oxford University Press, 1992), p. 12.

[25]Francis Crick and Leslie E. Orgel, "Directed Panspermia," *Icarus* 19 (1973): 341-46.

[26]Cf. Hubert Yockey, *Information Theory and Molecular Biology* (Cambridge: Cambridge University Press, 1992), p. 335.

[27]See Numbers, *Creationists,* p. 250.

[28]Frederick Grinnell, "Radical Intersubjectivity," in *Darwinism: Science or Philosophy?* ed. Jon Buell and Virginia Hearn (Richardson, Tex.: Foundation for Thought and Ethics, 1994), p. 105.

[29]Gerald Skoog, "A View from the Past," *Bookwatch Reviews* 2 (1989): 1-2.

[30]A David Kline, "Theories, Facts and Gods: Philosophical Aspects of the Creation-Evolution Controversy," in *Did the Devil Make Darwin Do It?* ed. D. B. Wilson (Ames: Iowa State University Press, 1983), p. 42.

[31]Robert Root-Bernstein, "On Defining a Scientific Theory: Creationism Considered," in *Science and Creationism,* ed. A. Montagu (New York: Oxford University Press, 1984), p. 73.

[32]Stephen Jay Gould, "Evolution as Fact and Theory," in *Science and Creationism,* ed. Montagu, p. 59.

[33]Philip Kitcher, *Abusing Science* (Cambridge, Mass.: MIT Press, 1982), pp. 126-27, 176-77.

[34]Committee on Science and Creationism, National Academy of Sciences, *Science and Creationism: A View from the National Academy of Sciences* (Washington, D.C.: National Academy Press, 1984), pp. 8-10.

[35]Richard Dawkins, *The Blind Watchmaker* (New York: Norton, 1986), p. 141.

[36]Ibid., p. 13.

[37]Michael Ruse, *Darwinism Defended* (Reading, Mass.: Addison-Wesley, 1982), p. 322. Strictly speaking, Ruse was here criticizing scientific creationism rather than intelligent design. Nonetheless he regularly applies the identical criticism to intelligent design.

[38]Eugenie Scott, "Keep Science Free from Creationism," *Insight* 21 (February 1994): 30. Strictly speaking, Scott was here criticizing scientific creationism rather than intelligent design. Nonetheless she regularly applies the identical criticism to intelligent design.

[39]Elliott Sober, *Philosophy of Biology* (Boulder, Colo.: Westview, 1993), pp. 49-52.

[40]Carl Sagan and Ann Druyan, *Shadows of Forgotten Ancestors* (New York: Random House, 1992), p. 387.

[41]This was the upshot of Newton's famous remark *"Hypotheses non fingo"* (I feign no hypotheses). Isaac Newton, *Isaac Newton's Papers and Letters on Natural Philosophy*, ed. I. B. Cohen (Cambridge, Mass.: Harvard University Press, 1958), p. 302. Nancy Pearcey and Charles Thaxton elaborate: "[Newton] insisted that the concept of force he had introduced was not an ultimate explanation at all—either occult *or* mechanistic. It was merely a postulate used to explain observations. Ultimate explanations, Newton said, should be left out of science. This is the context in which he uttered his famous expression *hypotheses non fingo*." Nancy R. Pearcey and Charles B. Thaxton, *The Soul of Science* (Wheaton, Ill.: Crossway, 1994), p. 90.

[42]Ruse, *Darwinism Defended*, p. 58.

[43]See Thomas Kuhn, *The Structure of Scientific Revolutions*, 2nd ed. (Chicago: University of Chicago Press, 1970). On page 151 Kuhn cites with approval Max Planck, who wrote: "A new scientific truth does not triumph by convincing its opponents and making them see the light, but rather because its opponents eventually die, and a new generation grows up that is familiar with it." Quoted from Max Planck, *Scientific Autobiography and Other Papers*, trans. F. Gaynor (New York: Philosophical Library, 1949), pp. 33-34.

[44]Ernst Mach actually did make such an argument. See Lawrence Sklar, *Physics and Chance: Philosophical Issues in the Foundations of Statistical Mechanics* (Cambridge: Cambridge University Press, 1993), pp. 32-34, 131-32.

[45]Dawkins, *Blind Watchmaker*, p. 316.

[46]Daniel Dennett, *Darwin's Dangerous Idea* (New York: Simon & Schuster, 1995), p. 153.

[47]Dawkins, *Blind Watchmaker*, p. 13.

[48]See David Berlinski, *On Systems Analysis: An Essay Concerning the Limitations of Some Mathematical Methods in the Social, Political and Biological Sciences* (Cambridge, Mass.: MIT Press, 1976).

[49]Stefan Helmreich, *Silicon Second Nature: Culturing Artificial Life in a Digital World* (Berkeley: University of California Press, 1998), p. 44.

[50]Methodological naturalism is defined and critiqued in the articles by Stephen C. Meyer and J. P. Moreland in J. P. Moreland, ed., *The Creation Hypothesis* (Downers Grove, Ill.: InterVarsity Press, 1994), as well as in Alvin Plantinga, "Methodological Naturalism?" *Origins & Design* 18, no. 1 (1997): 18-27.

[51]Stephen Meyer develops this point much more extensively in "Demarcation and Design: The Nature of Historical Reasoning," in *Facets of Faith and Science*, vol. 4, ed. Jitse van der Meer (Washington, D.C.: University Press of America, 1996).

[52]Sklar, *Physics and Chance*, pp. 32-34, 131-32.

[53]Cf. Bas van Fraassen, *The Scientific Image* (Oxford: Oxford University Press, 1980).

[54]John Horgan takes this approach in *The End of Science* (New York: Broadway Books, 1996).

[55]Percy Bridgman, *Reflections of a Physicist*, 2nd ed. (New York: Philosophical Library, 1955), p. 535.

[56]Paul Feyerabend, *Against Method*, rev. ed. (London: Verso, 1988).

[57]William Paley, *Natural Theology* (1802; reprint, Boston: Gould & Lincoln, 1852).

[58]Cf. van Fraassen, *Scientific Image*.

[59]Ludwig Wittgenstein, *Culture and Value*, ed. G. H. von Wright, trans. P. Winch (Chicago: University of Chicago Press, 1980), p. 18e.

[60]Henry Petroski, *Invention by Design: How Engineers Get from Thought to Thing* (Cambridge, Mass.: Harvard University Press, 1996), p. 30. Petroski is a professor of civil engineering as well as a professor of history at Duke University.

[61]For a critique of Gould's objections to design based on optimality, see Paul Nelson, "The Role of Theology in Current Evolutionary Reasoning," *Biology and Philosophy* 11 (1996): 493-517.

[62]Ibid.

[63]Francis Darwin, ed., *The Life and Letters of Charles Darwin* (New York: D. Appleton, 1888), 2:105.

[64]Charles Darwin, *On the Origin of Species*, (1859; reprint, Cambridge, Mass.: Harvard University Press, 1964), pp. 242-44.

[65]Stephen Jay Gould, *The Panda's Thumb* (New York: Norton, 1980), pp. 20-21.

[66]See Boethius, *The Consolation of Philosophy*, Loeb Classical Library (Cambridge, Mass.: Harvard University Press, 1973), p. 153. Alvin Plantinga's free will defense is a resolution of the problem of evil that has provoked much response from philosophers of religion. For a synopsis see Kelly James Clark, *Return to Reason* (Grand Rapids, Mich.: Eerdmans, 1990), chap. 2. Finally, a significant number of contemporary philosophers of religion resolve the problem of evil by denying traditional accounts of divine omniscience and omnipotence. Process theologians have taken this view for some time, but more traditional philosophers and theologians are now taking this line also. See William Hasker, *God, Time and Knowledge* (Ithaca, N.Y.: Cornell University Press, 1989).

[67]For more in this vein see Diogenes Allen, *Spiritual Theology* (Cambridge, Mass.: Cowley Publications, 1997).

[68]See Hugh Ross, *The Fingerprint of God*, 2nd ed. (Orange, Calif.: Promise, 1991), pp. 121-22.

[69]See Hugh Ross, "The Big Bang Model Refined by Fire," in *Mere Creation: Science, Faith & Intelligent Design*, ed. William Dembski (Downers Grove, Ill.: InterVarsity Press, 1998).

[70]See part 1 of Michael Denton, *Nature's Destiny: How the Laws of Biology Reveal Purpose in the Universe* (New York: Free Press, 1998).

[71]Roger Penrose, *The Emperor's New Mind* (New York: Oxford, 1989), p. 344.

[72]See Dembski, *Design Inference*, pp. 214-17.

[73]George Greenstein, *The Symbiotic Universe: Life and Mind in the Cosmos* (New York: William Morrow, 1988), pp. 26-27.

[74]Quoted in Paul Davies, *The Accidental Universe* (Cambridge: Cambridge University Press, 1982), p. 118.

[75]For a description—though not an endorsement—of this argument, see Lee Smolin, *The Life of the Cosmos* (Oxford: Oxford University Press, 1997), pp. 202-10.

[76]John Leslie, *Universes* (London: Routledge, 1989); John Earman, "The Sap Also Rises: A Critical Examination of the Anthropic Principle," *American Philosophical Quarterly* 24, no. 4 (1987): 307-17; and Richard Swinburne, *The Existence of God* (Oxford: Oxford University Press, 1979).

[77]Francis Crick, *Life Itself: Its Origin and Nature* (New York: Simon & Schuster, 1981), chap. 7; Bernd-Olaf Küppers, *Information and the Origin of Life* (Cambridge, Mass.: MIT Press, 1990), chap. 6; Yockey, *Information Theory and Molecular Biology*, chap. 9. Strictly speaking, Yockey is an information theorist who works in biology.

[78]Swinburne, *Existence of God*, p. 138.

[79]For a detailed treatment of selection effects and their failure to account for specified complexity (or "specified improbability" as it's put there), see Dembski, *Design Inference*, chap. 6.

[80]Paul Moorhead and Martin Kaplan, eds., *Mathematical Challenges to the Neo-Darwinian Interpretation of Evolution* (New York: Alan R. Liss, 1967), pp. 73-80, a symposium held at the Wistar Institute of Anatomy and Biology, April 25-26, 1966.

[81]I'm ignoring bonding affinities here, just as I ignored the conditional probabilities of one

Roman letter succeeding another (in English, for instance, *u* always follows *q*). I'm concerned here strictly with sequencing.

[82]Yockey, *Information Theory and Molecular Biology,* chap. 5.

[83]Thomas Schneider, "Information Content of Individual Genetic Sequences," *Journal of Theoretical Biology* 189 (1997): 427-41; J. U. Bowie, J. F. Reidhaar-Olson, W. A. Lim and R. T. Sauer, "Deciphering the Message in Protein Sequences: Tolerance to Amino Acid Substitution," *Science* 247 (1990): 1306-10; and J. U. Bowie and R. T. Sauer, "Identifying Determinants of Folding and Activity for a Protein of Unknown Structure," *Proceedings of the National Academy of Sciences* 86 (1989): 2152-56.

[84]There is a way to strengthen the argument from analogy, and that is to make its conclusion follow as an inductive generalization: when objects U and V both possess properties A, B, C and D, and when U also possesses property Q, the conclusion that V possesses Q follows inductively if in every instance where an object possesses A, B, C and D, and where it can be determined whether the object also possesses Q, the object actually does possess Q. Alternatively in this strengthened argument from analogy the appearance of A, B, C and D has yet to be divorced from the appearance of Q. This strengthened form of the argument therefore has an additional premise and can be formulated as follows:

> U has property Q.
> U and V share properties A, B, C and D.
> There is no known instance where A, B, C and D occur without Q.
> Therefore, V has property Q.

Granted, this is still not a deductive argument. But for the conclusion to fail, V would have be the first known instance of an object that possesses A, B, C and D without possessing Q. It is possible to formulate the design argument in biology as such a strengthened argument from analogy (U corresponding to machines; V to living systems; A, B, C and D to such properties as functional interdependence, storage of information and processing of energy; and Q to the property of being designed by an intelligence). Such a revamped argument from analogy, to my mind, goes a long way toward addressing Hume's objections to design. Nevertheless, since I cash out the design argument as an inference to the best explanation, I shall not pursue this line of inquiry further.

[85]Elliott Sober, *Philosophy of Biology* (Boulder, Colo.: Westview, 1993), p. 33.

[86]Ibid. Although Sober is right to treat the design argument as an inference to the best explanation, it should be recognized that inferences to the best explanation need not be formulated in terms of probabilities, likelihood principles or Bayesian decision theory. At the heart of inference to the best explanation is the notion of explanatory power. Although explanatory power can be cashed out probabilistically as Sober does so that the hypothesis H has greater power explaining the data D according to how closely the probability $P(D|H)$ approaches its maximum possible value of one, explanatory power remains a notion that makes sense more generally and without the probabilistic formalism. Explanatory power was taken up in chapter seven.

[87]Ibid., p. 52.

[88]Ibid., pp. 35-36. The citation in this quotation is to L. Alvarez, et al., "Extraterrestrial Cause for the Cretaceous-Tertiary Extinction," *Science* 208 (1980): 1095-108.

[89]Thomas Reid, *Lectures on Natural Theology,* ed. E. Duncan and W. R. Eakin (1780; reprint, Washington, D.C.: University Press of America, 1981), pp. 51-59.

Index